RUN TO WIN

HOW TO FINISH STRONG IN THE RACE OF LIFE

RUN TO WIN

HOW TO FINISH STRONG IN THE RACE OF LIFE

GREG **LAURIE**

Published by: Kerygma Publishing–Allen David Books
www.kerygmapublishing.com

Coordination: FM Management, Ltd.
Contact: fmmgt@cox.net
34332 Port Lantern
Dana Point, CA 92629

Cover design: Ty Mattson
Interior design and production: Highgate Cross + Cathey

Printed in the United States of America.   ISBN: 978-0-9834004-6-2

CONTENTS

INTRODUCTION

I am a runner.

I can't believe I just wrote those words, because I fought it for years, even decades. Sure, as a kid I loved to run and even went out for track and field in high school. But as the years passed and the waistline grew, running became less appealing. For years I sat in wonder as I listened to those who spoke almost euphorically of the endorphins their brains released as they ran.

I had never experienced any endorphin release. Just pain and more pain. Runner's high? Where did it go?

I had to acknowledge, however, that those who did jog regularly dropped quite a few pounds. So I decided to start again.

Someone watched me run a bit and told me that I "pronated."

"Pro-what?"

In other words, I ran on the inside edges of my feet, causing more strain on shins, knees, and so on. This was surprising to me, as I had the ultimate running shoes—or so I thought. I ended up with a less-expensive, but firmer, pair of shoes.

Other runners told me music helped them as they jogged.

So I loaded up my iPod and was ready to go. My first time out was more walking than running. After a while, it became about equal periods of both. Soon it was primarily running. And that is what I'm doing as of this writing. It takes discipline to run, but the results are worth it.

There's another kind of running that requires discipline. But the results are worth it in that race too. If you are a Christian, you are in a spiritual race, as Paul made clear in his New Testament letters. No doubt you've felt the occasional strained muscle, days when the track seemed too long and the sun too hot—and hopefully moments of victory, too, that made all the pain worthwhile.

What's great about being in a race is that you are a participant, not a spectator. You have something to say about how you're going to do spiritually. Make no mistake about it: people fall away from their faith and quit the spiritual race only because they choose to do so. It's up to you.

It's a well-proven truth that we can learn from one another's mistakes as well as each other's successes. You may be wondering, *What is the secret to spiritual longevity? What steps can I take to assure I will make it across the finish line? How can I know I will hear the Lord say to me, "Well done, good and faithful servant"?*

We should all be asking these questions, because one day, every one of us will complete this race we're running, and each of us will be either a winner or a loser. One day, we all are going to die. (The statistics on death are quite impressive: one out of every one person will die!)

Let me ask you this: what would you like written on your tombstone? How about something that would tell us a bit about you, what you believed and stood for? Larry King authored a book called *Remember Me When I'm Gone*. It contains the epitaphs the rich and famous have written for themselves—things for which they want to be remembered.

Some are humorous, some bizarre, some touching. Here are a few samples:

Here lies Stacy Keach.
A Georgia peach.
Lived at the beach.
Now out of reach.
—*Stacy Keach, actor*[1]

I am speechless. Trust me.
—*Milos Forman, filmmaker and director*[2]

I seem to have run out of tomorrows.
—*Arte Johnson, comedian*[3]

Calvin Klein by Eternity.
—*Calvin Klein, clothing designer*[4]

Hugh Hefner, founder and publisher of *Playboy* magazine, noted in King's book, "I'd like to be remembered as someone who played some part in changing our hurtful and hypocritical views on sex—and had a lot of fun doing it."[5]

Sometimes tombstones describe how the person died. In memory of an accident in a Uniontown, Pennsylvania, cemetery, one tombstone reads:

Here lies the body of Jonathan Blake.
Stepped on the gas instead of the brake.

Sometimes tombstones are painfully blunt. I read about one for a man named John Starkweather. It says:

Here is where friend Starkweather lies.
Nobody laughs. Nobody cries.
Where he goes, how he fares,
nobody knows. Nobody cares.

A tombstone in a Thurmont, Maryland, cemetery contains a more telling statement:

Here lies an atheist.
All dressed up and no place to go.

What would your friends or family write on your tombstone? What statement could they make to sum up your life? Would you like what it says?

When we finish this race of life, we will stand at the judgment seat of Jesus Christ. There we will receive our rewards, if we have run well. Some of us have acquired the great awards this world has to offer over the years. Perhaps you excelled in sports, and your shelves were lined with trophies and plaques. Personally, I always had a lot of those Honorable Mention ribbons (which means I showed up but came in last place). But in heaven there will be many rewards for those who have been faithful to God over the years.

The Lord doesn't overlook even the smallest and most insignificant gesture on behalf of His kingdom. Jesus said that our service to God, though not seen by people, is seen by God: "Your Father who sees in secret will Himself reward you openly" (Matthew 6:4). Speaking of this day in the future of all believers, the Bible says, "For we must all appear before the judgment seat of Christ, so that each of us may receive what is due us for the things done while in the body, whether good or bad" (2 Corinthians 5:10 NIV).

Paul further developed this concept:

> For no one can lay any foundation other than the one already laid, which is Jesus Christ. If anyone builds on this foundation using gold, silver, costly stones, wood, hay or straw, their work will be shown for what it is, because the Day will bring it to light. It will be revealed with fire, and the fire will test the quality of each person's work. If what has been built survives, the builder will receive a reward. If it is burned up, the builder will suffer loss but yet will be saved—even though only as one escaping through the flames. (1 Corinthians 3:11–15 NIV)

According to this and other passages, the promises of God guarantee our presence in the kingdom. But the quality of service we render here and now will determine what position we will have in the kingdom. Salvation is a gift through faith *in* Jesus Christ. Honor is a reward for service *to* Jesus Christ.

When Paul wrote of "wood, hay or straw," he was basically speaking not of gross sin as much as putting more importance on the passing things of this world than on the things of God. It might be a career, some sport or hobby, endless hours spent in front of a TV, and so on. I've heard more than once that the average American spends somewhere around fifteen years of his or her life in front of the TV set! What a waste. Things such as these will pass.

On that final day, God will want to know what you did with your gifts (talents and abilities) and your time. He will want to know what you did with the sacred charge of spreading the gospel, which He entrusted to you.

I can't tell you how important this is.

When a person dies and I am asked to speak at the memorial service, I always try to find out as much as I can about the person. Sometimes, the person was a friend, or someone I knew, so I can talk about what I personally observed. But when I don't know the person, I ask family members and friends to tell me about him or her.

I never point out how successful the person was in business because at a funeral, frankly, nobody cares. I don't talk about how handsome or beautiful he or she may have been. I try to find the enduring qualities of such people's lives: acts of kindness, sacrificial acts, or a story that might sum up what really mattered to them.

I can't tell you how sad it is to find nothing of this kind. Then I realize I am dealing with a person who largely wasted his or her life, and that is just pathetic!

But it happens far too often.

This reminds me of the prophet Daniel's words to the irreverent King Belshazzar: "You have been weighed in [God's] balances, and found wanting" (Daniel 5:27). In other words, Daniel was saying, "Belshazzar, you are a spiritual lightweight. You have no substance. And guess what? Your life is required of you!"

Let me ask you this: if someone were to honestly sum up your life at your funeral service, for what would he or she remember you?

It's sad for us when someone dies. But if that person dies in the Lord, and if he has served Him for his whole life, it's really a glorious thing in many ways. The Bible says, "Precious in the sight of the Lord is the death of His saints" (Psalm 116:15).

We all know death will come. What we need to do—what we need to focus on—is finishing well and making every single day count. We all want a life that's worth living. The tragedy of life isn't that it ends so soon, but that we wait so long to begin it—or that we live our lives in a way that seems to go nowhere fast.

In Florence, Italy, a young artist labored long and hard over a marble statue of an angel. When finished, he asked the great artist Michelangelo to examine it. No master looked over the work more carefully than Michelangelo. It appeared perfect in every way.

The young artist waited for Michelangelo's response. His heart nearly broke when he heard, "It lacks only one thing."

But the great artist didn't tell him what it lacked. For days the artist couldn't eat or sleep, until finally a friend called on Michelangelo at his studio and asked him to please tell what he thought it lacked.

He said, "It lacks only life."

That could be said of so many today. They have everything they should to supposedly be happy—a good job, a family, a beautiful home—but they "lack only life."

Most of us could well say somewhere down the road of life, "If I had known what I know now, I would have lived differently. I would have done things differently in order to have a better life." Remember, some die earlier than expected. Somehow we think we're all going to make it into our eighties or nineties. We may, we may not. Some of us may have shorter courses to run. That makes every minute count—for all of us.

One man who lived his life well was Jim Elliot. He was in his early twenties when he felt called to take the gospel to the Auca tribe in Ecuador. He, along with some friends and his new bride, Elisabeth, followed God's leading. Jim paid with his life when the very people he had been trying to reach turned on him. He and his missionary colleagues died from spear wounds. Wrapped around one spear was a gospel tract they had given the Aucas.

Jim gave his life for the gospel. It seems like a tragic thing, but he lived for the glory of God. He did what he was supposed to do. And he finished well. He understood the importance of that; in fact, he wrote in his journal some eight years before his death, "I seek not a long life but a full one, like Yours, Lord Jesus."[6] He lived that full life.

Time is passing by, and we don't want to squander this precious thing God has given us called life. And we don't want anything less than a spectacular finish.

In this book I'd like to share some examples of godly people who managed to lead not just blessed and productive lives, but who finished victoriously as well—people like the martyr Jim Elliot. In contrast, I will also share stories of people who failed in life, death, or both. We can learn from them as well. And finally, I'd like to look at the most important life ever lived, the earthly life of Jesus himself, to see how He ran His race . . . and how He finished.

Life is certainly filled with surprises. Some people I thought were going to do great things for God started out tremendously—but then veered off course. They have actually fallen away and no longer walk with Christ. Other people I thought would never even make it as Christians are not only making it, but also serving the Lord gloriously and with great effectiveness.

It all boils down to the finish line, doesn't it?

No matter how or when we started this race, we want to finish well. I want to be one of those people who hit that final tape with flying colors, don't you? Let's take a run together and find out how.

THE RACE OF YOUR LIFE

When I was a kid, I always wanted to be an athlete. I always admired the guys with strength, coordination, and athletic abilities. Unfortunately, I never was one of those guys. I was the guy who always wanted to hit the homerun . . . and usually struck out. I was the guy who backpedaled in the outfield to catch that high pop fly . . . and then let it dribble out of my mitt.

When I was in high school, I noticed that football players always seemed to get the cute girlfriends, so I decided to go out for football. I wasn't big or brawny enough to be great at blocking and tackling, but one thing I did fairly well was run.

In a pinch, I could run pretty fast.

So I went out for the team, endured the miseries of late-summer daily doubles, and actually won a place on my high school team, which was a pretty big deal to me. When all the other players shaved their heads, I did too. (That was back when I had hair.) I even ordered a team jacket, so everyone would know that I was a football player.

Early that fall, however, I got called into the school office, and a counselor told me, "Greg, I'm sorry, but you can't be on the team. Your grades are too low."

I remember my reaction to this day. I said, "Couldn't you have told me this *before* I shaved my head?"

So after working on my grades, I went out for track and field in the spring, where I thought I could put my running abilities to good use. While I was pretty good at the short-distance runs, I didn't seem to have the stamina for those longer distances. As time went on, I realized that I needed to pace myself.

And now? Well, the years have passed, and I don't run a whole lot anymore. I just walk most of the time. I buy nice running shoes, but I don't actually *run* in them. I'm not alone in that. I read in the paper the other day that 89 percent of those who purchase running shoes never use them for running. A number of us have the idea and the *intention* of running, but somehow we never get around to it.

Why is this? It's really not rocket science. The fact is, many of us are just naturally lazy. I actually hate exercise. Even so, I go the gym every day of the week. (I know a route that takes me right by the Krispy Kreme doughnut store.)

Real athletes understand that success depends on commitment. An Olympic athlete has to work out an average of four hours a day, 310 days a year for six years to compete for a gold medal. Discipline? I can't even imagine how much discipline that would take.

No matter how we may feel about running, if we belong to Jesus Christ, we're in one race up to our eyebrows.

It's the spiritual race.

And it is the race of our lives.

The Race of Our Lives

Again and again, the New Testament uses the metaphor of running a race to describe our relationship with God. You have probably heard it said, "It's not whether you win or lose, but how you play the game." That may be true in checkers or cricket or softball, but in the spiritual race of life, it's all about winning.

This is not a race you want to lose. We're all running for the gold here.

But it's also important that we play by the rules. The apostle Paul zeroes in on these things in 1 Corinthians 9:

> Don't you realize that in a race everyone runs, but only one person gets the prize? So run to win! All athletes are disciplined in their

training. They do it to win a prize that will fade away, but we do it for an eternal prize. So I run with purpose in every step. I am not just shadowboxing. I discipline my body like an athlete, training it to do what it should. Otherwise, I fear that after preaching to others I myself might be disqualified. (vv. 24–27 NLT)

Paul not only uses the athletic metaphor of running in this passage, but he talks about fighting too. When we think about fighting, we probably think about a boxing match with those big padded gloves. But in the New Testament days, they would sometimes fight to the death. It probably could be most closely compared to what we call "ultimate fighting" or "cage fighting" today.

Have you ever seen that? I was flipping through the TV channels the other night and caught a few minutes of it. They literally put these men in a cage to do battle. They have very little padding around their fists and are allowed to wrestle, punch, kick—and do maximum damage to each other.

In this particular match, I noticed that although one of the guys was taller and seemed to be in great shape, his blows kept missing the opponent. He threw a powerful punch, but he kept whiffing. He never could quite connect with his adversary, who was shorter and stockier. It was the shorter man who kept darting in and out, landing blow after blow.

After a few minutes, I'd seen all I wanted to see. But I could tell that unless that bigger man found a way to connect with his punches, he was going to lose that match—and take a terrible beating in the process.

Some people may not like that fight imagery, but the fact is, the Christian life *is* a fight—as well as a race. And Paul emphasized that we must play by the rules, or we'll end up disqualified.

We've all read stories about Olympic athletes who have had to endure the humiliation of returning their medals, because it was discovered they used some illegal, performance-enhancing substance to give them an extra edge. In the Olympics, there are established rules, and to enter the competition, you must agree to play by those rules.

So it is in the race of life: there are rules, and we must heed those rules to stay in the game.

There are also opponents in the race of life.

When I say "opponent," that doesn't mean that I am competing with you or that you are competing with me. My opponent isn't my fellow Christian. In fact, if anything, we're part of a *team*, running this race together.

No, our opponents are the world, the flesh, and the devil. And the devil doesn't want us to complete this race that we have begun. Paul wrote to the believers in Galatia and said, "You were running the race so well. Who has held you back from following the truth?" (Galatians 5:7 NIV)

There are those who would want to cut in on us or stop us from running this race well—or even finishing at all.

In his second letter to young Pastor Timothy, Paul writes,

> I have fought the good fight, I have finished the race, I have kept the faith. Finally, there is laid up for me the crown of righteousness, which the Lord, the righteous Judge, will give to me on that Day, and not to me only but also to all who have loved His appearing. (2 Timothy 4:7-8)

This isn't a race we want to just start; it's a race we must also finish. It's not a race where we want to make a good showing for the first nine laps and then drop out in the final lap. No, we want to cross the finish line. We want to finish what we've begun.

Here's how Paul expressed it from a dark Roman dungeon, every word ringing with passion—and sheer determination.

"I Press toward the Goal . . ."

> But what things were gain to me, these I have counted loss for Christ. Yet indeed I also count all things loss for the excellence of the knowledge of Christ Jesus my Lord, for whom I have suffered the loss of all things, and count them as rubbish, that I may gain Christ and be found in Him, not having my own righteousness, which is from the law, but that which is through faith in Christ, the righteousness which is from God by faith; that I may know Him

and the power of His resurrection, and the fellowship of His sufferings, being conformed to His death, if, by any means, I may attain
to the resurrection from the dead.

Not that I have already attained, or am already perfected; but
I press on, that I may lay hold of that for which Christ Jesus has
also laid hold of me. Brethren, I do not count myself to have
apprehended; but one thing I do, forgetting those things which
are behind and reaching forward to those things which are ahead,
I press toward the goal for the prize of the upward call of God in
Christ Jesus. Therefore let us, as many as are mature, have this
mind; and if in anything you think otherwise, God will reveal even
this to you. (Philippians 3:7–15)

So what principles can we learn from these words of Paul on how
to win the most important race we will ever run?

1. You must be dissatisfied with where you are

In verse 12, Paul said, "Not as though I have already attained, or am
already perfected." Or, as another translation puts it, Paul says, "I'm
not saying that I have this all together, that I have it made. But
I am well on my way, reaching out for Christ, who has so won-
drously reached out for me" (MSG).

Paul certainly was satisfied with Christ . . . but he wasn't satisfied
with *himself*. Here is one of the greatest Christians of all time saying, "I haven't obtained my goal. I'm not there yet."

I find myself thinking, *Well, if Paul didn't hit the mark, then
who in the world has?* Just think about the accomplishments of
this man! He established countless churches, preached amazing
sermons, endured terrible persecutions for Christ, and penned
letters that we rightly regard today as the very Word of God. And
miracles? God gave him amazing gifts of healing, including raising a man from the dead.

If ever there was a guy who had bragging rights, it was Paul. If
anyone could have legitimately kicked back a little and rested on his
laurels, it was Paul. But he didn't. He wouldn't. He refused to stop
reaching, straining, and pressing toward the goal. And he lived that
way right up to the very end of his life.

Sometimes as believers, you and I may get hung up on an experience we had with God, once upon a time. We attain some emotional or spiritual mountaintop and say to ourselves, "Well, that's wonderful. That will last me for days. I'll just bask in the glow of that great time I had with the Lord." But God never intended for us to coast or take it easy in the spiritual life. He wants us to keep pressing on, pressing forward.

Experiences in the Christian life are like the manna that was given to Israel. You can't store them up, or they'll go stale! You have to gather fresh "manna" every day. No matter how much we may grow spiritually, there is always room for more and more growth. We all need to look at ourselves and say, "Am I where I ought to be? How can I grow even more?"

It's that way in my life. Even after thirty-eight years of walking with Jesus, I realize more and more just how far I have to go. I don't say that to appear humble. We *all* fall short. We *all* have a long way to go. And if we don't see that about ourselves, then something is wrong.

One of the problems we have as believers is that we're often satisfied with where we are. We don't see the need for more growth and more transformation. Many Christians are self-satisfied because they compare their progress in the race of life with that of other Christians. "Well," we might say to ourselves, "at least I'm doing better than *her*. At least I'm not struggling with the same things as *him*."

The truth is, you can always find someone who isn't doing as well as you are. You can always look over your shoulder and see someone struggling along behind you. The objective, however, isn't to pace yourself alongside Christians who are almost at a standstill; the objective is to become all that God intended and empowered you to be. We need to ask ourselves, "Am I being the man—or the woman—that God has called me to be?" Paul didn't compare himself with others; he compared himself with Jesus Christ.

Obviously, the plan for this life isn't perfection, but *progress*. We are imperfect people surrounded by other imperfect people in the midst of an imperfect world. We never will be perfect, this side of heaven. But we can, as Paul says, "Press toward the mark."

I was reading a little cartoon strip in the paper not long ago. The strip, by Stephen Pastis, is called "Pearls Before Swine." A little rat and a little pig were having a conversation.

The pig said, "Hey, what are you doing here, Rat?"

"People are always letting me down," the rat replied. "So I wanted to find a place where I could be around people who would never disappoint me, never lie, and never let me down."

Then in the next frame, you see that the two little friends are in a graveyard. And the rat says, "Eureka."

The point? You'll never find a perfect place with perfect people. And if you did, you would only spoil it.

Paul isn't calling for perfection, but he is calling for progress. Are you making progress?

2. Get rid of extra weight and things that would hinder you

In verses 7–8, Paul writes, But what things were gain to me, these I have counted loss for Christ. Yet indeed I also count all things loss for the excellence of the knowledge of Christ Jesus my Lord, for whom I have suffered the loss of all things, and count them as rubbish, that I may gain Christ."

Paul is saying, "Those things that used to be so important to me now mean nothing. *Nada*. They're like so much garbage to me." His encounter with Christ changed everything about him—and especially his priorities.

Over in Hebrews 12:1 we read: "Let us throw off everything that hinders and the sin that so easily entangles. And let us run with perseverance the race marked out for us" (NIV).

When you're running a race, you don't want to be dragging something with you. You don't want to run a race towing a wagon full of barbells, do you? For that matter, you don't want to run a race wearing heavy coveralls and logging boots. Those things will only slow you down. Throw them off!

I'm reminded of the tendency I have to overpack when I travel somewhere. Even though I've been traveling for years, this problem persists. Somehow, I always end up hauling around a bunch of stuff I don't need. I'll cram the suitcase full of clothes and never need them or wear them. Invariably, I'll ask myself, *Why do I do this every time?* Packing lighter is especially important these days, because the airlines will make you pay dearly for overweight bags.

It's the same in the race of life. Sometimes we travel with too much weight. By that I mean that we drag along things that shouldn't be in our lives—things that slow us down or trip us up. The writer of Hebrews basically says, "Get rid of those weights. Get rid of those entanglements. Throw them off, so that you can run the race God has given you to run."

That weight might even be a person. It might be someone you hang around with who continually trips you up, pulls you off course, or keeps you from running your best race.

Whenever Franklin Graham comes out to visit me in Southern California, he invariably will say, "Come on, Greg. Let's go for a run in the morning."

I always try to be a good sport and go with him, but frankly, he'd be a lot better off going without me. Why? Because I run about four minutes and then I'm tired and have to walk. But Franklin doesn't want to walk after four minutes, because he could keep on running for an hour.

So the fact is, I slow Franklin down. I keep him from running the race he really wants to run—and is fully capable of running.

We have people like that in our spiritual race too. When we're with them, they slow us down, because they really don't have an interest in the things of God.

You'll say, "Hey, let's go to church today."

And they might reply, "Oh, I don't know. It's raining. It's kind of miserable outside. Why don't we go to the mall instead?" (Why is it easier to go to the mall on a rainy day than it is to go to church?) Or maybe when you're around that person, you stop reading the Bible, don't pray as much, or don't tune into Christian music like you usually do. You know that person isn't comfortable with spiritual things, so you stop doing them . . . and they begin to drag you down to their level.

The Bible tells the story of Abraham, who had a nephew named Lot. Lot made the trip with his uncle to the Promised Land, but he didn't have the same relationship with God as Abraham did. He came along on the journey, but he never had the same level of commitment or devotion to God. And whenever Lot was around, it seemed to drag Abraham down.

Finally, God told Abraham to part company with his nephew, which he eventually did—with reluctance. But it wasn't until he unloaded Lot that the Lord really began to speak to him and bless him again, because Lot was slowing him down.

We all know people like that, don't we?

The fact is, there are certain people with whom we're better off not spending a lot of time.

In 2 Timothy 2:22 (NLT), Paul writes to his young friend, "Run from anything that stimulates youthful lusts. Instead, pursue righteous living, faithfulness, love, and peace. Enjoy the companionship of those who call on the Lord with pure hearts."

Find people who want to run toward the same goal that you do. In the spiritual sense, keep fast company! And be wary of those who continually slow you down, drag down your attitude, or lead you into things that cause you to stumble.

3. Run with the right motive

In the Olympics, everyone wants to receive the gold. But obviously, not everyone does. Have you ever seen an Olympic gold medal? I have. I've even held it and . . . put it around my neck! But no, I didn't win it. The fact is, it was for the women's softball team, so that would be a little embarrassing to win that medal as a guy. But a young woman in our church went to the Olympics, and her team won the gold for the United States. When she returned home, she let me hold her medal.

It's a beautiful thing. Very impressive. If I ever won a gold medal, I think I'd wear it the rest of my life. Thirty years later, I'd still have it hanging around my neck!

It's an impressive accomplishment to win a gold medal. For that matter, it's an amazing feat to win a silver or a bronze. The fact is, however, we don't celebrate bronze medal winners very much. You don't see a bronze medal winner on a box of Wheaties. But if you win the gold, you might end up on a million breakfast tables.

Paul tells us that he is running the race of life, looking forward to a reward that will last forever—long after every Olympic gold medal has dissolved into dust.

The apostle said: "Finally, there is laid up for me the crown of righteousness, which the Lord, the righteous Judge, will give to me on that Day, and not to me only but also to all who have loved His appearing" (2 Timothy 4:8).

Crowns—whatever they may be—sound appealing, and the thought of heavenly rewards may provide some extra motivation. But in the final analysis, we're not running the race for a crown or for a reward. We're running the race for Jesus. That is the motive.

In Philippians 3:8, Paul said: "I also count all things loss for the excellence of the knowledge of Christ Jesus my Lord, for whom I have suffered the loss of all things, and count them as rubbish. . . ." In verse 10, he speaks of his strongest desire: "That I may know Him and the power of His resurrection, and the fellowship of His sufferings. . . ."

Paul is saying, "Listen, I am running this race for Jesus. He's the One who called me out on the Damascus Road. He's the One who has transformed my life. And He's the One for whom I'm running this race."

That is what will get you through the race of life, friend. People— even loved ones—may let you down. Circumstances may press in, seemingly squeezing you from all sides. In the face of these things, however, the Book of Hebrews urges us to "lay aside every weight, and the sin which so easily ensnares us, and let us run with endurance the race that is set before us, looking unto Jesus, the author and finisher of *our* faith, who for the joy that was set before Him endured the cross, despising the shame, and has sat down at the right hand of the throne of God" (Hebrews 12:1–2).

Looking to Jesus. . . . As Corrie ten Boom said years ago, "Look within and be depressed. Look without and be distressed. Look at Jesus and be at rest." The simple truth is, when you have your eyes on the Lord, you can get through every lap and weather any storm. But if you have your eyes on people—if you're running to impress others—it will be very, very difficult to stay on course.

That's why we need to look to Jesus. Jesus himself will keep you going through the race of life. Paul says that his determined purpose in life was that he might "know Him" (see Philippians 3:10). Note that Paul didn't say it was to "know *about* Him."

We live in a celebrity-obsessed culture today. Our media breathlessly follows every step—and misstep—of the rich and famous. We know all *about* them (and much more than we need to know), but we don't really know them. We might think we do, but we don't.

It can be the same with God. There are people who know a great many things about Him. They may have even taken college or seminary courses about God. But that doesn't necessarily mean they *know* Him.

Paul was determined to know Jesus. He never could be satisfied with simply knowing about Him. Paul was saying, "My determined purpose in life is to know Him. That is why I run the race of life."

4. Have a clear objective

In Philippians 3:13, the apostle said, "But one thing I do. . . ." He didn't say, "These fourteen things I dabble with." Paul had one purpose, one overarching goal that shone out of his eyes as he looked at the remaining years of his life. He was extremely focused.

David had the same concept when he wrote,

> One thing I ask from the Lord, this only do I seek: that I may dwell in the house of the Lord all the days of my life, to gaze on the beauty of the Lord and to seek him in his temple. (Psalm 27:4 NIV)

One thing. Do you know what that "one thing" is in your life?

One day Jesus went to Bethany to visit His friends, Mary and Martha. I would imagine that Martha was a terrific cook and that Jesus and men liked to pop in now and then for a meal. Like most men, they probably showed up unannounced, saying, "Hey, Martha, what's for dinner tonight? Do you have any extra? Throw another bone in the soup. We're hungry!"

It's also easy to imagine the Lord and the disciples relaxing in the living room while Martha runs into the kitchen to create something special for dinner. It wouldn't be like her to put out some crackers and cheese or heat up leftovers. She would want to whip up a feast fit for a king (which only makes sense, since He *is* a King).

On one such occasion, she was frantically working away in the kitchen, growing more frustrated by the minute because she needed some help. Glancing out into the front room, she noticed her sister, Mary. And what was Mary doing? Prepping the food? Setting the table? Plating the meal?

No, she was seated at Jesus' feet, completely absorbed in every word He was speaking.

Martha thought to herself, *What's wrong with this picture? This just isn't right! She should be in here slaving away with me.* So in frustration, she strides out of the kitchen (probably wiping her hands on a dishtowel). Upset, agitated, and angry, she basically says, "Lord, tell my sister to come help me."

Jesus looks at Martha and says, in essence, "Now Martha, you're upset over all of these details, but there is really only *one thing* worth being concerned about. Mary has discovered it, and I won't take it from her. I appreciate all you do, Martha, but there is a time and a place for everything. And Mary understands that this is a time to listen to My words. And you should understand the same thing. I value your work, Martha, but what I want is your heart."

Mary, like David the psalmist and Paul the apostle, was focused on one thing.

There are so many diversions that can distract or confuse us in the race of life. Periodically, you and I ought to take the time to sit ourselves down and ask ourselves questions like these: *What must I not do? What could I do? What must I do?*

The answer to that triplet of questions might surprise you. You may find that instead of doing what you must do, you're merely doing what you could do—or even what you must not do.

What must I not *do?* Obviously, we must not do those things that are sin. As we noted earlier, Hebrews says, "Let us throw off everything that hinders and the sin that so easily entangles . . ." (Hebrews 12:1, NIV). In other words, get rid of anything that slows you down, trips you up, dulls your spiritual appetite, or becomes detrimental to your walk with God. These things are sin for you, and you must not do them.

What could *I do?* I could do any number of things. I could involve myself with a million details that would keep me occupied and busy for every waking hour. I recently heard about a man who was unemployed for over two years, all the while, taking care of his "Farmville" virtual farm on a computer all day. At ten o'clock every day, no matter what he was doing, he would break off to go feed his virtual chickens!

Obviously, that is a total waste of time. The truth is, however, we can involve ourselves in many good, useful, and worthwhile things that are, nevertheless, *not the main thing*. Sometimes we spin our wheels like Martha—busy, busy, busy, but missing the main thing—the thing for which we were created and placed here on the earth. As someone has so wisely said, the good is often the enemy of the best, and the greatest danger in life is permitting the "urgent" things to crowd out the truly important things.

What must *I do?* The main thing is to keep the main thing the main thing. And what is the main thing? It is knowing God and walking with Him. Paul understood that, and it's true for every one of us. Cultivating our relationship with the living God is that one thing we must do!

5. Don't look back in the race of life

Anyone who has ever run a race understands this, especially when you're getting close to that finish line. Resist every temptation to steal a glance over your shoulder to see how your opponent is doing. Why? Because if you do, you'll break your stride and possibly lose the race. You need to keep looking forward. You need to focus on that tape at the finish line.

Paul underscores this in Philippians 3:13 when he says, "Forgetting those things which are behind. . . ." To forget doesn't mean to fail to remember. *It means to no longer be influenced or affected by that memory.*

Sometimes we're tripped up—or even crippled—when we try to live in our past. That's no way to run a race! We have a much better shot at finishing strong in our race if we can put our past behind us.

As we entered into a new year, I read in the newspaper about a new tradition someone is trying to start at the annual Times Square festivities in New York City. Some people brought out a giant shredder, and everyone was invited to shred those things they no longer wanted in their lives. Many people responded to that invitation. They brought unpaid bills, bad medical reports from the doctor, pictures of ex-boyfriends or girlfriends, medical records, and on and on it went.

The article described one woman who fed a photo of her ex-fiancé (with his new girlfriend) into the industrial-sized machine, and said, "I feel liberated!" Another lady, visiting from Ecuador, seized the opportunity to banish her unpleasant thoughts, her high cholesterol, her blood pressure, and her bills.

I will admit that it's great symbolism and a nice sentiment, but it's a funny thing about bills. You can shred them, but they'll keep coming. Nice, fresh, new ones will continue to land in your mailbox, because the bills still need to be paid. And though you might grind your medical records to powder, those medical issues still will be on the table. You might feed an old photograph into the shredder, but the broken shards of an old relationship—the hurts, failures, and regrets—really don't go away.

But here's the good news for those of us who have put their faith in Jesus Christ. We really can put our past behind us. How do we do it? By receiving God's forgiveness of our sins. The fact is, to effectively forget the past, I must first be *forgiven* of it. There is no forgetting without forgiveness.

The Bible says, "If we confess our sins, He is faithful and just to

forgive us our sins and to cleanse us from all unrighteousness"
(1 John 1:9). Scripture tells us that God forgives our sins and *forgets*
them—and we must do the same. God promises in Hebrews 10:17,
"Their sins and their lawless deeds I will remember no more." God
is saying, in essence, "I will not hold these sins and transgressions
against you any longer. Your sins are now in the past."

For this reason, we should not choose to remember what God
has chosen to forget! Our God has a big eraser, and He knows how
to use it.

"Fine, Greg," someone might say, "I'm glad God can forget things.
But I have a hard time with that. What am I supposed to do when
those hurtful memories keep coming back?"

The only answer I can give to that is, "Just do what you need
to do." Forgive yourself and forgive others, even if you don't feel
like it. For instance, if I see somebody walking toward me who
has wounded me in the past, should I be mean and harsh toward
that person? Should I be cold and hostile? No, I should be loving—
whether I feel like it or not. I should love that individual in obedience to the Word of God. And if I don't *feel* forgiving or forgiven,
I should act as though I am forgiving and forgiven.

I'm not talking about mind over matter here; I'm talking about
obedience over feelings.

I make the declaration, "I have been forgiven, and God has forgotten my sin." But then the devil whispers in my ear, *"Oh no, you're
not getting off so easy. You're a miserable failure. You sinned, and you
know you did."*

But wait a second here!

Do I have to listen to that? No, I don't! I'm under no obligation to
listen to that destructive voice. (It's not for nothing that Revelation
12:10 calls Satan "the accuser of our brethren.") God has said that
He has forgiven and forgotten your sin. So why do you need to relive
it again and again and again? That's part of what Paul means when
he speaks of "forgetting those things which are behind and reaching forward to those things which are ahead." Jesus said something
similar: "No one who puts a hand to the plow and looks back is fit

for service in the kingdom of God" (Luke 9:62 NIV).

But not only should you forget past failures, you should also forget past *successes*. At different points in our lives, you and I may find ourselves tempted to drag out our old scrapbooks and press clippings, or we find ourselves living in the so-called "glory days" of our past. The fact is, successes are often harder for people to get over than failures. Somewhere I heard it said, "Self-satisfaction is the death of progress."

So don't live in your past. "Well," you say, "I remember when God did thus and so. Those were great days!"

Well and good. Thank Him for that encounter, that miracle, that divine intervention. But now . . . what does the Lord want to do in your life *today*?

6. Press on, even when the way is hard

In Philippians 3:13, Paul says, "I press toward the goal for the prize of the upward call of God in Christ Jesus."

Paul was picturing an athlete exerting himself—going all out. The Greek word for "press" is *agonizo*, from which we get our words "agony" and "agonize." This is a term that points to strong exertion, as with a runner heading into the final stretch of his race. Every muscle is straining, pain racks his body, his lungs are on fire, but he can see the ribbon up ahead. He's saying, "Yeah, it hurts, but I know I'm going to finish! I'm going to complete this race of life!"

As Paul was bidding farewell to the elders at Ephesus, knowing that he never would see their faces again this side of heaven, he told them that he knew very well that tribulations and suffering awaited him on the road ahead. Then he added, "But none of these things move me; nor do I count my life dear to myself, so that I may finish my race with joy . . . " (Acts 20:24).

You see, it's not enough just to run the race, or even to run the race well. You must finish the race, and finish it with joy.

Wherever you are in your race today, refocus your eyes on Jesus and the race He has set before you. It's not enough for you to run well six out of ten laps, or even nine out of ten laps.

You need to finish well.
And that's where you'll find the joy.

RUNNING UP A MOUNTAIN

Caleb is one of the unsung heroes of the Bible. He stands as a shining example of one who never lost his edge spiritually. He was faithful to the very end. He himself said at age eighty-five, "I am as strong this day as on the day that Moses sent me; just as my strength was then, so now is my strength for war, both for going out and coming in" (Joshua 14:11).

Let's try to identify where he got this true grit, this spiritual *chutzpah* to live so strong for so long. His story is in Joshua 14. At that point in the history of God's people, the Israelites had finally made it to the long-awaited Promised Land, and Joshua was dispersing portions of it to the various tribes. Caleb suddenly spoke up, saying,

> "You know the word which the Lord said to Moses the man of God concerning you and me in Kadesh Barnea. I was forty years old when Moses the servant of the Lord sent me from Kadesh Barnea to spy out the land, and I brought back word to him as it was in my heart. Nevertheless my brethren who went up with me made the heart of the people melt, but I wholly followed the Lord my God."
> (Joshua 14:6–8)

In response, Joshua granted faithful Caleb what he asked: Caleb would inherit the land he had surveyed. Yet the old man proved he had not yet exhausted his courage, for then he said:

> "Here I am this day, eighty-five years old. As yet I am as strong this day as on the day that Moses sent me. . . . Now therefore, give me this mountain [the land of Hebron] of which the Lord spoke in that day; for you heard in that day how the Anakim were there, and that the cities were great and fortified. It may be that the Lord will be with me, and I shall be able to drive them out as the Lord has said." (vv. 10–12)

The other guys must have thought old Caleb was senile. Hebron was not some beautiful green pasture; it was one of the most treacherous, mountainous areas of the Promised Land. Worse, formidable adversaries, identified as the three sons of Anak, lived there. They would have to be routed before the old man could take possession. No one wanted to take them on except eighty-five-year-old Caleb, holding up that muscular old arm, saying, "Give me this mountain."

I love his boldness.

Caleb *ran* up that mountain, blowing away his adversaries. He was victorious. He had been strong all those years, and he finished well.

A Strategy for Strength—Courtesy of Caleb

Let me share some principles with you from Caleb's life that can give us this spiritual stamina we all need to run and indeed finish in the race of life.

1. Follow the Lord 100 percent

Scripture says again and again that Caleb "wholly followed the-Lord." It's in Joshua 14:8–9 and verse 14 too: Joshua blessed Caleb and gave the old man what he asked because "he wholly followed the Lord God of Israel."

This is clearly a key to Caleb's spiritual success. But what does it mean to "wholly follow the Lord"? It means that you must fully follow the Lord not halfheartedly, but completely—one hundred percent.

What does that mean? It means that you give everything to God. Many people don't do this—the way they live provides the evidence. It all starts with priorities. When crisis hits, they expect God to drop everything and get them out of the mess they are in. But when it comes to honoring Him by just going to church on Sunday, they are too busy: "I don't know if we should go to church. The weatherman said it might rain today. There is no rain out there right now, but we don't want to risk our lives and tempt the Lord. We'd better not go. How about the mall or the movies?"

The real problem here is lack of total commitment. There will always be a hundred convenient excuses to hide behind, but the fact is you will make time for what matters to you.

We see the priority problem in their resources and giving as well. They ask God to provide for them and take care of their needs. Even though He does, they don't even think about giving when the offering plate passes.

What is wrong with these pictures? Are you wholly following the Lord your God? Are you fully following Him?

Let me tell you something. If you're not, you will be picked off eventually. It's only a matter of time until you become a casualty in the race of life. You can see this in the lives of the Israelites.

Caleb mentioned a very important place in his little speech called Kadesh Barnea. Forty-five years earlier, Caleb, Joshua, and Moses, along with the children of Israel, had come to the brink of the Promised Land, a point of entry known as Kadesh Barnea.

You remember God had gloriously delivered the Israelites from their slave masters in Egypt, in answer to their prayers. He had opened up the Red Sea for them to cross through, then drowned the Egyptian army as it pursued them. When the Israelites arrived at the new land God had promised them that was flowing with milk and honey, God instructed Moses to send twelve representatives to check it out.

After forty days, the spies returned and gave their report. It happened that they had divided into two groups. The majority—ten of them—said there were these huge, walled cities and giant adversaries. They exaggerated, saying, "Next to them we felt like grasshoppers, and that's what they thought, too!" (Numbers 13:33 NLT). The consensus: there was no way they should go in.

Joshua and Caleb gave the minority report, in essence saying, "Yes, it's true there are some big obstacles there, but so what? God is bigger than any obstacles, and He will be with us. *Let's go for it.*" But the Israelites were so upset with Joshua and Caleb for suggesting this that they clamored about heading back to Egypt.

The Lord was angry with the Israelites for failing to honor Him. He had brought them that far, had done great things to deliver them, yet they didn't believe He would preserve them in the new land. So God basically declared, "Of those that have come this far, only Joshua and Caleb are going into the land. The rest of you are not going in."

In other words, those who followed the Lord wholeheartedly won the race; the others were disqualified.

I guess it's all in how you look at things.

You could say two were optimists and the others were pessimists. It is more than that. Joshua and Caleb looked at the Promised Land—remembering it was the *Promised* Land—through the eyes of faith.

I once heard the story of an American shoe salesman who was sent to a foreign country. He had been there just a week when he e-mailed the company for money to come home. They asked why. He said, "Nobody here wears shoes."

That man returned, but the company quickly sent another salesman in his place. After a couple of days, he e-mailed back, saying, "Send me all of the shoes you have. Absolutely no one here has shoes. There are unlimited opportunities!"

Caleb saw God's promise where others saw only trouble and defeat. It isn't that Caleb had great faith in God as much as he had faith in a great God. He knew God had delivered them from one enemy, and He would deliver them from others as well.

2. Don't compromise—stand your ground

How easy it would have been for Caleb to go along with the crowd, not ruffling anybody's feathers. But he knew what was right, and so he stood his ground. At the risk of being personally ostracized, he took a stand for what he knew was true. He knew he needed to be more concerned with God's approval than man's. And he was rewarded.

As you walk with the Lord, you will face many temptations to cave in to peer pressure, to do what everybody else does. I know what you're thinking: if you take a stand with your family, neighbors, or coworkers, they may ostracize you. They may mock you. They might even harm you physically. But if you're going to fully follow the Lord, then, like Caleb, you must make this principle operative in your life. Stand firm. Seek God's pleasure—no one else's.

3. Take God at His word

Caleb didn't win immediate entrance to the Promised Land. First he had to wander around with those ungrateful, complaining Israelites for forty years. They said things like, "We remember the good old days back in Egypt, where we had garlic, leeks, and onions." Now, when you read about life for the Israelites in Egypt, you don't see anything about their having great food. You read about their being miserable slaves who cried out to God, day and night, to be delivered. The Israelites conveniently forgot all of that.

Isn't it interesting how the devil helps us exaggerate our pasts when he wants to pull us back? The devil will whisper in our ears, "Remember the good old days?" *Yeah. That was good,* we think.

The devil is clever. He doesn't say, "Remember when you were so miserable that you actually considered suicide? Remember the times you were so drunk that you didn't even know where you were when you woke up? Remember when your marriage almost fell apart?" He will remind you only of the few "good times" you had in order to draw you back. He did exactly this to the Israelites, and they went right along with it—except for Caleb.

Despite the Israelites' childish clinging to fictitious memories about "good ol' Egypt," Caleb hung on to the promises of God. It didn't matter to him that he had to wait forty years. He knew God would be faithful, regardless of the time frame.

We need to do the same. Some who have been walking with us will turn away and go back to the old life. Crises will hit. Hardship falls on everyone. But like Caleb, we have to believe God's promise that we are going to make it across that finish line.

Fortunately, we don't have to do this in our own strength. Jude referred to "Him who is able to keep you from stumbling, and to present you faultless before the presence of His glory with exceeding joy" (1:24).

Scripture reminds us that the Lord is "the author and finisher of our faith" (Hebrews 12:2).

Caleb trusted God's word to him. We can do the same.

4. Long for fellowship with your God

Caleb asked for a place in the Promised Land called Hebron. There's something interesting about the name Hebron, which, in the original language, means "fellowship, love, and communion." Hebron is where Abraham met with God face-to-face and received the promise of the new land in the first place.

Here's my point: Caleb yearned for fellowship with God. While the other Israelites longed for Egypt, Caleb longed for Hebron. While the others looked back, Caleb looked forward. While others wanted to please themselves, Caleb wanted to please God. Of Caleb, Chuck Swindoll once said: "Every new sunrise introduced another reminder that his body and rocking chair weren't made for each other. While his peers were yawning, Caleb was yearning."[1]

This is an essential key to spiritual longevity. *You must always move forward.* You must always seek to grow spiritually and never look back. That's what will keep you going. You have to follow the Lord, even if your friends aren't there with you. As the song says, "Though none go with me, still I will follow." If you're living this Christian life for others' applause, you won't make it. People certainly will let you down. Circumstances will inevitably challenge you. You have to run, empowered by your love for God.

Is that why you're running the race right now?

I already told you that in high school, I ran track and field. I found a little secret back then about running faster. Whenever a pretty girl was watching, I somehow had a new burst of energy to run a bit longer and faster!

I have a better motivation for you than an attractive onlooker: the Lord himself is watching you. He is the only One for whom you need to run the race. That's what kept Caleb going. And that longing for fellowship and communion with God resulted in his finishing well. We need to apply Caleb's principles in our lives.

The author of Hebrews reminded us of this motive in running the race of life well in the twelfth chapter of the book:

> Therefore we also, since we are surrounded by so great a cloud of witnesses, let us lay aside every weight, and the sin which so easily ensnares us, and let us run with endurance the race that is set before us, looking unto Jesus, the author and finisher of our faith, who for the joy that was set before Him endured the cross, despising the shame, and has sat down at the right hand of the throne of God. (Hebrews 12:1–2)

Another Who Finished Well

Let me share with you a contemporary story about a man who operated on these principles.

On September 11, 2001, flight attendant Al Marchand hugged his wife, Rebecca, in Boston's Logan Airport and told her he loved her. He was heading off to a plane bound for Los Angeles.

Marchand, forty-four, had retired from the police force only eight months prior and landed a new job with United Airlines. Rebecca had questioned a career change that pulled him away from the family, but Al insisted that God wanted him to take the job for a reason. Sixty-four minutes after takeoff, Al Marchand's plane, flight 175, plowed into the World Trade Center's South Tower.

Rebecca said she knew it wasn't a mistake that her husband was on flight 175, calling it a lifetime of planning on God's part.

Just four years earlier, Al Marchand had first heard about having a personal relationship with God—at a pub. When he wasn't working as a policeman, he moonlighted as a brewer. The people who cleaned the pub listened to my messages on tape while they worked.

Al tried to avoid hearing the tapes, but some of what I was saying caught his ear anyway. Eventually Al left his office door open just a bit so he could hear more.

Al enjoyed a lively drinking relationship with his girlfriend, Rebecca, and they visited club after club every night. But when Rebecca found Jesus, she gave Al an ultimatum: "Follow Jesus with me, or let me go." Al resisted, but the words he heard me say haunted him, and he found himself visiting a church the next weekend. A week later, he gave his life to Jesus. A week after that, he and Rebecca were married.

The couple became enthusiastic believers. Al made a point of talking about Jesus with everyone he met. He loved to share this life-giving relationship.

Then Al received a new call from God, and it beckoned from an Internet advertisement: "Become a flight attendant." Al was certain he had found God's plan for his life, seeing it as an opportunity to share the gospel if ever there was a time when his fellow crew members and passengers were facing an emergency on board.

Then came September 11.

The night before, he had been asked to take the place of another flight attendant who had become ill. For her part, Rebecca believes Al was supposed to be on that fatal flight and that her husband shared the gospel with other passengers.

Though now in heaven, Al is still impacting people as a result of his relationship with Jesus.

When you read a story like that, you say, "How tragic." On one hand, it is. But on the other hand, I think it's glorious! I am confident that Al did what he loved to do: share the gospel. Who knows how many came into eternity as a result of his being in the right place at the right time to finish the course that God had set for him?

This man finished well. We need to do the same.

Kept, Preserved, Protected

Though you are the only person who can run your spiritual race, you don't have to run alone. The Bible says that God will keep you and preserve you. Jude addressed his letter "to those who are called, sanctified by God the Father, and preserved in Jesus Christ" (v. 1).

How secure is that? The original language uses the perfect tense. The nearest equivalent of that is "continually kept by Jesus Christ." It is a continuing result of a past action.

You need to know that whatever difficulties you face today as a believer, you are being watched over and protected by Christ. God will always protect His own, because He loves us.

Even we careless humans don't lose something we love. We keep our eyes on it. If I have a cheap pair of sunglasses, I may not be all that concerned about their whereabouts. But if I have a more expensive pair, I will tend to know where they are. We protect that which is dear to us.

Look at it this way: you are loved by God. He's going to protect His investment. Imagine: if it were not for God's intervention on our behalf, every one of us would experience vapor lock on the spot. None of us would make it across the finish line.

Fortunately for all of us, Jesus Christ is in heaven, loving, preserving, and interceding for us before the Father. Hebrews 7:25 says, "He is able to save completely those who come to God through him, because he always lives to intercede for them" (NIV). We are preserved, protected, and kept by the power of God. That is good—no, great—news!

What is our part in this powerful equation? The Bible says we are to "keep [ourselves] in the love of God" (Jude 1:21). Is that a contradiction? On one hand, the Bible says God will keep us. On the other hand, it says we need to keep ourselves. A contradiction? No, not at all. These two verses complement one another. They merely show us there is God's part, and then there is ours. We don't keep ourselves saved, but we can keep ourselves safe.

That is why Jude reminded us to keep ourselves in the love of God. God's love is unconditional. It is undeserved. But we are capable of stepping out of harmony with His love. Jude was saying to keep ourselves away from all that is spiritually destructive. In other words, consciously avoid any influence that would violate God's love and bring sorrow to His heart. Maintain a position where God can actively show His love to you. Keep yourself in the love of God.

We all know of situations, activities, and places where we would find ourselves more vulnerable to the devil's enticements. Now that we have been delivered from his power, we don't want to put ourselves into a position of vulnerability again, right?

Why do I bring this up? Because Scripture tells us that "some will turn away from the faith, giving attention to deluding and seducing spirits and doctrines that demons teach" (1 Timothy 4:1 AMP). In these critical days, the devil is walking about "like a roaring lion," looking for people he can pull down (see 1 Peter 5:8).

The Book of Hebrews warns us of the perils of throwing in the towel and turning back spiritually. Hebrews 3:12 says, "Beware, brethren, lest there be in any of you an evil heart of unbelief in departing from the living God." Notice the writer did not direct this admonition to nonbelievers. He said, "Beware, brothers." Christian, be careful—you can depart from the living God.

Don't Stop Short of the Goal

Then the writer added, "[So] exhort one another daily, while it is called 'Today,' lest any of you be hardened through the deceitfulness of sin. For we have become partakers of Christ if we hold the beginning of our confidence steadfast to the end" (Hebrews 3:13–14).

Did you catch that? You become a partaker of Christ if you hold your confidence all the way to the end.

In other words, you have to cross the finish line.

It's not enough to do well for the first five years or the next twenty. You have to cross the finish line in order to finish well.

That is why Paul, when he was leaving the elders of Ephesus, said,

> "None of these things [such as the threat of imprisonment] move me; nor do I count my life dear to myself, so that I may finish my race with joy, and the ministry which I received from the Lord Jesus, to testify to the gospel of the grace of God." (Acts 20:24)

My question to you is this: are you doing what God has called you to do? Are you finishing the course? Like Caleb, like Al, let's keep moving forward spiritually, maintaining our love for God, taking Him at His word, seeking His approval alone. If indeed we wholly follow Him, we will, without a doubt, finish well.

That's what we all should be hoping for right now.

This is not the time for slowing down.

This is not the time for easing up.

This is not the time for resting on your laurels.

This is the time to pour it on!

Keep yourself in the love of God. Pick up the pace!

WALK LIKE A MAN

I'm glad the Bible not only compares the Christian life to running a race, but also to walking a walk.

Isaiah 40:31 pulls it together:

> But those who wait upon the Lord
> Shall renew their strength;
> They shall mount up with wings like eagles,
> They shall run and not be weary,
> They shall walk and not faint.

What we see here are different levels of movement, but the same strength in God.

In Genesis we read about a man who walked—not ran—with God. In his story we will discover more secrets for winning the spiritual race of life. We will discover how we can learn to endure—and not do what athletes call "bonking." That's when you are running and just don't feel as though you can go any farther. It's as if you have hit a wall.

Certainly this happens in the spiritual race. We think, *I can't make it another inch. I'm worn out. I'm stopping here.* But we need to learn how to press on and endure, because in our relationship with God, we're in it for the long haul. We want to finish this race well. It is more than a journey of feeling; it is a journey of faith.

The Longest Day

Let's look at the story of a man who took that journey. Talk about taking a long walk: this man's was the longest possible. It lasted three hundred years. His name was Enoch. He walked with God for—that's right—three centuries.

It's interesting how in the whole Bible, only five passages refer to Enoch. One is in Hebrews 11: "By faith Enoch was taken away so that he did not see death, 'and was not found, because God had taken him'; for before he was taken he had this testimony, that he pleased God" (v. 5).

Though the Bible contains little information about Enoch, what we do have is significant. His story appears in Genesis 5:21–24:

> Enoch lived sixty-five years, and begot Methuselah. After he begot Methuselah, Enoch walked with God three hundred years, and had sons and daughters. So all the days of Enoch were three hundred and sixty-five years. And Enoch walked with God; and he was not, for God took him.

It's a short passage of Scripture for such an interesting character. Understand that Enoch lived in a very dark time in human history. It was just before God's judgment, which would come in a great flood. At this time, the twin sins of violence and sexual perversion characterized mankind. Man was so wicked that God essentially said, "I am sorry that I even made him because the thoughts and intents of his heart are wicked continually" (see Genesis 6:6). Judgment was on its way to cleanse the earth. It was a miserable era in the history of our world.

In the midst of all of this stood a man who walked with God. This was no small feat. The people of this day were largely wicked, and Enoch walked alone with his God. Consider the spiritual and moral climate he confronted—and overcame—every day.

It's clear Enoch was a godly man, but what about him so touched God that He "took" him so he would not see death? Certainly he was a man of passions like all other humans. He didn't live in a monastery. Yet he managed to walk with God for three hundred years in an extremely wicked time in human history. How? He wasn't perfect, but he gave us a model to live by.

How to Finish the Race, by Enoch

I want to identify for you three principles of Enoch's life. These are three keys that will help us finish the race as winners, not losers.

1. Enoch walked with God

In short, Enoch continued on. "Walking" speaks of making progress. You are headed toward a destination, and you are moving toward it, slowly but surely. There is no mention of stopping or giving up.

The idea of walking with God appears constantly in the Bible. Some examples:

- "Therefore, as you received Christ Jesus the Lord, so walk in him, rooted and built up in him and established in the faith." (Colossians 2:6–7 ESV)
- "Walk in the Spirit, and you shall not fulfill the lust of the flesh." (Galatians 5:16)
- "Let us walk properly as in the daytime, not in . . . sexual immorality and sensuality, not in quarreling and jealousy." (Romans 13:13 ESV)
- "And walk in love, as Christ loved us and gave himself up for us, a fragrant offering and sacrifice to God." (Ephesians 5:2 ESV)

Over and over again, the Bible tells us to walk with God, walk in love, and walk in the light. What does it mean practically to "walk with God"? Let me tell you what it *doesn't* mean: it is not merely living by rules, regulations, and daily resolutions that you quickly break. It's more than that—much more.

Malachi 2:6 gives us God's description of one who walks with Him: "True instruction was in his mouth, and no wrong was found on his lips. He walked with me in peace and uprightness, and he turned many from iniquity" (ESV).

Think about this: God himself says, "True instruction was in his mouth. . . . He walked . . . in peace and uprightness, and he turned many away from iniquity."

Let me ask you: are you walking with God?

What does it mean for us to be walking with God? Let's take a look at some of the elements.

Walk as a single unit. Amos 3:3 is another key verse for unlocking the principles of walking with God. It's a short passage, but it's action-packed: "Can two walk together, unless they are agreed?" All sorts of subtle nuances and shades of meaning from the original language help us to flesh out what it means to walk with God. The original meaning spoke of God and man walking as a single unit, as though they were one.

We could compare it to riding a tandem bicycle. Let's say that you and I went out for a ride. You were in the front, pedaling away. I was in the back, hitting the brakes. Is that going to help you? No, it's going to slow you down and impede your performance. We need to ride in tandem. We need to ride with the same rhythm and pacing so we can make progress. The two of us together can go even faster than one can.

We could compare it with rowing a boat. If everybody is rowing a large boat, people are paddling on the left and the right, and somebody is in the back, barking out the commands. If one guy in the back is digging his paddle in on the wrong side, it's going to impede the performance of the vessel.

We could compare it to singing. When we all sing together, the sound is beautiful. But there's always someone who has no rhythm or pitch whatsoever. He sings out of harmony, and people cringe (because you know people who are off-key usually sing louder than everyone else!). The beauty of the song is marred by one person's jarring notes.

The idea is to get into harmony with God. You are moving in tandem with God. You are paddling in the direction God wants you to take. You are singing in harmony with Him.

Live in communion with God. When that happens, the Christian life starts firing on all cylinders. That's also the secret to getting prayers answered. How many times have you been frustrated because you pray consistently for something, yet your prayers seem to reach only to the ceiling? God never seems to answer your prayers in the affirmative. Why? Maybe because you are praying outside of His will. Maybe you are praying for something God doesn't want you to have.

We need to tap into Jesus' promise in John 15: "If you abide in Me, and My words abide in you, you will ask what you desire, and it shall be done for you" (v. 7). Another translation says, "If you maintain a living communion with me and my words are at home with you, you can ask at once for yourself whatever your heart desires and it is yours" (WET).

I really like that translation. It makes the conditions clear: "If you maintain a living communion with me and my words are at home with you...." When you live in communion with God, your desires will change. So will your prayers! You'll get into sync with the will of God. You will discover the important truth that prayer is not getting Him to do what you want Him to do; prayer is getting you to do what God wants you to do. It's not bending God your way; it's bending you God's way. It's not getting your will in heaven; it's getting God's will on earth.

If you want to see your prayers answered in the affirmative, you need to get into harmony with God. Or, as we have said, you need to be like Enoch and walk with God.

Keep your appointment with God. Amos 3:3 is also translated, "Do two men walk together except they make an appointment...?" (AMP). The original language implies that meaning: you have an appointment with God.

Some people are late for everything. One guy I know, no matter when I tell him to be somewhere, is always fifteen to twenty minutes late. I try to help him; I tell him to leave early because the last time (and the time before) he was late. Nothing changes. He is consistently inconsistent.

It's one thing to be late for an appointment with a friend. It's another thing to be late for an appointment with God himself.

Adam had an appointment with God every day. After the sun set, the Lord God and Adam met and conversed. One day Adam didn't show up for his appointment. Why? Because he had sinned. He was hiding. The Lord God walked through the garden "in the cool of the day," asking, "Where are you?" (Genesis 3:8–9).

I wonder if the Lord is saying that to some of us: "Where are you? I wanted to speak with you this morning. You didn't have time for Me. You had time for newspapers . . . for telephone calls . . . for TV . . . for e-mails. You had no time for prayer. You had no time for Bible study. I wanted to talk to you at lunch, but your prayer was so fast. Later on I wanted to speak to you, but you didn't have the antenna up. Where are you? We had an appointment."

Make time for God each and every day.

Pool your resources. Again, this is the implication of the original text in Amos 3:3. Think of it this way: Maybe you want to start a business, but you don't have investment capital. You call a friend and ask him to go into business with you. If you do this together, the business is a go. You draw up a contract and get started.

God says He wants to go into business with you, but He needs you to bring your resources to the table. If you do that, He will bring His as well. Do you understand what a great deal this is? This is like Bill Gates wanting to go into business with someone who has only a dollar to invest.

Bill says, "We will be equal partners."

You say, "That sounds good."

"How much do you have?"

"Umm . . . one hundred pennies."

"Okay, so you have one dollar. Put it on the table."

"There it is, Mr. Gates. How much do you have?"

"Billions. I may be worth a billion dollars more than I was an hour ago. I am the richest man in the world. And when we go into business together, I will bring my resources, and you bring yours."

Sound like a good deal?

God essentially says, "I want to go into business with you. Let's pool our resources. What do you have?"

"Well . . . I have my talents. They aren't many, but here they are."

"What else do you have?"

"I have my life."

"What else do you have?"

"I have these resources and—a few problems."

"Put it all there. Is that it?"

"That's it."

"Let me bring all of My power and glory and resources to this as well, and let's go into business together."

Walking in harmony with God, keeping your appointment with God, and pooling your resources with God are what it means to walk with God.

I ask you today: are you walking with God?

Oh, by the way . . . late bloomers are welcome. Exactly when did Enoch start walking with God? Look at Genesis 5:21–22: "Enoch lived sixty-five years, and begot Methuselah. After he begot Methuselah, Enoch walked with God three hundred years. . . ." It appears that the birth of Methuselah brought about the conversion of Enoch. That is when his walk with God began.

This should give incredible hope to late bloomers. There are a lot of them. For instance, we all know Ronald Reagan was sixty-nine years old when he was elected president of the United States, and he was seventy-seven when he left office. That's blooming late!

I heard about a late bloomer named Jim Ward. He was one of the best-known triathletes in the world. What's unusual about Jim is that he started triathlons at the age of sixty-eight. He recently died at the age of eighty-three—five miles into a bike race! It was Jim's goal to complete the Ironman Triathlon as an octogenarian, and he almost made it.

Do you know what the Ironman is? It's a contest held in Hawaii once a year. The challenge includes these sports in this order: a 2.4-hour swim in the ocean; a 112-mile bicycle race; and a 26.2-mile run. You don't do these over a week. You do them in a seventeen-hour span, one right after the other.

Jim Ward was a ten-time triathlete world champion in his age group. In his seventies, he became the oldest athlete to finish the Ironman. He was planning on doing the same in his eighties.

He was quoted as saying, "I'm just not going to quit." It reminds me of Caleb who said, at age eighty-five, "Give me this mountain." It reminds me of Enoch, who hung in there for three hundred years. Enoch didn't start walking with God until Methuselah, his son, was born. The name Methuselah has a profound meaning: "When he is dead, it shall be sent."

God revealed to Enoch, because he walked with the Lord, that when the child Methuselah died, judgment would come upon the earth—He would send it. This was fair warning to Enoch. In other words, "Neither you nor your son will face this judgment. I will initiate it after you both are gone."

That speaks volumes about the grace of God.

As we look at our world today, we might wonder why the Lord hasn't come back and established His kingdom. Why does He allow wicked people to prosper? God's answer is in 2 Peter 3:

> Knowing this first: that scoffers will come in the last days, walking according to their own lusts, and saying, "Where is the promise of His coming? For since the fathers fell asleep [the beginning of time], all things continue as they were from the beginning of creation." . . . With the Lord, one day is as a thousand years, and a thousand years as one day. The Lord is not slack concerning His promise, as some count slackness, but is longsuffering toward us, not willing that any should perish but that all should come to repentance. (vv. 3–4, 8–9)

God has not yet brought judgment upon the earth because He is waiting for more people to believe. He wants more people to come into His kingdom.

Imagine being Enoch. You had this child, Methuselah. You knew that when he died, judgment would come. Every time that kid got the sniffles, you would think, *Oh, man, this is it. Judgment's coming!*

What would this do to you practically? It would cause you always to be ready. You would live in recognition of the temporary nature of life on earth and the nearness of eternity. That is exactly what Methuselah did. It was his birth that got Enoch right with the Lord.

2. Enoch was well-pleasing to God

Jesus said He always did the things that are pleasing to God (see John 5:30). Can you imagine making such a statement—that you always please God? I certainly couldn't claim that. Neither could you. Yet Hebrews 11:5 says, Enoch "had this testimony, that he pleased God."

Enoch was a man who walked with God and lived a life that was well-pleasing to Him. What are those things that God specifically says are pleasing to Him? Let's take a look.

• *Patient endurance.* First Peter 2:19–20 says,

> For God is pleased with you when you do what you know is right and patiently endure unfair treatment. Of course, you get no credit for being patient if you are beaten for doing wrong. But if you suffer for doing good and endure it patiently, God is pleased with you. (NLT)

Have you ever been misrepresented? Have you ever been mistreated? Has anyone ever told a lie about you, and you just endured it? That pleases God. You need to know that.

• *Worship and helping others.* Hebrews 13:15–16 says,

> Therefore by Him let us continually offer the sacrifice of praise to God, that is, the fruit of our lips, giving thanks to His name. But do not forget to do good and to share, for with such sacrifices God is well pleased.

When you engage your heart and lift up your voice to praise the name of the Lord, it pleases Him. Notice that this verse says it is the "sacrifice of praise." Sometimes offering our praise to God is indeed a sacrifice. We may not be in the mood because we're distracted or having trouble of some kind. But that is the *best* time to worship God—not because we necessarily feel like it, but because He is worthy.

The Bible says "Oh, give thanks to the Lord, for He is good! For His mercy endures forever" (1 Chronicles 16:34). That verse doesn't say, "Give thanks to the Lord when you feel good," but rather because He *is* good.

• *Giving to the work of the kingdom of God.* In Philippians 4:17–18 Paul wrote,

Not that I desire your gifts; what I desire is that more be credited to your account. I have received full payment and have more than enough. I am amply supplied, now that I have received from Epaphroditus the gifts you sent. They are a fragrant offering, an acceptable sacrifice, pleasing to God. (NIV)

Paul was saying to those believers, "This gift you sent for the work of the kingdom—I know it was hard. I know you sacrificed. But this pleases God."

When you invest your financial resources into the work of the kingdom, you delight the Lord. When you lift your voice in praise, you honor the Lord. When you are mistreated but just take it without becoming bitter or retaliating, you please God. These instructions are so clear that we have no excuse for not following them.

Enoch walked with God. He was well-pleasing to God.

3. Enoch had a witness for God

Hebrews 11:5 says, "Enoch was taken away so that he did not see death, 'and was not found, because God had taken him'; for before he was taken he had this testimony, that he pleased God."

Do you have a good testimony? Are you being an effective witness? When you get down to it, every Christian is a witness in some way, shape, or form. Even if you never open your lips and speak about your faith, you have a testimony. The question is, is that testimony a good one, or is it a poor one?

Believe me, people do say something about you and your faith after observing you. It's up to you to affect what they say.

When you walk with God and Jesus overflows from you and someone asks, "What makes you different? What makes you joyful and peaceful? I want to know more," you can say, "Let me tell you about my faith in Jesus Christ." What a glorious thing that is. As Augustine once said, "Preach the gospel, and when necessary, use words."

Maybe sometimes we aren't good witnesses because we don't

walk with God, or enjoy fellowship and communion with Him. We don't move in harmony, in tandem, with Him. God wants to change us so we will be pleasing to Him and be witnesses for Him.

What is the end result of our good testimony and witness? Genesis 5:24 says, "Enoch walked with God; and he was not, for God took him." The phrase "took him" could be translated "carried over or across." God carried Enoch over death.

The Bible says, "It is appointed for men to die once, but after this the judgment" (Hebrews 9:27). In the case of Enoch, God made an exception and took him straight to heaven. He picked him off of one shore and put him on the other.

The fact of the matter is that when you walk with God on earth, you also will walk with Him in heaven. Revelation 3:4 says, "They will walk with me, dressed in white" (NIV). Enoch is representative of those believers who will not die, but will be caught up to heaven, as mentioned in 1 Corinthians 15:51–52, where Paul said, "I tell you a mystery. We shall not all sleep [die], but we shall all be changed— in a moment, in the twinkling of an eye . . ." (ESV).

Let me ask you this: if the Lord were to come back today, would He take you along? He took Enoch. Why? Enoch walked with God. He was well-pleasing to God. He was a witness for God.

Keep Your Eyes on the Prize

We see from Enoch's life that in the spiritual race, speed doesn't matter nearly as much as distance does. Sure, run fast if you want, but definitely run (or walk) *long*. In other words, finish the race. That is the objective. Paul said as much in Philippians 3:12–14:

> Not that I have already attained, or am already perfected; but I press on, that I may lay hold of that for which Christ Jesus has also laid hold of me. Brethren, I do not count myself to have apprehended; but one thing I do, forgetting those things which are behind and reaching forward to those things which are ahead, I press toward the goal for the prize of the upward call of God in Christ Jesus. (NIV)

Nowhere did Paul say to sprint. He said to keep pressing on.

Hang in there, and complete the course you have begun.

Paul concluded that statement by saying, "All of us, then, who are mature should take such a view of things. And if on some point you think differently, that too God will make clear to you" (Philippians 3:15 NIV). In other words, Paul was saying that if we want to grow up spiritually, we need to pace ourselves—because we're in this for the long haul.

Are you walking with God? Are you well-pleasing to Him and a consistent witness for Him? God wants you to come into harmony with Him. He wants to reveal His plan and purposes to you. He wants you to walk with Him—even if it is for less than three hundred years.

By imitating Enoch, you can guarantee that you'll survive the long haul and finish well.

You will win the race.

TRIPPING UP IN THE RACE OF LIFE

People often ask what my favorite Bible passage is, and I have to say that's a tough call. But if you allow me to say what some of my favorite passages are, one comes to mind quickly:

> "For I know the thoughts that I think toward you, says the Lord, thoughts of peace and not of evil, to give you a future and a hope. Then you will call upon Me and go and pray to Me, and I will listen to you." (Jeremiah 29:11–12)

Isn't that encouraging?

It's true. God loves you. God has a good plan for you. God has a future and a hope for you.

What's more, God wants to use you. He wants you to make your mark in some way. You may be known to millions, thousands, hundreds, or maybe only a handful, but God has a purpose for your life. You are significant.

The question is, do you want to reach your potential as a Christian? Do you want to cross the finish line in the spiritual race, or are you going to self-destruct? You might be surprised to know that you have everything to say about that. In the spiritual race, we can see many who started with such great promise but somehow crashed and burned.

Paul wrote to the believers in Galatians 5:7, "You were running a good race. Who cut in on you to keep you from obeying the truth?" (NIV). We can all do better in this race of life. Much better.

The Bible offers us a story of a man who had incredible potential, but largely wasted it. God gave him amazing physical strength, and this man had God's blessing and anointing on his life. The fact is that he could have been one of the greatest leaders in the history of Israel.

Instead, his life became a proverb—an example of how *not* to live. His was a life of squandered resources and dissipated potential and ability. He threw it all away because of some subtle but serious mistakes—something we're all capable of doing. His name was Samson, and this is his story.

Long on Hair, Short on Sense

The life of Samson illustrates the ancient truth that a good beginning doesn't necessarily guarantee a good ending. That is why Solomon wrote in Ecclesiastes 7:8, "The end of a matter is better than its beginning . . ." (NIV). American poet Henry Wadsworth Longfellow said, "Great is the art of beginning, but greater is the art of ending."[1]

When we think of Samson, our minds immediately race to his compromised involvement with the wicked Delilah. The truth is a number of smaller compromises ultimately led to his fall with that woman.

It's a fact that seemingly insignificant choices can create disaster and destruction. Remember the horrific explosion of the Space Shuttle, *Challenger,* in January 1986? You might have been watching the takeoff live on television when the shuttle exploded on its ascent.

NASA's extensive research finally concluded that the explosion was the result of a faulty O-ring. When this ring failed to seal in hot gases, they escaped, caught fire, and blew up the spacecraft. This incredible vessel, on which we had spent millions of dollars, completely self-destructed—along with its precious human cargo—because of something as small and seemingly insignificant as a defective, ten-dollar O-ring.

In the same way, it's the little things in life that often bring us down. This is certainly what happened with Samson. He had all the potential to be someone great for God and lead the people of Israel out of their backslidden state.

Humanly speaking, no one was stronger than Samson. He also had spiritual sharpness and mental ability. An angel of the Lord predicted of Samson before he was born, "He shall begin to deliver Israel out of the hand of the Philistines" (Judges 13:5).

Note the word "begin."

The angel didn't say Samson would *complete* the task. God knew he would never reach his full potential.

As in Enoch's day, this was a dark era in Israel's history. The Bible says that in the time prior to Samson's ascent, "Israel did evil in the eyes of the Lord" (Judges 13:1), and He consequently turned them over to their enemies, the Philistines. God's people did what they wanted without regard for the One who made them. Then God raised up one man, Samson, to make a difference.

This is often how the Lord works. When times are especially dark, God brings forth a leader. He designates someone to turn the light on . . . someone to stand in the gap . . . someone to turn the tide—someone like you.

The angel of the Lord declared Samson was to live a life separated from the sinful compromise of Israel. He would be a Nazirite. This meant, among other things, that he would never partake of fermented drink—never come under the influence of alcohol. As well, no one could ever cut his hair. Some wrongly think Samson's strength was a result of his long hair, but the reality is that his strength came from God; the long hair symbolized his being set apart by God.

Immediate Enemies

In the beginning, it was clear that God's hand was upon Samson. Scripture tells us, "The Lord blessed him. And the Spirit of the Lord began to move upon him . . ." (Judges 13:24–25 NIV). No sooner did this happen than we find Samson marrying a Philistine woman—against the wishes of his parents, I might add. Samson's marriage led to a series of conflicts with the Philistines in which he came up victorious because of the superhuman strength God gave him. But the Philistines bore a grudge. And all was not well with God's hero. Look at Judges 16:1–3:

> Now Samson went to Gaza and saw a harlot there, and went in to her. When the Gazites were told, "Samson has come here!" they surrounded the place and lay in wait for him all night at the gate of the city. They were quiet all night, saying, "In the morning, when it is daylight, we will kill him." And Samson lay low till midnight; then he arose at midnight, took hold of the doors of the gate of the city and the two gateposts, pulled them up, bar and all, put them on his shoulders, and carried them to the top of the hill that faces Hebron.

Samson made a choice. Gaza was an enemy city with ungodly people in it. Samson was self-confident, thinking, *I've gotten myself out of messes before. I can get myself out of another if one arises.*

While Samson spent time with the prostitute, his enemies found out that the famous strongman was in their little city. They thought to themselves, *We're going to take this guy out once and for all. We've had enough of him.* Then they figured, *Why do it at night? Let's wait until the sunrise.*

They posted a guard by the house and set an ambush. His enemies went to sleep that night, thinking that annihilating their enemy would be like shooting fish in a barrel.

But around midnight, Samson decided to skip town. He walked to the gates of the city and looked at them for a minute. We know from archaeological studies that these massive gates were covered with studded nails as well as metal to make them fireproof. They weighed thousands of pounds.

To any normal man, this would have been an insurmountable obstacle. For Samson, it was a mere inconvenience. The mighty judge of Israel reached down and ripped them out of their foundation and then toted them along as he left town. It would have been enough to lift them up and simply drop them. But I guess old

Samson decided to get a little cardiovascular with his weight training that day as he carried these incredibly heavy gates some twenty miles from where he found them.

Needless to say, when his enemies woke and saw that, no one went after him. Samson was far too intimidating. The incredible strength God had given him made him a formidable opponent, to say the least.

This is what makes the story tragic. Samson had power without purity. He had strength without self-control.

God extended His grace to Samson for twenty long years, and Samson experienced the thrill of victory time after time. Whenever his enemies came against him, he handily destroyed them. On one occasion he killed one thousand Philistines with a donkey's jawbone that he randomly picked up. They just couldn't stop this man who was so blessed and empowered by God himself. He seemed indestructible.

A Fatal Flaw

After observing Samson's weakness for sexual lust, the Philistines decided there was only one way to subdue this powerhouse: with a woman. Samson was a he-man with a she weakness.

If the Philistines could not prevail on the battlefield, they would do so in the bedroom. And Samson's enemies took full advantage of this sizable chink in his armor. Let's read about it:

> Afterward it happened that he loved a woman in the Valley of Sorek, whose name was Delilah. And the lords of the Philistines came up to her and said to her, "Entice him, and find out where his great strength lies, and by what means we may overpower him, that we may bind him to afflict him; and every one of us will give you eleven hundred pieces of silver."

> So Delilah said to Samson, "Please tell me where your great strength lies, and with what you may be bound to afflict you." And Samson said to her, "If they bind me with seven fresh bowstrings, not yet dried, then I shall become weak, and be like any other man." So the lords of the Philistines brought up to her seven fresh bowstrings, not yet dried, and she bound him with them.

Now men were lying in wait, staying with her in the room. And she said to him, "The Philistines are upon you, Samson!" But he broke the bowstrings as a strand of yarn breaks when it touches fire. So the secret of his strength was not known. (Judges 16:4–9)

The Philistines enlisted Delilah to do their dirty work: find out the secret of Samson's strength so they could overpower him. They offered her the equivalent of fifty thousand dollars to do this.

The deck was stacked against the unsuspecting he-man. There is no question that Delilah was a very attractive and enticing woman. For temptation to be tempting, it has to be appealing.

That's the rub.

Temptation will promise you life, but ultimately brings death. It will promise you fulfillment, but ultimately result in emptiness. It promises freedom, but ultimately brings bondage.

Delilah began her strategic attack. Samson had shown his vulnerability—women—and the devil exploited it. He had a willing victim in Samson.

This is important. Sometimes we think the devil can pretty much pick us off at will. I remember once hearing a preacher who had fallen into sin say, "The reason I fell is because the devil did it to me. I was being so used of God that Satan just pulled me down." That's partially true. Of course the devil wants to pull you down, especially if God is using you, but the adversary needs your cooperation.

Satan cannot take you against your will. You have to give in to the temptation. As James wrote, "Each one is tempted when he is drawn away by his own desires and enticed. Then when desire has conceived, it gives birth to sin; and sin, when it is full-grown, brings forth death" (James 1:14–15). For Satan to succeed, we must listen, desire what he offers, and *yield*.

The devil is no fool. He will vary his bait depending on whom he is tempting. As those who fish know, you use different kinds of bait for different kinds of fish. But keep this in mind: It's not the bait that constitutes sin; it's *the bite*. It's not a sin to be tempted, but it is a sin to surrender to that temptation.

Samson took it hook, line, and sinker . . . and paid a terrible price.

The Games People Play—to Death

Why didn't Samson realize what was going on? Look at how crazy it was. Delilah was pretty explicit in declaring her objectives to the foolish Samson: "Please tell me where your great strength lies," she cooed into his ear, "and with what you may be bound to afflict you" (Judges 16:6).

This is the first clue that this was not a healthy relationship. The woman was saying, "I want to afflict you."

For Samson, it was a game. He probably was thinking, *As if you could afflict me. I am Samson, who kills Philistines for entertainment. I rip huge gates out of their foundations and carry them for sport. I am the Samson whom no one can stop, and you, little Delilah, are going to afflict me?*

I think he found it humorous and toyed with her. He started telling lies, but—this is important—he got closer and closer to the truth as she continued to press him.

Sometimes we think, *I can handle this. I won't fall. I'm stronger than that.* You have all heard the rationalizations and maybe even used them. *I'll go only so far, and then I'll stop. I promise.*

Or how about this one: *I'll return it. I'm only borrowing it.*

Here's another: *Just one time. We'll never do it again.*

How many people have ended up in a pit of bondage because they took the bait of temptations like those? The Bible says, "Can a man scoop fire into his lap without his clothes being burned?" (Proverbs 6:27 NIV).

Answer: Probably not!

Really, Samson should have realized Delilah offered a trap from the devil. The fact that she said, "The Philistines are upon you," and his enemies lurched at him from the shadows should have clued him in.

But Samson wasn't thinking clearly—not at all. People never

do when under the intoxicating effects of lust. Delilah leaned in for the kill:

> Then she said to him, "How can you say, 'I love you,' when your heart is not with me? You have mocked me these three times, and have not told me where your great strength lies." And it came to pass, when she pestered him daily with her words and pressed him, so that his soul was vexed to death, that he told her all his heart, and said to her, "No razor has ever come upon my head, for I have been a Nazirite to God from my mother's womb. If I am shaven, then my strength will leave me, and I shall become weak, and be like any other man." (Judges 16:15–17)

When Delilah realized she had finally gleaned the essential information, she sent for the Philistines. They paid her, and she finished the job:

> Then she lulled him to sleep on her knees, and called for a man and had him shave off the seven locks of his head. Then she began to torment him, and his strength left him. And she said, "The Philistines are upon you, Samson!" So he awoke from his sleep, and said, "I will go out as before, at other times, and shake myself free!" But he did not know that the Lord had departed from him.

> Then the Philistines took him and put out his eyes, and brought him down to Gaza. They bound him with bronze fetters, and he became a grinder in the prison. (Judges 16:19–21)

This is such a sad story. If Samson were a runner in a race, we would say he fell and fell hard—so hard it looked as though he never would get up again. Ironically, if anyone had the ability to win the gold, it was Samson. But instead, he was disqualified. Certainly he is one of the losers in the spiritual race.

Delilah basically said to him, "If you love me, you will do this." Warning: If you ever find yourself in a relationship with someone who asks you to compromise your values as a believer to prove your love, that is not a good relationship. That's exactly what Delilah did, and Samson took a one-way trip to Delilah's barbershop.

Talk about sleeping with the enemy! This woman had positively declared she wanted to destroy him, yet he felt comfortable enough to doze off in her lap.

Here is the truly tragic part: "He did not know that the Lord had departed from him" (Judges 16:20). Samson had lost touch with God. This happens. When someone starts compromising with sin, other believers may warn him, "Friend, what you are doing isn't right. The Bible clearly says so. You really shouldn't." But how does this person often respond? "Hey, man, don't judge me. The Bible says, 'Judge not lest you be judged.' Who are you to judge me? You have no right to do that."

The fact of the matter is that we are to make evaluations and, yes, judgments as believers on our own lives and on the lives of fellow Christians. How else are we to heed biblical warnings to beware of false prophets or not "cast our pearls before swine" (see Matthew 7:6, 15)? I obviously need to make some judgment or evaluation to determine whether a person is teaching false doctrine or isn't open to the gospel.

Now, the word Jesus used for "judge" means "condemn" (see Matthew 7:1). I am not to *condemn* a fellow Christian, but if I observe or judge that he is going in the wrong direction, then I need to warn him.

The Bible says, "Because the sentence against an evil work is not executed speedily, therefore the heart of the sons of men is fully set in them to do evil" (Ecclesiastes 8:11). Allow me to loosely paraphrase that: Because we don't get busted immediately, we think we can get away with sin forever. The Bible warns, "Be sure your sin will find you out" (Numbers 32:23).

Sin Blinds, Finds, and Grinds

Samson was about to find out the truth of that. The Philistines captured him. When he needed his strength to escape their clutches, that strength was no longer there. The Lord was no longer with him as He once was, so Samson could no longer shake them off like rag dolls. They pinned the mighty warrior to the ground and heartlessly gouged out his eyes. The Philistines then put Samson to work as a grinder in prison. It was a cruel and tragic end to a brilliant reign.

This shows us that sin blinds us, it finds us, and it grinds us. Let's take a closer look at how this happens.

1. Sin blinds us

Sometimes we do completely irrational things. We all know of men and women who have great families, loving spouses and children, and have enjoyed great blessings from the Lord. But then they go out and have an affair with a coworker. These men and women are *blinded*. They deceive themselves into thinking that it's somehow okay.

This kind of immorality usually starts with a fantasy: *I would never do this, but . . . what would it be like if I did?* Then you take it to the next level and start flirting with that person. After that, you start having intimate conversations, maybe sharing some of your marital problems. You become very close friends. Too close. The next thing you know, you're embroiled in a soul-destroying sexual affair.

Adultery is what the Bible calls it. It blinds you. You have been deceived by sin.

2. Sin finds us

Sure, there is that euphoric excitement when you get away with sin. You've made your decision, you've followed through, and you think you've gotten away with it. You feel unrestrained by rules. But in the end, sin will find you. As we saw earlier, the Bible says, "Your sin will find you out." We can't escape it or its consequences. Samson couldn't. You won't.

3. Sin grinds us

You will pay the miserable price: The broken marriage. The betrayed trust. The damaged witness and reputation. The devastated children with deep wounds they often carry for the rest of their lives—not to mention other problems such as HIV, venereal disease, and, depending on what you have done, maybe even jail time. Your sin will find you out and grind you down, and you'll be left with nothing.

Or will you?

Hope among the Ashes

Samson found out the hard way what a horrible and devastating thing sin could be. Yet even in his mess, there was hope. Look at Judges 16:22: "However, the hair of his head began to grow again after it had been shaven."

Do you know what this verse is about? It tells us that God gives second chances.

You might be thinking, *Greg, you're warning me about divorce, adultery, and other things, but it's too late. I am a divorced man [or woman]. I've already had the affair. I've been caught. I feel horrible. You're hitting me hard, and I'm already overwhelmed with guilt.*

But look at this: "The hair of [Samson's] head began to grow again. . . ." Yes, I am warning those who haven't fallen in this way not to fall. But I'm also saying to you, if you have fallen into sin, learn from it and know that God gives you another opportunity to serve Him.

Maybe you're in a second marriage now, after a failed first marriage. Well, make this one work! Don't let it fall apart. If you are estranged from your children, try to reconnect with them. Try to make up for the wrongs you've done. Make the best of what you have. God has given you a second chance. Try to fail forward.

Aren't you glad God gives second chances? I certainly am. Samson was as well. As his hair grew, his strength began to return. While Samson helped push the grinding rock, day in and day out, the Philistines laughed at him. They felt powerful. The mighty man was a blind mouse.

Then one day the Philistines had a big feast. Everybody was in town—about three thousand in number—to celebrate their god, Dagon, for giving them victory over Samson. They said, "Let's bring Samson out. Let's have a laugh at his expense. Let him perform for us."

They led the former mighty man of Israel out, deeming him so harmless that they gave the job of leading him to a little boy. Samson asked the boy to put his hands on the foundational pillars of the pagan temple, so that he could "lean on them." Then Samson prayed: "O Lord God, remember me, I pray! Strengthen me, I pray, just this once, O God, that I may with one blow take vengeance on the Philistines for my two eyes!" (Judges 16:28).

With all of his might he pushed, and those pillars gave way and the roof collapsed. All of those Philistines, blaspheming and worshiping their false god, were killed that day. In fact, Samson "killed many more when he died than while he lived" (Judges 16:30 NIV).

Maybe you're being tempted right now. Maybe you've already acted on it. Learn the lesson of Samson. Look at what can happen to you! Heed the warnings God is giving you. And remember, if you already have failed, God will forgive you if you will repent. Acknowledge that you have done wrong, and God will give you a second chance. You may not be allowed to win the gold, but continuing on with God's redeeming grace is better than giving up completely.

Remember David's many sins. And remember that to this day, he is still known as "the man after God's own heart."

DISQUALIFIED!

The moment we put our faith in Jesus Christ, we are enrolled in a spiritual race. One of the mandates of any competition is that we play by the rules or we will be disqualified. This is true in every race, but perhaps especially in the spiritual one.

I base this on 1 Corinthians 9:24–27, where Paul said,

> Don't you realize that in a race everyone runs, but only one person gets the prize? So run to win! All athletes are disciplined in their training. They do it to win a prize that will fade away, but we do it for an eternal prize. So I run with purpose in every step. I am not just shadowboxing. I discipline my body like an athlete, training it to do what it should. Otherwise, I fear that after preaching to others I myself might be disqualified. (NLT)

First Samuel gives us the story of a man who did not play by the rules. Ironically, he could have done very well. He had all the makings to be someone great for God. Like Samson, this man before us might have succeeded incredibly, but because he did not play by God's rules, he was disqualified. His name was Saul.

Another Great Start, Tragic Ending

The life of King Saul, the first king for the nation Israel, is a study in contrasts. He began his reign in victory and ended in humiliating defeat. He lost his character, power, crown, and, in the end, his very life.

Saul's life stands as a warning, much as Samson's does, that you can't rebel against God and get away with it. It will catch up with you. It may not be today or tomorrow. But as we saw in the last chapter, sin will blind you, find you, and grind you.

Saul's life was a tragic waste.

The epitaph on King Saul's tombstone might have been the words that came out of his own mouth: "I have played the fool and erred exceedingly" (1 Samuel 26:21).

Tragically, it didn't have to be that way. Saul was a young man with seemingly limitless potential.

It all started when Israel demanded a king. Judges such as Samson had been ruling God's people, and God spoke to the Israelites through such prophets as Samuel. The judges and prophets revealed the will of God to the nation. It was a glorious arrangement, because God himself directed them.

The Israelites, however, grew discontented with this arrangement. They wanted to be "like all the other nations" and have their own king. So they approached the prophet Samuel and made their request.

Samuel took it to the Lord, and the Lord said He would give Israel exactly what it requested. This is a reminder to be careful what you ask for, because God just might answer your prayer with a yes.

As we are going to see, Israel's request was fraught with peril. This is one reason Jesus taught us in the Lord's Prayer to say, "Your kingdom come. Your will be done . . ." (Matthew 6:10). In other words, "Lord, if what I am about to pray is in any way outside of Your will, overrule it. Your will be done. Your kingdom come. I want Your will more than I want my own."

God gave the Israelites a man named Saul, and they got what they deserved. You have heard of the People's Choice Awards—Saul was the people's choice. But he wasn't necessarily God's.

Don't get me wrong. At first, Saul had many fine qualities, traits that were admirable in a leader for a nation. He was an obedient son from a good family. He was humble enough to tackle the little as well as the large tasks. He looked to be someone great who would do wonderful things for the nation of Israel. But as we will see, he squandered his resources and opportunities. He ignored the rules. He played the fool, and, because of that, he was disqualified. He was a man who had a tremendous beginning but a tragic ending.

A Promising Start

Let's look at his story. The son of a rich man, Saul was doubly blessed; the Bible calls him "the most handsome man in Israel" (1 Samuel 9:2 NLT). That was important then. Maybe it's even more important now, in our visual age.

I think back to the debate between John F. Kennedy and Richard Nixon for the presidency. People who listened to that debate on the radio felt Nixon won, and people who watched it on television felt Kennedy won. It was all because of how telegenic Kennedy was. Presidential debates have not been the same since then.

That is typical of our culture. We celebrate attractive people. We prefer style over substance.

For instance, *People* magazine doesn't publish an annual issue called "The Most Ordinary People." It is called "The World's Most Beautiful People." Certainly Saul would have been included. He might even have made the cover of *People's* "Sexiest King Alive." He was an attractive man.

Even good-looking people, however, have to do chores. One day Kish's donkeys ran off, so he told Saul to find them and bring them home. Saul enlisted a servant's help, and the two set out. They searched everywhere with no success. But while they were out on this errand, they walked right into the middle of the will of God. Saul's servant said, "I have heard that there is a man of God around here—the prophet Samuel. Maybe he will know where the donkeys went."

They found the legendary Samuel. When the men met, the Lord suddenly spoke to the prophet, "That's the man I told you about! He will rule my people" (1 Samuel 9:17 NLT).

Imagine Saul's surprise when "Samuel took a flask of olive oil and poured it over Saul's head. He kissed Saul on the cheek and said, 'I am doing this because the Lord has appointed you to be the leader of his people Israel...'" (1 Samuel 10:1 NLT).

Saul was just out looking for a donkey, and he ended up being anointed as the king of Israel!

There is an important lesson for us to learn from this story. It is simply this: we need to be willing to do the small, seemingly insignificant things before God will call us to do the larger ones. You never can be too small for God to use—only too big.

As Saul was faithful in the little things, God opened a great door for him. It's worth noting that God often selects people for His service who are going about the ordinary, mundane, everyday activities of life.

Consider the fact that the great Moses was tending sheep when God spoke to him through the burning bush and told him to deliver the people of Israel. He was just going about his business when he found out the course of his life was to change forever.

Elisha was plowing a field when the prophet Elijah called him to be his successor. David was running an errand for his father when the Lord used him to conquer the mighty Goliath. Peter, James, and John were fishing when Jesus came to them and said, "Follow Me, and I will make you fishers of men" (Matthew 4:19). *You never know what great doors may turn upon small hinges.*

Look at what happened next: the Spirit of the Lord came upon Saul and "gave him another heart" (1 Samuel 10:9).

God took this young man who had so much natural potential—a striking appearance, a strong background, an obedient heart—and He anointed him. Then he had everything he needed to be a great leader. He had the whole package. Everything was going Saul's way.

The Bible says God then raised up some good men to assist Saul. First Samuel 10:26 says, "When Saul returned to his home at Gibeah, a group of men whose hearts God had touched went with him" (NLT).

In his race, Saul was off the blocks with a bang. So far so good.

Failing the First Test

Then the first test came. One of Israel's enemies, the Ammonites, had surrounded an Israeli city. The enemy's wicked king, Nahash, ordered the occupants to surrender. Israel asked for a peace agreement instead: "We will be your servants." Nahash agreed but added, "On this condition I will make a covenant with you, that I may put out all your right eyes, and bring reproach on all Israel" (1 Samuel 11:2).

The Israelites wisely said, "Can we get back to you on that?"

Among themselves they reasoned, "Let's see if anyone will come and back us up. If not, we'll surrender." They sent word to the other tribes, and when Saul heard was happening, he was rightfully outraged. He said, "Now is the time for the tribes of Israel to come together." Rallying an army of more than three hundred thousand men, he sent word back to the little Israeli city: "Help is on the way."

When Saul and his army showed up, they completely wiped out the Ammonites. Israel had a new hero, because Saul had more than risen to the occasion. Saul was not only brave, but he was compassionate. After his triumph over the enemy, he refused to put to death those who questioned whether he should be king (because, of course, some did). Again, it was a very good beginning.

The prophet Samuel then reaffirmed Saul as the king of Israel. He called the people and said:

> "Now therefore, here is the king whom you have chosen and whom you have desired. And take note, the Lord has set a king over you. If you fear the Lord and serve Him and obey His voice, and do not rebel against the commandment of the Lord, then both you and the king who reigns over you will continue following the Lord your God.
>
> "However, if you do not obey the voice of the Lord, but rebel against the commandment of the Lord, then the hand of the Lord will be against you, as it was against your fathers." (1 Samuel 12:13–15 NLT)

There was the condition: worship and honor God. Do what He tells you to, follow Him, and everything will be fine. Samuel warned that if they rebelled and disobeyed, they would reap what they sowed.

Isn't the same true for us today? God tells us how to live our lives. He tells how to have successful marriages. He tells us how to conduct ourselves in business, how to live life to its fullest. He says, "Here are My rules and standards. Here is My power to help you live them. If you go this way, all will be well. If you disregard what I say, then you will regret it."

It's true.

Essentially, God was giving Saul fair warning: "Listen to Me: you have the potential. You have the power. I have given it all to you. Now the ball is in your court. *If you follow Me, all will be well.* But if you rebel, you will have trouble."

You know the rest of this story. Saul started immediately to rebel. He went into a free fall, starting with one error that eventually led to his complete decline.

It happened like this. Another enemy of Israel's, the Philistines, mounted an attack. The Philistine armies were huge, and Israel was paralyzed with panic. Saul tried to rally the troops to go into battle, but the Lord told him, through Samuel, to wait until the prophet showed up and offered a burnt offering. Saul, however, grew impatient when the prophet seemingly delayed his coming, and "his men were trembling with fear" (1 Samuel 13:7 NLT).

Saul thought, *Why do I have to wait for some prophet? I know how to present a burnt offering. How hard could it be? I've watched him do it so many times. I'll just do it myself. Surely God will make an exception under such circumstances.*

And then he proceeded to directly disobey the Lord.

Samuel appeared just as Saul was finishing the offering, and he confronted him: "What is this you have done?" (v. 10 NLT). Saul explained his need to proceed. "'How foolish!' Samuel exclaimed. 'You have not kept the command the Lord your God gave you. Had you kept it, the Lord would have established your kingdom over Israel forever. But now your kingdom must end . . .'" (vv. 13-14 NLT). In fact, he said, the Lord had already chosen Saul's successor.

I know that at first blush, this may seem a bit extreme on God's part, but the Lord could see that Saul's heart had already turned away. Saul had determined to follow his own rules, not God's.

Giving in to "Little" Sins

We may not like some of the rules God sets forth in His Word. "Why can't I do thus and so? I still have to live in the real world. Why does God say I can't do that? It doesn't seem fair. What's wrong with a little bit? Just a few drinks. A little flirting. A small white lie. I'll know when to stop."

Famous last words.

What you need to realize is that it's always the "little" sins that lead to the big ones.

I read a bizarre story in the paper some years ago about an eighteen-year-old young man in London. The article said he was hospitalized after his pet scorpion stung him on the tongue. It turns out this young man kissed the scorpion (its name was Twiggy) good night every evening before bed. One night Twiggy stung him on the lip. He opened his mouth in pain, and Twiggy jumped inside and stung him on the tongue. The young man had to be hospitalized as a result.

In the same way, some of us are giving sin a little good night kiss. We think, *It's just a little thing. So trivial. How much harm could this do?* We should know better.

Partial Obedience Is No Obedience

Let's get back to Saul. What happened after he disobeyed God with the sacrifice is even sadder. God commanded King Saul to settle accounts with an old enemy, the Amalekites. God said to completely destroy them. Instead, Saul partially obeyed the Lord: he defeated the enemy in battle but kept some livestock. He also only captured, but didn't kill, the king.

Again Samuel confronted Saul, and Saul lied: "I really planned on giving it all to the Lord anyway. That's why I kept it."

Samuel replied,

> "What is more pleasing to the Lord: your burnt offerings and sacrifices or your obedience to his voice? Listen! Obedience is better than sacrifice. . . . Rebellion is as sinful as witchcraft, and stubbornness as bad as worshiping idols. So because you have rejected

the command of the Lord, he has rejected you as king."
(1 Samuel 15:22–23 NLT).

Saul confessed, "Yes, I have sinned. I have disobeyed your instructions and the Lord's command, for I was afraid of the people and did what they demanded. But now, please forgive my sin and come back with me so that I may worship the Lord" (vv. 24–25 NLT). Samuel refused. He knew Saul wasn't interested in worshiping the Lord. All he wanted was a photo op.

Repentance Must Be Real

Let's say you have a friend who betrays your confidence. You tell him something in secret, and the next thing you know, Larry King is talking about it on his show. How did this happen?

You confront him: "I shared with you a struggle I was having. I asked you to pray, and instead you told everyone. That offends me."

He says, "I'm so sorry. Can you find it in your heart to forgive me? I'll never do it again."

Okay—you forgive him. A little time passes. And then it gets back to you that this same friend has gone out and told complete lies about you. You confront him again. He says, "I am so sorry. I don't know why I did it. I'll take you out to a nice dinner. Will that even the score?"

You go to dinner. But another day passes, and it gets even worse. He says, "I'm sorry. But look, I bought you a new shirt."

So, you are discovering something about your so-called friend. He's no friend at all. The fact of the matter is that you don't want him to take you to dinner or buy you a new shirt. What you want is for him to keep your confidence and be what he claimed to be: a true friend.

In the same way, many of us today say we are friends of Jesus. We claim to be Christians. But if we don't do what He tells us to do, then we really have no right to call ourselves His friend. We may lift our hands in praise at church and proclaim, "Lord, I love You so much. You are so good. I will do whatever You want me to do!" Then we go out and break His commandments left and right. Then we pray, "God, I am so sorry. Let me make up for it. I'll put more money in the offering. I'll go to a couple of midweek Bible studies. Here, Lord, let me show You my love in some way."

Newsflash: God doesn't want your money or your attendance at another service if it is all for the wrong reason. *God wants your heart.* Jesus said in John 15:14, "You are My friends if you do whatever I command you." That means we need to do it.

Off-Key Worship

Worship music has become very popular today. It's not uncommon to see commercials on TV offering the latest collection of songs of praise to God, and in many ways, I applaud that. But at the same time, true worship is not about how catchy the tune may be or even how well it's performed.

It's all about the heart.

Did you know that if your lifestyle contradicts what you believe, your worship can actually be offensive to God? Amos 5:23–24 says, "Away with your noisy hymns of praise! I will not listen to the music of your harps. Instead, I want to see a mighty flood of justice, an endless river of righteous living" (NLT).

I bring this up because I know people who have a yo-yo-like relationship with God. They're either really up or really down. They're either fully backslidden or passionate to the point of being obnoxious. One day all they can talk about is how much Christ means to them. The next day they're engaged in something that's clearly sinful. What happened? A week later they're back in church, singing louder than anyone else. A week after that, they're back in sin again.

It's ridiculous.

This is why David prayed in Psalm 51, "Create in me a clean heart, O God, and renew a steadfast spirit within me" (v. 10). The word David used for "steadfast" means "to be consistent." This is more important than your roller-coaster spiritual highs and lows.

You might see someone singing beautifully to the Lord. *What a voice, you think. How that must please God.*

Well, if the singer's heart is in the right place, it *does* honor God.

(Let me add that if someone has the worst voice you have ever heard, but she loves the Lord, her singing honors Him as well.) But if that person with a beautiful voice is contradicting what she sings by the way she lives, then her song offends God. Again, God looks on the heart.

God looked in Saul's heart, and spiritually speaking, his songs were off-key.

The Torment of Disobedience

Tragically, Saul went from bad to worse. It wasn't long before David emerged on the scene to take over, by God's command. Saul began to hunt him relentlessly. Paranoia and jealousy filled the wicked king. Saul even tried to murder David on more than one occasion. After Samuel's death, Saul was so desperate that he consulted a witch to try to make contact with the departed prophet. Ultimately he died a pathetic death on the battlefield: realizing he was defeated, Saul committed suicide.

His life had so much promise, potential, and talent, and it ended like that. God had blessed him. He had everything he needed, but he threw it all away.

If Samson was defeated in the race of life by lust, then Saul was defeated in the race of life by pride.

Saul is great proof of the fact that you never know how someone is going to turn out. Think of when you were in school: certain kids you knew would never amount to anything. They weren't the star athletes, the great quarterbacks, the brilliant scholars, the cheerleaders, or the most popular people on campus. Maybe for all practical purposes, they were nobodies. They may have had a few too many pens in their shirt pockets or wore their pants a bit too short. We laughed at them, calling them "geeks" or "nerds." It's quite possible that today we call them "Boss," isn't it? People can come out of nowhere and suddenly make their mark.

Then there were those whom we expected to be great successes in life, whatever their fields of endeavor, and none of them ever made a name for themselves.

The spiritual life carries the same kinds of surprises. I think of those I knew as a younger believer, people God was so mightily using. They were impacting others. I was so excited that I could say I knew them! I knew they would make their mark on the world for the Lord Jesus Christ. Some of those people, though, self-destructed. They got tripped up in the race of life. You probably know some people like that too.

Epitaph for a Fool

I've mentioned that Saul himself summed up his life with these words: "I have played the fool and erred exceedingly." That would have been a fitting epitaph for this man.

As I asked earlier in this book, if you were to create a phrase that summed up your own life, what would you say? Let me ask you this: What *should* be said? What you would like may be different from what ought to be said about you.

Could you imagine if we told the truth on tombstones? We always see things like "Loving father and wonderful husband." But what if he was really a failure as a man? Maybe that tombstone should read: "Total screw-up" or "What a waste!"

I wonder what someone will write on your tombstone . . . or mine.

Saul played the fool. He started the race well, but once he fell, he never got up again. At least in the end, Samson made a comeback. Saul never did. He was disqualified in the race of life. He foolishly threw his life away, and in the end, he knew it.

Let me share a few principles Saul might have written based on his life. These are things to do if you want to fail and lose the race of life.

1. Ignore the little things

Spiritual decline is gradual. Saul's failure wasn't immediate. At first he was humble, but pride soon set in. Then pride turned into envy, and he took matters into his own hands. He ignored what God had plainly told him to do.

It's not for us to pick and choose what parts of the Bible we like and then dispense with the others. We are to obey God even in the smallest matters, because "small" sins turn into big sins. They certainly did for Saul.

2. Never take responsibility for your actions

More than once Saul blamed others for his own bad choices. When Samuel confronted Saul about the burnt offering, the king answered, "I saw my men scattering, and you didn't arrive when you said you would, and the Philistines are . . . ready for battle. . . . So I felt compelled to offer the burnt offering myself . . ." (1 Samuel 13:11–12 NLT).

In other words, "It's the Philistines fault. It's my men's fault. It's your fault." Saul just wanted to save face. He forgot that no matter what we try to say about ourselves and our motives, God knows the truth.

3. Don't just get mad; get even

Saul's animosity ultimately destroyed him. He was jealous when God placed His anointing upon the young shepherd boy, David, and began to use him. We need to understand that there always will be people who will do better than we will. We will meet people who are smarter, more attractive, more talented, and younger. The Lord God may raise up a certain person, and we will say, "Why him [or her]? Obviously I'm the right choice. I'm better-looking, gifted, dedicated, and so humble." Maybe it's because you think so much of yourself that He doesn't choose you. God gets to choose whom He will use. Don't let hatred make you a victim.

The Rules Work for Everyone

God has given you, like Saul, potential. God has given you certain talents and enabled you to perform certain tasks well. He has put His hand upon you. The call of God is the enabling of God; He has not asked you to do anything that He won't give you the strength to do.

Maybe as you read Saul's story, you felt as though you were reading your own. You feel like you are on your way down. If you can heed Saul's example, you can change your ways. But if you continue in the way you're going, you will find it a slippery slope. One day you may end up like Saul, saying, "I have played the fool and erred exceedingly." Don't let that happen. Make a recommitment if you need to.

It's up to us to run the race well and play by the rules. Don't be disqualified. Don't be prideful. Don't play the fool. Don't crash and burn. It is such a waste of life.

HIGH HURDLES

He came from the most humble of beginnings and rose to be the greatest king in the history of his nation. In battle he was fearless. In wisdom and ruling, he was without peer. Yet for all this, he wasn't some macho dude; he was a guy who had a tender, even sensitive, heart. He was both a warrior and a poet, a clear-thinking ruler and talented musician. He was someone God described uniquely as being a man after His own heart.

Of course, you know I'm talking about David.

In the last chapter, we saw that the Lord ruled Israel through the various judges, and He spoke to them through the prophets. But because the other nations had human kings Israel wanted one too. For all practical purposes, God gave them exactly what they asked for: a man after their own heart.

Saul was the first king of Israel. We saw that on one hand, he had many wonderful attributes. He started off very well, but then he began to unravel and self-destruct. What seemed to be relatively small sins led to very large sins. Saul crashed and burned.

The Lord chose someone to take his place. With David, it was as though the Lord was saying to Israel, "You've had your turn. I gave you the man with all of the characteristics and attributes that you wanted in a leader. Now let Me give you a man I want." Saul was the man after "man's own heart." David was the man after "God's own heart."

God's selection was so unexpected that we need to pay careful attention to it. In David, the Lord is showing us the kind of person He is looking for today.

God's Eyes versus Man's

As our story begins, Saul's failures have devastated the prophet Samuel.

Yet the Lord said to him, "You have mourned long enough for Saul. I have rejected him as king of Israel, so fill your flask with olive oil and go to Bethlehem. Find a man named Jesse who lives there, for I have selected one of his sons to be my king" (1 Samuel 16:1 NLT).

It's interesting that the Lord didn't tell Samuel who was to be the king—yet. He didn't say which son of Jesse He had chosen. This is typical of the Lord—He leads us one step at a time. Just take that step the Lord has told you to take.

When a man of the magnitude and stature of the prophet Samuel showed up in Bethlehem, the people were understandably concerned and even alarmed.

"Do you come in peace?" they asked (1 Samuel 16:4 NLT).

The prophet reassured them and invited them to attend the sacrifice he was about to make to the Lord. He wanted to scope out the crowd and see if he could identify God's anointed.

When they arrived, Samuel took one look at Eliab and thought, "Surely this is the Lord's anointed!"

But the Lord said to Samuel, "Don't judge by his appearance or height, for I have rejected him. The Lord doesn't see things the way you see them. People judge by outward appearance, but the Lord looks at the heart."

Then Jesse told his son Abinadab to step forward and walk in front of Samuel. But Samuel said, "This is not the one the Lord has chosen." Next Jesse summoned Shimea, but Samuel said, "Neither is this the one the Lord has chosen." In the same way all seven of Jesse's sons were presented to Samuel. But Samuel said to Jesse, "The Lord has not chosen any of these." Then Samuel asked, "Are these all the sons you have?"

"There is still the youngest," Jesse replied. "But he's out in the fields watching the sheep and goats."

"Send for him at once," Samuel said. "We will not sit down to eat until he arrives."

So Jesse sent for him. He was dark and handsome, with beautiful eyes.

And the Lord said, "This is the one; anoint him."

So as David stood there among his brothers, Samuel took the flask of olive oil he had brought and anointed David with the oil. And the Spirit of the Lord came powerfully upon David from that day on. . . . (1 Samuel 16:6–13 NLT)

God's Choice

When Jesse said David, "the youngest," was out in the fields, he used an interesting phrase. "The youngest" didn't just mean David was younger in years than the others, but that he was least in his father's estimation—so much so that Jesse wouldn't have even acknowledged David's existence had the prophet not persisted.

Fortunately, God the Father had more sense than Jesse the father. Maybe you can relate to David on this point. Maybe your parents didn't appreciate you or show you affection. They may have foolishly favored your siblings over you, heaping praise on them and little to none on you. Know this: those whom man rejects often become beloved of the Lord. You need to know that in spite of your parents' lack of love for you, you have always had a heavenly Father who cares for you.

Alan Redpath wrote in his wonderful book on David, *The Making of a Man of God,* "The thought of God toward you began before He ever flung a star into space. Then He wrote your name on His heart; it was graven in the palms of His hands before the sky was stretched out in the heavens."[1] God always has been thinking about you.

God chose David in spite of the fact that his father did not show much love toward him. David later wrote, "Even if my mother and father abandon me, the Lord will hold me close" (Psalm 27:10 NLT).

The Lord rejected all of the magnificent seven, and Jesse called David. Picture it: he came bounding in, a young kid—a teenager.

A good-looking boy, but still wet behind the ears, David had reddish hair, maybe some freckles on his face. No doubt he smelled like the sheep he faithfully attended.

In biblical days, no one admired shepherds. People looked down on them. In fact, a court of law did not allow the testimony of a shepherd. They were at the bottom of the social ladder. So whom did God select as His man? He selected a young boy who had the lowliest profession and whose father didn't appreciate him.

I'm sure the brothers were thinking, *What is our little brother doing in here? This has nothing to do with him.* Then, to their shock and surprise, the prophet took out oil, poured it on David's head, and said he was the new king of Israel. I think the brothers suspected that aged Samuel had gone senile. You can be sure they felt resentment and anger. *How could he possibly say our little brother, David, is the new king of Israel? There must be some mistake here.*

David took it so well. He didn't boast about it. He just went back to watching his sheep. As Chuck Swindoll points out in his great book on David,

> He did not go down to the nearest department store and try on crowns. He didn't order a new set of business cards, telling the printer, "Change it from shepherd to king-elect." Didn't have a badge saying, "I'm the new man." Didn't shine up a chariot and race through the streets of Bethlehem, yelling, "I'm God's choice . . . !"[2]

David just went back to doing what he had been doing before and waited for further direction.

The Person God Will Use

Let's look a bit more closely at the account of David's rise to the throne. From it we can identify some principles about the man or the woman whom God will use.

1. God uses ordinary people

David was in many ways the opposite of King Saul. Saul came from a family who loved him; David came from a family who neglected him. Saul was the most handsome man in all Israel; David was a handsome enough guy, but relatively ordinary. Saul was attractive on the outside, but on the inside he was vain, shallow, and devoid of true integrity.

In contrast, David had a deep spiritual life and an intense devotion to God. (If you want to know about David's spirituality profile, just read some of the Psalms. They're like windows into his soul.) Saul's problem was that he was full of himself. The Lord rejected him. David was full of the Lord, and God accepted him.

This reminds us of the truth of the Scripture in 1 Corinthians 1:26–29:

> Brothers and sisters, think of what you were when you were called. Not many of you were wise by human standards; not many were influential; not many were of noble birth. But God chose the foolish things of the world to shame the wise; God chose the weak things of the world to shame the strong. God chose the lowly things of this world and the despised things—and the things that are not—to nullify the things that are, so that no one may boast before him. (NIV)

The Lord seems to go out of His way to use ordinary people to do extraordinary things; then people give credit to the Lord rather than to human beings. Just as surely as God plucked David from obscurity, He is looking for men and women He can use in these critical days in which we are living. God is looking for people to touch this generation. He is looking for people to change this world. Second Chronicles 16:9 says, "The eyes of the Lord run to and fro throughout the whole earth, to show Himself strong on behalf of those whose heart is loyal to Him."

What kind of person does He look for? Someone strong? No. The previous passage says He is looking for someone to whom He can show *His* strength—someone whose heart is turned toward Him. Is your heart totally turned toward God?

One of the men God used mightily in his generation was D. L. Moody. Moody was the Billy Graham of his day. Dwight Moody was a shoe salesman when he came to faith. You might say that Moody went from selling soles to saving souls. He was just a run-of-the-mill guy.

Do you know what got Moody pointed in the right direction after his conversion? A man went up to him once and said, "The world has yet to see what God can do through one man totally committed to Him."[3]

Moody said, "When I heard that, I said to the Lord, 'I want to be that man.'"

Do you know what Billy Graham was when God called him? He was a farm boy living in North Carolina. He came to faith at a meeting held by a traveling evangelist. Young Billy Frank, as they called him, dedicated his life to the Lord. Who could have imagined what God would do with that young man?

The most godly people I know are also the most down-to-earth. God is looking for ordinary people to use. David was an ordinary man.

2. God uses spiritually-focused people

David had a real insight into who God was and set his heart to follow him. In Psalm 57:7, he wrote, "My heart is fixed, O God, my heart is steadfast and confident!" (AMP). This means that David's heart was totally focused on who God was. He was locked in to what was right. He wasn't fickle. He was meditative. Yet he was brave and courageous.

In Psalm 27:4, David laid out the focus of his life, as we considered earlier:

One thing I have desired of the Lord,
That will I seek:
That I may dwell in the house of the Lord
All the days of my life,
To behold the beauty of the Lord,
And to inquire in His temple.

David said, "This is my heart. It is my one thing." Everybody is living for something. The main thing is to keep the main thing the main thing.

Many of us, if we're honest, could say the one thing we are most focused on right now is a career: "I want to get established. I want to make a good living. I want to provide for my family." The other thing many of us might say is, "My main priority is my family. I want to be a good husband [or wife]. I want my family to stay strong." I am not criticizing either of these. It's fine to want to have a good career and family. These are worthy goals.

But neither of these should be the one thing. The one thing should be Christ.

In Matthew 6:33, Jesus said, "Seek first the kingdom of God and His righteousness, and all these things shall be added to you." Let me translate that into the modern vernacular: put the things of God number-one in your life, and everything else will work out just fine. Seek first the rule and reign of Christ in your life.

God may not give you everything you hoped for in life. Then again, He may give you more. You just leave that up to Him and put Him first. That's what David did.

3. God uses people who are willing to act in faith

At that particular time in his life, David's primary responsibility was to watch sheep. If lions or bears attacked his sheep, he fought to the death to protect them. He spent hours ensuring their safety. No doubt that's when he came up with Psalm 23. He probably was watching the sheep munching contentedly in a lush green field one day when he thought, *The Lord is my shepherd; I shall not want.*

David figured if that was what God wanted him to do, then those were going to be the best-fed and most-protected sheep around. In fact, he would, if necessary, lay his life down for them.

Did the young shepherd boy dream of one day doing great things for God? Did he ever think he would be crowned as the king of Israel? We can't know for sure. But one thing we do know is that David had a clear focus and a proper sense of what his priorities should be in life.

What God Can Do through the Willing

Divine opportunity usually, if not always, comes unexpectedly.

The Lord was about to open a big door for David. Faithfulness on an errand for his father would result in David's greatest victory. Big doors swing on small hinges. His brothers were all away, fighting for the Israeli army. They were facing off with the Philistines at the Valley of Elah. The Philistines had a warrior known as Goliath.

This guy was big. Not just NFL or NBA big, but a real monster. He stood nine feet six inches tall in his socks—a wall of a man, all muscle. The Bible tells us that his armor alone weighed two hundred pounds. He carried a javelin that weighed more than twenty-five pounds.

This oversized Philistine challenged the Israelites every day. He would growl "Who is going to come and fight me? Who has the courage to face off with me?" He did this for forty days.

Then the redheaded youth showed up in town. He was on an errand for Dad, taking cheese sandwiches to his brothers. (Though announced as king, David had yet to take his throne. Saul was still in power.) He heard all the commotion. He scurried down to the front to see for himself who was making all this noise. And there in the Valley of Elah was this frightening, oversized man, bellowing his threats.

David was amazed—not at Goliath's incredible size, but that the man was blatantly and openly blaspheming God, and no one was lifting a finger to stop him. David's blood began to boil with righteous indignation, and he asked for an audience with King Saul. When he came into Saul's presence, he confidently said, "Don't worry about this Philistine. I'll go fight him!" (1 Samuel 17:32 NLT).

Can you imagine? There probably was a lot of eye-rolling going on in the king's tent at that moment. Everyone probably had a good laugh at David's expense.

Amazingly, Saul agreed to let the boy try. What did he have to lose? Perhaps the giant would laugh himself to death. Little did he realize that he was preparing the way for David's ultimate ascent to the throne of Israel.

Saul clothed David with his massive coat of armor. It was so heavy and cumbersome that David couldn't even move. He left it behind, choosing instead his staff and his slingshot. David was ready, if necessary, to lay it all on the line. If you want to play it safe, keep everything predictable, maintain your routine, then have a nice time on Easy Street. You never will be a man or a woman God will use. If you're going to make a difference, you will have to take some steps of faith.

David risked everything he had to honor God. Look at 1 Samuel 17:

> He picked up five smooth stones from a stream and put them into his shepherd's bag. Then, armed only with his shepherd's staff and sling, he started across the valley to fight the Philistine.
>
> Goliath walked out toward David . . . , sneering in contempt at this ruddy-faced boy. "Am I a dog," he roared at David, "that you come at me with a stick?" And he cursed David by the names of his gods. "Come over here, and I'll give your flesh to the birds and wild animals!" Goliath yelled.
>
> David replied to the Philistine, "You come to me with sword, spear, and javelin, but I come to you in the name of the Lord of Heaven's Armies—the God of the armies of Israel, whom you have defied. Today the Lord will conquer you, and I will kill you and cut off your head. And then I will give the dead bodies of your men to the birds and wild animals, and the whole world will know that there is a God in Israel! And everyone assembled here will know that the Lord rescues his people, but not with sword and spear. This is the Lord's battle, and he will give you to us!" (vv. 40–47 NLT)

Talk about going for broke. There was now no turning back for the shepherd-boy-anointed-king. If God didn't come through, he was dead.

Look at what happened in verse 48—this is important: "As Goliath moved closer to attack, David quickly ran out to meet him." You would expect David to perhaps hold his ground, or, at the most, take some cautious steps in the direction of his adversary. But instead, he sprinted full speed at Goliath.

Talk about running a race!

Reaching into his shepherd's bag and taking out a stone, David placed it in his sling. He no doubt shot up a silent prayer. Then he hurled that stone with all the might a young shepherd boy could muster. Like a guided missile, the stone found its target: the fore-head of the rapidly approaching Goliath.

The giant was stopped in his tracks, and, like a massive redwood, he went crashing to the ground with a mighty thud.

Victory was David's!

Since he had no sword, he ran over and pulled Goliath's from its sheath. He whacked off Goliath's head, and as he did, fear shot through the ranks of the Philistines as quickly as David's stone had felled the giant.

When the Philistines saw that their champion was dead, they turned tail and ran.

Strategy for Giant-Killing

We all face giants in life. You might be facing one right now—some-thing that looms so large, something so frightening or so powerful that you don't think you can ever win against it. Maybe it's the giant of addiction. You find yourself under the power of a drug habit or alcohol dependency, or you are hooked on pornography. Then again, it could be the giant of fear and worry or the giant of jealousy. You have tried to overcome and conquer it, but it smacks you down again and again. This giant lords its power over you. It taunts and terrifies you.

You might face a different kind of giant altogether: an incurable illness, a lawsuit, a marriage that seems doomed for failure, or a prodigal son or daughter. David gives us a four-step model for slay-ing giants and running the spiritual race.

1. Remember that the battle is the Lord's

Look at verse 47: "This is the Lord's battle, and he will give you to us!" (NLT). We sometimes forget, when circumstances fill us with fear, that we are fighting a spiritual battle. Ephesians 6:12 says, "For our struggle is not against flesh and blood, but against the rul-ers, against the authorities, against the powers of this dark world and against the spiritual forces of evil in the heavenly realms" (NIV).

The fact is, you need to fight fire with fire. You need to fight spiritual battles with spiritual weapons, utilizing the weaponry God has made available to you. As Paul wrote in 2 Corinthians 10:4, "The weapons we fight with are not weapons of the world. On the contrary, they have divine power to demolish strongholds" (NIV).

What are those weapons? One of them is prayer. When we pray, we remind ourselves of who God is. In the Lord's Prayer, Jesus taught us: "In this manner, therefore, pray: Our Father in heaven, hallowed be Your name" (Matthew 6:9).

Before personal petition, just contemplate the fact that you are talking to God Almighty. He is all-powerful, all-knowing, and everywhere-present. There is nothing God cannot do. If you seek God for who He is, then you will see your giants for what they are. Suddenly your giants will be transformed to pygmies. God is more powerful than anyone or anything else.

David said to Goliath, "You come to me with sword, spear, and javelin, but I come to you in the name of the Lord Almighty—the God of the armies of Israel . . ." (v. 45 NLT). He put his enemy into perspective.

You are on the winning side. God is stronger than the devil. Your God is mightier than any vice, addiction, or problem. Your God is greater. First John 4:4: "You are of God, little children, and have overcome them, because He who is in you is greater than he who is in the world."

2. Take the attack to your enemy

Earlier in the story, the Israelites said, "Have you seen this man who has come up?" (1 Samuel 17:25). Goliath had crossed the ravine and was climbing up Israel's side. If you tolerate a Goliath, he will take over your territory. He will come right up on your doorstep. That's why you can't make any deals with the devil.

Of course you try, right? You say, "I can control this. I can handle this. I can manage this. I can keep this under control." Yeah, right. It's like a wildfire—it gets out of control. It will run over your life. You won't know how it ever happened.

That's why you don't run from giants. You *attack* them.

You don't negotiate with them. You *eradicate* them.

You don't yell at them. You *kill* them.

Verse 48 says, "As Goliath moved closer to attack, David quickly ran out to meet him" (NLT). I like that. As his enemy grew closer, David raced right at the guy. There was no bobbing and weaving, darting back and forth, or evasive maneuvers. He took it right to that lumbering giant. And you need to do the same with your giant.

3. Get your giant out of hiding

You need to force your giant out into the light of day. Stop allowing this sin to enjoy the comfort of darkness. Stop rationalizing it. Stop blaming other people for it. Admit it, not only to God but to someone else—a responsible Christian, such as a pastor, a spouse, or a close Christian friend. Come right out and say it: "I have a problem. I have never revealed this to anyone before. I am sick of it. I want to slay my giant. I need your help. I am asking you to keep me accountable. Call me every day and ask me what steps I am taking to deal with this. I want you to confront me about it. I need prayer. I need help."

4. Trust only God

David put no trust in Saul's armor. This is a temptation we all face: trusting in our own resources. Sometimes the Lord will reduce us to nothing so He, and He alone, will get the glory.

Has that happened to you?

That's good! Then God can get the glory and show you what He is really capable of. That's what David did. Don't wear Saul's armor.

Are You Ready for God to Use You?

Are you ready to go for it? You're just an ordinary person, you say? No matter. Are you a person who is willing to be faithful in what God has set before you today, no matter how small and insignificant? Are you willing to take chances and leaps of faith? Are you willing to run toward your giants in this spiritual race?

I am telling you that God can and will use you. Just make yourself available and say, "Lord, here I am." You can be like David: an ordinary man God used to do extraordinary things. The power was all

God's; the courage was all David's. Like David, you can, with God's help, overcome every hurdle and begin to run well the race of life.

We've seen how David handled the early laps of his race. In the next chapter we'll see how he fared as he settled into his pace.

FORGIVE OR FALL

In 2 Samuel 9 we find one of the most beautiful messages on forgiveness in the pages of the Bible. David extended it toward a potential enemy, a man he could have eliminated had he chosen to do so. Instead, David graciously forgave.

The obstacle before David on the track of life could have ultimately destroyed him. The same obstacle certainly destroyed David's predecessor, King Saul, who harbored a grudge like nobody's business. One of the reasons God described David as a man after His own heart is because he forgave.

If you want to be a man or woman after God's own heart and run this spiritual race well, you have to learn how to forgive others. Why? Because as fatally flawed people, we will sin against people, and people will sin against us. We will hurt one another from time to time, whether intentionally or not. Husbands will hurt wives, and wives will hurt husbands. Children will hurt their parents, and parents will hurt their children. Family members will offend one another. Friends will hurt friends. That is why we need to learn how to forgive.

Only as forgiving people can we run, instead of limp, through our race.

Let's pick up where we left off looking at David. We will see how he demonstrated that he was indeed a man after God's own heart.

God's People Forgive

You recall that God had rejected Saul as king over Israel because of repeated disobedience. The Lord told the prophet Samuel to go to Bethlehem, where God identified David as the next king of Israel.

In the battle that had broken out between the Israelis and the Philistines, you'll recall that King Saul should have faced off with Goliath. Instead, he hid in his tent. David basically told King Saul, "Don't worry about anything. I'll take care of that guy for you."

Saul and the members of his court probably had a good chuckle. "You and what army? You're just a boy." But when David succeeded in killing the giant, Israel had a new hero. There was a new hit song on Israeli radio: "Saul has slain his thousands, and David his ten thousands" (1 Samuel 18:7).

David was the man.

And King Saul wasn't a bit happy about it.

In that moment, the jealous king saw the son of Jesse as a potential threat to his throne: "So Saul eyed David from that day forward" (v. 9).

In the interim, David forged a very strong relationship with Saul's son, Jonathan, and it lasted a lifetime. Jonathan, in contrast to his wicked father, understood David was a good and a godly man. He knew David would one day become the king of Israel. Back in that culture, when one king took over for another, he often destroyed all that king's descendants, because they might try to take the throne. So Jonathan asked David to make a deal with him, to pledge himself to looking out for Jonathan's offspring.

David agreed. Meanwhile, Saul hunted David like a wild dog. He was determined to kill his replacement. David had to hide in caves. It was a difficult life. He might have said, "Lord, what's this all about? I choose to follow You. I responded to Your call, and yet here I am, living like a hunted animal. I thought I was supposed to be the king. Why do I have to live this way?" Instead, David hung in there and trusted God.

He had a couple of shots himself at killing King Saul. One time David was hiding in a cave and King Saul walked in to relieve

himself. Some of David's men said, "God is giving you an opportunity. Kill him right now." David said no. He would not harm the
Lord's anointed, but he "arose and secretly cut off a corner of Saul's
robe" (1 Samuel 24:4).

Saul left the cave, and David called out from a distance, saying,
"I just wondered if you were feeling a draft, King Saul. I cut a little
bit of your robe off. I could have killed you, but I didn't do it." Then
he threw in a holy promise: "May the Lord avenge the wrongs you
have done to me, but my hand will not touch you" (v. 12 NIV).

Evidently this moved Saul, who wept and said, "You are more
righteous than I. You have treated me well, but I have treated you
badly. . . . I know that you will surely be king" (vv. 17, 20 NIV).

Of course, we know that this rare moment of candor didn't last
long. Saul still pursued David from pillar to post, all over Israel. But
he failed. Ultimately Saul and his son Jonathan died on the battlefield, and David ascended to the throne.

This would have been the time to strike out all potential enemies. David could have destroyed, justifiably, any offspring of Saul's
or Jonathan's. But David would have none of that. Imagine what
you would have done if you had been in David's shoes. Would you
have extended kindness to the relatives of one who had abused—
in fact, tried to kill—you, not once, but many times?

Let's read about it in 2 Samuel 9:

> One day David asked, "Is anyone in Saul's family still alive—any-
> one to whom I can show kindness for Jonathan's sake?" He sum-
> moned a man named Ziba, who had been one of Saul's servants.
> "Are you Ziba?" the king asked.
>
> "Yes sir, I am," Ziba replied.
>
> The king then asked him, "Is anyone still alive from Saul's family?
> If so, I want to show God's kindness to them."
>
> Ziba replied, "Yes, one of Jonathan's sons is still alive. He is crip-
> pled in both feet."
>
> "Where is he?" the king asked.
>
> "In Lo-debar," Ziba told him, "at the home of Makir son of
> Ammiel."

So David sent for him and brought him from Makir's home. His name was Mephibosheth; he was Jonathan's son and Saul's grandson. When he came to David, he bowed low to the ground in deep respect. David said, "Greetings, Mephibosheth."

Mephibosheth replied, "I am your servant."

"Don't be afraid!" David said. "I intend to show kindness to you because of my promise to your father, Jonathan. I will give you all the property that once belonged to your grandfather Saul, and you will eat here with me at the king's table!"

Mephibosheth bowed respectfully and exclaimed, "Who is your servant, that you should show such kindness to a dead dog like me?" (vv. 1–8 NLT)

God's Love for the Down-and-Out

This isn't just a story of David extending grace to a young boy named Mephibosheth; it is a picture of God extending grace to us as well.

In 2 Samuel 9:1, the word "kindness" is important. A better translation would be "grace." Grace is a very important word to us as Christians. One definition of grace is "God's unmerited favor."

Let me further define grace by contrasting it with a couple of other words: justice and mercy. Justice is getting what you deserve. Mercy is not getting what you deserve. Grace is getting what you don't deserve.

Let's say you try to steal a car and you are arrested. That's *justice*. That means you got what you deserved, and you serve a sentence. But let's say the judge decided to show you mercy. Instead of prosecuting you to the full extent of the law, maybe he put you on probation and told you never to steal another car again. That was *mercy*.

Grace means that not only were you not charged with the crime, but the judge gave you the keys to his car and told you it was now yours!

This is what David wanted to do for Mephibosheth. He wanted to show grace to a member of Saul's household.

When David sent for Saul's former servant, Ziba, the servant said, "One of Jonathan's sons is still alive. He is crippled in both feet" (2 Samuel 9:3 NLT). Ziba seemed to be saying, "There is someone, but . . . you might not want him because he's defective. He may not be worth the trouble. I don't know if this young man would fit into your beautiful palace. Maybe you ought to rethink it."

David's response was beautiful. He said only, "Where is he?" (2 Samuel 9:4 NLT). He wasn't taken aback. He didn't ask for details. He just wanted to know where the man was so that he might show grace to him.

In the same way, God doesn't base His grace and love on the recipient's worthiness.

Ziba answered that Mephibosheth was living in Lo-debar. Lo-debar looked the way it sounds: dry and dead. Its name means "the name of no pasture." It was barren—a place where no one wanted to live. It certainly wasn't an appropriate hometown for a grandchild of the former king.

Why was Mephibosheth there? Probably because he was in hiding. He was, by then, an adult, and he had a son himself. He lived in fear of King David's reprisal. To make matters worse, he was isolated and separated from the tabernacle where God's people met. He was living apart from fellowship, in a barren place, unable to walk.

What a perfect picture of all of us living in Lo-debar, feeling unloved, unwanted, unneeded, and undeserving. And just as David reached out to Mephibosheth, God reaches out to us. Romans 5:8 says, "While we were still sinners, Christ died for us."

Active Compassion

Remember the story of those four men who brought their friend to Jesus? Jesus was teaching in a room that was tightly packed with people. Those guys were so determined that they climbed up on the roof and dug away. They lowered the guy down on a cot right in front of the Lord. All four worked together so the Lord could deal with the man's need. He rewarded their persistence and touched the man. I love that.

We need that kind of persistence. We need to reach out. Right now we know people who are living in Lo-debar. By that I mean we know Mephibosheths out there who are hurt. They are perhaps angry with God. They feel they have been mistreated. They live in isolation and fear. They need someone to reach out to them with the love of Jesus Christ.

As Mephibosheth might have thought, they think, *All that has gone wrong in my life is God's fault. Why did God let this happen?* It's a lie of Satan that persuades people to keep their distance from God. Satan doesn't want us to know God's love. Mephibosheth kept his distance from David, which is exactly what Satan wanted. But David listened to what God wanted, and it was he who ended up seeking out Mephibosheth.

In the same way, it is God who makes the first move in our lives. I know we as Christians like to refer to "the day I found the Lord." The truth is that He wasn't lost; *we* were. Certainly one day we discovered a God who loved us. But God found us before we found Him. He chose us before we chose Him. was Jesus sought us out as a shepherd looks for lost sheep.

This what David was doing: "You tell Mephibosheth that the king wants him to come into the palace."

A Kindly King, a Good God

Imagine how Mephibosheth felt when that knock came on his door and he heard, "Open the door in the name of the king."

A sense of dread must have washed over him. His heart sank. He had feared this day, and now it had finally come.

But the message wasn't what he thought it would be. The representatives at the door must have smiled at him, and said, "It's not what you think. King David wants show grace to you."

Mephibosheth probably was filled with doubt. *No, he wants to kill me.* But the moment he met David, this man after God's own heart, he was stunned to see a heart full of love and compassion.

David said, "I want you to come here. All of the land that belonged to your grandfather Saul, I want to give to you. I want you to live in the palace with me. I want you to eat at my table and be like a member of my own family. Let me show kindness to you."

That is exactly what God does for us. He extends kindness to us. Our relationship with God is based 100 percent on what Jesus Christ did for us. That doesn't mean we should not to seek to live godly lives. But a godly life doesn't bring the blessing of God; it is the blessing of God that produces the godly life. God loves you. He accepts you not because of who you are, but because of Jesus.

I heard a story about something that happened in the 1800s in London. A little boy wanted to hear the great American evangelist D. L. Moody, whom I referenced earlier. Moody had come to town to preach. This little street urchin made his way across the entire city of London, risking his very life, with no food or proper shoes. After a long journey, he finally came to the great church where Moody was scheduled to speak.

It was overflowing with people. He could hear the singing through the opened windows. The little guy was so excited. As he made his way up to the door, an old usher scowled at him and asked, "What are you doing, young man?"

The boy said, "I am going to go hear the great evangelist D. L. Moody."

"Not looking like that! You're filthy. Go away!"

The little boy was crushed. He was sitting on the steps, crying, when a black carriage pulled up in front of the church. Out of it stepped a large man. He saw the sad little boy on the steps and asked, "Young man, what is wrong?"

The boy answered, "I came here to hear the great preacher D. L. Moody, but they won't let me in the church."

"Is that so?" the big man said. "You just put your hand in my hand, and I will see what I can do to help you."

The little boy put his dirty little hand into the man's big, clean hand. The man led him right down the middle aisle, past the usher who wouldn't let him in, to the front row. The big guy sat him in a front-row seat. Then the man stepped up to the pulpit.

That man was, of course, D. L. Moody. That young boy couldn't get in on his own, but when he held Moody's hand, he walked through the front door.

So it is with us—because of Jesus. We are filthy in sin, but he takes our dirty hands in his clean one and leads us to the front-row seats in the palace.

David provided a marvelous and practical example of this in 2 Samuel.

Table for Two

Note that four times in thirteen verses, the writer of 2 Samuel 9 mentions that Mephibosheth sat at David's table. That may not seem significant to us, but in biblical times, dinner was the big event of the day. People then didn't have all of the entertainment and distractions we have today. Dinner was it. Not only did they have a great feast in the palace, but afterward they spent time talking and having fellowship.

Think about Mephibosheth. He had been living in that barren place called Lo-debar. The next thing he knew, he was in the palace in Jerusalem, sitting at the table of the king, just like a member of the royal family.

David's commitment to his friend Jonathan was what brought Mephibosheth to the king's table. We can glean several important principles from this.

1. We need to extend forgiveness to others

I don't care if they have wronged you or needlessly hurt you. I don't care if you would love to get back at them. God commands you to forgive, and that is what you ought to do. Don't let a root of bitterness ruin your life.

2. We need to reach out to the Mephibosheths of the world

These are people we know who may seem hostile to God or opposed to the gospel. We need to show them God's love and not give up on them. David did both these things. He listened to the will of God, and he determined that he would hold true to how he knew God wanted him to act. He showed forgiveness and compassion. And because of this, he prospered.

Remember: Saul harbored unforgiveness, and he fell. David did not. He not only started the race well, but he bounded into the lead.

In the next chapter, let's take a final look at just how David finished his race.

THE ART OF GETTING UP AGAIN

I've always loved reading biographies, and the Bible is, among other things, a biographical book. It tells us stories of some very great and some very wicked people. The authors added no "spin" to what we read in its pages. God's Word is just unvarnished truth, telling us what different persons were really like—flesh-and-blood people like you and me.

The Bible always gives us a hero, warts and all. God arranged this so we could learn from others' failures and successes. First Corinthians 10:11 says, "These things happened to them as examples for us" (NLT).

We're going to take a third look at the life of a man who certainly made his mistakes. As you recall, David was a young man whom God plucked out of obscurity to become the greatest king in Israel's history. It's worth noting the New Testament mentions David more than any other person in the Old Testament. Truly he made his mark.

In his biography, we look at how David ruled: his wisdom, his compassion, his great courage on the battlefield, his keeping a promise to an old friend to extend kindness to his son. We see such a beautiful example of a man after God's own heart.

Yet in the spiritual race, even the strongest runners sometimes fall. An easy stretch of track can lull a champion into relaxing the pace—so much so that he takes a disastrous tumble.

David Trips over a Bathing Beauty

As he was running the race of life, David was doing so well that he thought he could slow down a little, take a breather, and relax a bit. He didn't have to run with as much commitment.

He got sloppy.

It started with a lustful look, and it ended up as a nationwide scandal. Though the sin we are going to read about in David's life lasted only minutes, the repercussions of it lasted for the rest of his life.

I am speaking, of course, of the story of David and Bathsheba. This sin was so devastating to David's life, you might think that he could never survive such a fall. Amazingly, he did, though it cast a shadow over his life from which he never fully recovered.

Let's not forget, as sordid as the details are, that David was still a man after God's own heart. That is not to justify what he did in any way, but we should remember David was a godly man who made a big mistake. (Which, by the way, could happen to any one of us. If David had the potential to fall into sin like this, then you or I can fall as well.)

The story begins in 2 Samuel 11:

> In the spring of the year, when kings normally go out to war, David sent Joab and the Israelite army to fight the Ammonites. They destroyed the Ammonite army and laid siege to the city of Rabbah. However, David stayed behind in Jerusalem.
>
> Late one afternoon, after his midday rest, David got out of bed and was walking on the roof of the palace. As he looked out over the city, he noticed a woman of unusual beauty taking a bath. He sent someone to find out who she was, and he was told, "She is Bathsheba, the daughter of Eliam and the wife of Uriah the Hittite." Then David sent messengers to get her; and when she came to the palace, he slept with her. She had just completed the purification rites after having her menstrual period. Then she returned home. Later, when Bathsheba discovered that she was pregnant, she sent David a message, saying, "I'm pregnant." (vv. 1–5, NLT)

David was around fifty years old at that point in his life and had been ruling successfully for about two decades. He had distinguished himself as a man of God, a great musician, a poet, a writer, a warrior, and of course, a ruler.

No doubt about it, David was on a roll.

And that's always the time to put up your guard.

When things are going reasonably or even unreasonably well, when we are moving from glory to glory, we often find ourselves in a danger zone. That is exactly what David did.

He got lazy. Note the Bible says that when the time had come for kings to battle, David sent Joab instead. Instead of fighting the good fight, the king was sleeping in his bed. Instead of moving forward, he appeared to be moving backward.

There is no vacation from the spiritual battle. I wish there were. I wish we could kick back for a month or so. But the Christian life isn't a playground—it's a battleground. The moment you begin to slow down or relax your grip spiritually, you will begin to experience some serious problems.

David had set the scene for his own failure. He had compromised his duties as king not only by avoiding battle, but by gathering concubines (see 2 Samuel 5:13). He wasn't only lazy; he was lustful.

At that point in David's life, we don't read of his singing beautiful songs of praise to God. We don't read of his playing his stringed instrument. We don't read of his treasuring close fellowship and intimacy with God as he had done before. This fact made him far more vulnerable on the day he saw the beautiful Bathsheba bathing.

The sight of a lovely woman without her clothes would be a temptation for any man, but for David it was more intense than that.

Why? Because he had been feeding the fire of lust. So he took one look, and he crumbled. He swiftly took action to have the woman.

Again, we don't see David growing in his relationship with God at that time. This is usually what happens when we give in to temptation. We don't cease to believe in God—we just forget about Him. As Dietrich Bonhoeffer wrote that at this moment when lust takes control, "God . . . loses all reality. . . . Satan does not fill us with a hatred of God, but with forgetfulness of God."[1]

When David sent his servant to find out who she was, the servant returned and reported, "She is Bathsheba . . . the wife of Uriah the Hittite" (2 Samuel 11:3 NLT).

Apparently the servant understood why David inquired after the woman. He was warning the king: "Sire, she is a married woman. That means she's off limits."

You have to admire this servant for his boldness. Through him, the Lord was trying to warn David: "Go over—not under—this hurdle."

Caution Thrown to the Wind

Now, as you know, when a person comes under the power of sin, he does the most insane, irrational things. I've seen it many times. Often the person who commits the sin is the last to see how far he has fallen. In the same way, David, under the power of sin, wasn't thinking clearly. The man after God's own heart wasn't behaving as such.

Before we go further, let's talk a little about Bathsheba.

You might think of her as an innocent victim in this story. I disagree. Certainly the lion's share of guilt falls upon David, but we don't read of Bathsheba's necessarily protesting his request. It's true that if the king of the nation summoned you into his presence, you might submit out of fear of losing your life. On the other hand, one must ask if Bathsheba intentionally put herself in a place where she *knew* the king would see her.

A Jewish woman given to modesty, as she should have been, would not have normally bathed herself in a place where others could see her. It is possible that Bathsheba was trying to entice the king. Perhaps she, too, allowed her sin to make her irrational.

Soon Bathsheba was brought into the king's chamber. They had sex. They probably had some passionate pleasure that night. The Bible acknowledges there is pleasure in sin. If we deny that, we are fools. Would any of us sin if it were miserable? Let's be honest about it—sin can be enjoyable. The Bible even speaks of the "pleasures of sin," but says it lasts only a few moments (see Hebrews 11:25). And it comes with a hefty price tag. David found this out.

A Trickle Becomes a Flood

David at first must have thought he'd gotten away with it. Maybe he assumed, *It's just a one-night stand. No one will ever know.*

A little time passed. Then a message came to David from Bathsheba that said, "Tell the king I am pregnant."

David had a problem on his hands. What should he do? What he should have done was realize he had sinned and then *immediately* repent before God. Instead, David did what most of us do when we're caught in sin: he tried to cover it up.

David formulated an evil plan. He sent word to have Uriah, the husband of Bathsheba, come to the palace. Imagine Uriah for a moment. He seems to have been a pretty low-ranking soldier in the army. Suddenly he got a message that the king of Israel had summoned him to the palace. Imagine how exciting that must have been. It would be like getting a call from the White House saying the president wanted to see you immediately.

Imagine Uriah's anticipation as he made his way from the misery of the battlefield to the splendor of the palace. *I'm going to meet the man after God's own heart. What a great king I've heard he is. I admire him so. I'm so proud to be in his army and fight for him.*

When they met, David said, "Uriah, how are you? I wanted to hear how things are going out there in the battle."

"It's tough out there, but it's an honor to fight for you, King."

"I just thought you would like a nice meal and a night home with your wife." We read, "Then he told Uriah, 'Go on home and relax...'" (2 Samuel 11:8 NLT). We know, of course, his motives were completely impure. He was thinking that if Uriah slept with Bathsheba, Uriah would think the child she already had conceived with David was his.

Uriah, however, was such a committed soldier that he wouldn't go to his wife. The humble man "slept that night at the palace entrance with the king's palace guard" (v. 9 NLT).

The king's response? He called him back to the palace and got him good and drunk. Still, honorable Uriah refused to go home to his wife, saying, "Joab and my master's men are camping in the open fields. How could I go home to wine and dine and sleep with my wife? I swear that I would never do such a thing" (v. 11 NLT).

This was a man of integrity. He couldn't bear the thought of reveling in pleasure when his fellow soldiers were risking their lives for the king.

Again, David should have taken heed and repented. Again, he persisted in his sin. He put his murderous intentions in writing: "Station Uriah on the front lines where the battle is fiercest. Then pull back so that he will be killed" (v. 15 NLT). He sent Uriah back to the battle with this letter. Little did Uriah realize that he was carrying his own death warrant.

Joab obeyed and sent a message back to the king, which basically read, "Dear King: We led an attack against the city. We lost a few men, including Uriah the Hittite."

Again, David thought he had pulled it off. After Bathsheba mourned her husband, David ordered her back to the palace. They were married. Ultimately, everything seemed to work out.

There was one small problem. The Bible says, "But the Lord was displeased with what David had done" (v. 27 NLT).

Time to Pay the Price

It took awhile for David to realize this. Why? Because he'd shut God out. Once he had loved to worship God. He had loved to pray. He had loved to spend time in the presence of his God. During the time he was consumed with Bathsheba, however, it's as though he hung up on God. There was no communication, no communion. Granted, he still was in a relationship with God, but he wasn't living in fellowship with God.

When you live with unconfessed sin, your communication with God is shut down. Scripture says, "If I regard iniquity in my heart, the Lord will not hear" (Psalm 66:18). David experienced that. It broke his heart. He *missed* God. And God missed him. Do you know that when you are in sin, God misses fellowship with you?

The time finally came for David to come clean. Did he do so willingly and at his own initiation? No. The Lord had to direct the prophet Nathan to confront him.

This prophet was clever. He didn't play his hand with David right up front. He told a little story.

> So the Lord sent Nathan the prophet to tell David this story: "There were two men in a certain town. One was rich, and one was poor. The rich man owned a great many sheep and cattle. The poor man owned nothing but one little lamb he had bought. He raised that little lamb, and it grew up with his children. It ate from the man's own plate and drank from his cup. He cuddled it in his arms like a baby daughter. One day a guest arrived at the home of the rich man. But instead of killing an animal from his own flock or herd, he took the poor man's lamb and killed it and prepared it for his guest." (2 Samuel 12:1–4 NLT)

David's blood began to boil. His face was probably beet-red. He said, "That man should be put to death." That's pretty harsh. It's a bad thing to steal someone's lamb, but I don't think he deserved the death penalty.

Isn't it interesting how bad our sin can look in someone else's life? Isn't it amazing how people who are living in gross sin can be so judgmental of a seemingly small sin in the lives of others?

Remember the illustration that Jesus used in the Sermon on the Mount. He said, "Why worry about a speck in your friend's eye when you have a log in your own? How can you think of saying to your friend, 'Let me help you get rid of that speck in your eye,' when you can't see past the log in your own eye?" (Matthew 7:3–4 NLT).

In other words, "How can you be so critical of others when you are guilty of worse?" That was the case with David. He wanted to kill a guy for stealing someone's sheep.

Then the prophet pointed his finger at the king and said, "You are that man!" David realized he had stepped right into the trap. He had taken the noose and pulled it around his neck.

Fellowship Restored . . . at a Cost

David, at last, did the right thing. He said, "I have sinned against God." How do you think he felt? When you are living a sinful lifestyle and get busted, it's a horrible experience. But in some ways, it's a relief. You can stop hiding. You can stop lying. You can just say, "I did it. Hopefully now I can change my behavior."

I think David was relieved. Look at something he wrote during that time in Psalm 51: "Create in me a clean heart, O God, and renew a steadfast spirit within me. . . . Restore to me the joy of Your salvation . . ." (vv. 10, 12). In other words, "Lord, I've missed You. I want the joy back again. Give me a clean heart. Renew a right spirit."

The good news: God did forgive David in spite of the wickedness of his sin.

Still, the prophet Nathan reminded David, "By this deed you have given great occasion to the enemies of the Lord to blaspheme" (2 Samuel 12:14).

In other words, "David, you have given the enemy ammo to use against us. Couldn't you have thought about that?"

How I wish people would think about these things before they sin: their reputations, the cause of Christ, and the way their sin will affect others. I am amazed at what people who claim to be Christians will do. I have seen wives brazenly divorce their Christian husbands, though they had no scriptural grounds. I have seen husbands engaging in inappropriate, flirty relationships with women at the office. I've seen Christian young people willingly put themselves in places of vulnerability sexually or dabble with drinking and drugs.

I have confronted some of them, saying, "That is a sin against God."

They reply, "I know that."

"Why would you do something that's a sin against God?"

They say, "God will forgive me."

Technically, that is true. But every day a person continues in this attitude of disobedience, he is getting a harder heart. What about the cause of Christ? What about His reputation? What about His children? The sinner responds, "What about me?"

How tragic this is. How often it happens in our selfish culture, and how foolish to assume there are no serious consequences.

Nathan said that because of David's actions, "The sword shall never depart from your house" (2 Samuel 12:10). Does that mean God didn't forgive David? No. In spite of the wickedness of his sin, God forgave David. But he still paid a price for it. He saw his own sons behave exactly as he had. One son raped his half sister. Another son killed the brother who raped his half sister. The apples didn't fall far from the tree.

In addition, Nathan said, "Your child will die" (2 Samuel 12:14 NLT). Bathsheba and David had to go through the excruciating experience of the death of a child.

And finally, God gave David's wives to another man, who slept with them in public. "You did it secretly, but I will make this happen to you openly in the sight of all Israel" (2 Samuel 12:12 NLT).

For his actions, then, David experienced violence, death, and public humiliation. David's story is an excellent reminder that though you can console yourself with the hope of God's forgiveness, you may still, to some degree, reap what you have sown.

To put a contemporary face on this issue, let's say you rob a bank. You get arrested. You say, "God, I am so sorry. Forgive me." Now you hope no one will press charges. You appear before the judge and say, "Your Honor, I know it was wrong to rob that bank. I want you to know I am sorry. I have asked God to forgive me. I am asking you to forgive me. I would like to go home now for dinner."

The judge responds, "That's very touching, but no, you're going to prison."

You reap what you sowed. But look at the bright side: now you're going to have a prison ministry!

Just because you ask God to forgive you doesn't mean that you won't face some repercussions for the sin you have committed. This story is a warning for us to avoid getting apathetic in our spiritual lives. Keep up the pace—don't slacken. It could very well cost you everything.

Lessons for the Twenty-First Century

Let's rewind and see what we can learn from David's tragic mistake.

1. Learn to look away

I'm sure David wished he had never seen Bathsheba. The original language implies that when David saw her, he looked continuously. Now, when your eyes catch something you're not supposed to see, you can turn and not look. Or, you just keep looking . . . drink it in . . . commit it to memory. That's the way David looked: he locked in on her.

Jesus warned about that wrong look. In the Sermon on the Mount, the Lord told us how to deal with lust: "You have heard that it was said to those of old, 'You shall not commit adultery.' But I say to you whoever looks at a woman to lust for her has already committed adultery with her in his heart" (Matthew 5:27–28).

Here is the solution:

> "If your right eye causes you to sin, pluck it out and cast it from you; for it is more profitable for you that one of your members perish, than for your whole body to be cast into hell. And if your right hand causes you to sin, cut it off and cast it from you; for it is more profitable for you that one of your members perish than for your whole body to be cast into hell." (vv. 29–30)

Our Lord wasn't speaking literally, but figuratively. The heart of the matter is the matter of the heart. You can pluck out a right eye and still lust with the left one. You can cut off a right arm and still sin with the left. Jesus knew that. By using the phrases "right hand" and "right eye," He was making a point that the Jews listening immediately understood.

In their culture, the right hand always represented a person's best skills and most precious faculties. The right eye, in their culture, represented one's best vision.

Jesus' point is that we should give up whatever is necessary to keep from falling into sin.

2. Take heed

Look at your life and ask yourself, *Am I involved in anything that is feeding lust, impure thoughts, or setting the stage for sexual sin?* If David had practiced some careful and honest self-examination, he would not have fallen into this sin. Instead, he set himself up for the kill. Here is something to remember: Don't feed lust—*starve* it.

Conduct a rigorous self-inventory. Ask yourself, *Am I involved in a relationship that could lead to adultery?* Maybe it's a flirty relationship with someone. On occasion I've had a woman say to me, "I'm having marital problems with my husband, so I'm getting counsel."

I ask, "From whom are you getting counsel? A pastor?"

"No."

"A Christian woman from church?"

"Not exactly. I'm getting counsel from this guy I work with. He really understands."

Danger! You think nothing could ever happen between you. Stop that. You are setting yourself up. (And by the way, I've had men tell me the same thing about women in their lives.)

Let's say you're surfing the Internet, filling your mind with pornography, and you can't understand why you are always having lustful thoughts. What do you expect? Or you're listening to music that's incendiary and blatantly contrary to what you know God wants for you. Music is just a different kind of fuel that feeds uncontrolled fire.

As I said earlier, to kill lust, don't feed it—starve it. You have to recognize that it's a powerful force that can overtake you, regardless of whether you're a man or a woman, young or old, married two weeks or twenty-five years. Anybody can fall into devastating sin.

Remember, David was in his fifties. He'd been walking with God for over twenty years when he succumbed to sin. It can happen to you if you don't keep up your guard. It could happen to me if I don't keep up mine. We have to learn from David. "Let him who thinks he stands take heed lest he fall" (1 Corinthians 10:12). God has warned us.

Stumbling and Getting Back Up

In our spiritual race, if we want to win, we have to cope with failure. We have to get back up. We can't lie in the dirt, wallowing in guilt. We will be disqualified for quitting.

David recovered. He enjoyed many good years after his fiasco. Though he also faced the consequences of his sin, in the end, David made a beautiful comeback. He was like a runner who was sprinting, leaving everyone else in his dust—who then crashed. You would think he'd just admit defeat. But David got up and made it across the finish line.

So can you. Get back in the race and make it a beautiful finish.

STAY THE COURSE!

I want to tell you the story of a man who pretty much tried it all. If ever a person could say, "Been there, done that, bought the T-shirt," it was this man. You might describe him as a wealthy hedonist extraordinaire who makes Hugh Hefner look like a lightweight in comparison.

He was highly educated, yet he went on unbelievable drinking binges. On one hand, he chased pleasure like there was no tomorrow. On the other hand, he was an architectural genius who masterminded the building of incredible structures and a man known for his supernatural wisdom.

On one hand, he was a skillful runner who had all the muscle for a win. On the other hand, he wasted his energy, and it cost him the race.

Who was it? I'm not speaking of some contemporary billionaire. This man lived hundreds of years ago, yet the lessons and experiences of his life are as current as tomorrow's newspaper.

His name was Solomon. This is his story.

A Bubble That Bursts

Solomon was the son of David and Bathsheba. After their first infant died, as Nathan the prophet had predicted, the couple produced another child.

Solomon became the king of Israel after his father's death. Like many of the biblical characters we have studied, he had amazing potential to do great things. God had given him supernatural wisdom, an unlimited power to do good. He had a godly heritage (remember that in spite of David's lapse, he did make a strong spiritual recovery). In the beginning, Solomon ran the race of life powerfully and effectively.

Then, almost without warning, he chucked it all and crashed and burned. The Book of Ecclesiastes is the story of his fall, backslide, and prodigal days. The first three verses introduce the theme of the book, which he wrote in retrospect:

> The words of the Teacher, son of David, king in Jerusalem: "Meaningless! Meaningless!" says the Teacher. "Utterly meaningless! Everything is meaningless."

> What do people gain from all their labors at which they toil under the sun? (NIV)

You see, Solomon had gone on a search for the meaning of life. It wasn't enough for him to hear from others what right and wrong were. Nor was it enough for him to see the consequences of sin in the life of his father, King David. It wasn't enough for God to tell him what right and wrong were. He wanted to know for himself.

You don't have to wait for the last chapter to see what the results of that search were. He laid it out in verse 2. The New King James translation renders this verse, "Vanity of vanities."

Solomon liked the word "vanity." He used it thirty-eight times in the Book of Ecclesiastes. When Solomon used this word, he was not describing a person who spends a lot of time primping in front of a mirror. The word "vanity," as used in the Bible, has different shades of meaning, such as "emptiness," "futility," "meaninglessness," "the wisp of a vapor," or "a hollow, empty ring." One of my favorite translations is "a bubble that bursts."

In these opening verses, Solomon was saying, "I have looked at everything a person can experience in this life apart from God. I am telling you, it has an empty, hollow ring. It's a wisp of a vapor. It's empty. It's futile. It's like a bubble that bursts."

Solomon concluded that no possession, no relationship, no experience can satisfy the soul's deepest longing. He realized his quest had led him nowhere in life.

His pursuit of meaning was like riding a stationary bike. You pedal and pedal, but when you get off that thing, you have gone precisely nowhere. Solomon admitted he was just spinning his wheels. He was wasting his life.

A Godly Heritage Abandoned

Ecclesiastes 1 continues,

> One generation passes away, and another generation comes; but the earth abides forever. The sun also rises, and the sun goes down, and hastens to the place where it arose. The wind goes toward the south, and turns around to the north; the wind whirls about continually, and comes again on its circuit. All the rivers run into the sea, yet the sea is not full; to the place from which the rivers come, there they return again. All things are full of labor; man cannot express it. The eye is not satisfied with seeing, nor the ear filled with hearing. That which has been is what will be, that which is done is what will be done, and there is nothing new under the sun. Is there anything of which it may be said, "See, this is new"? It has already been in ancient times before us. There is no remembrance of former things, nor will there be any remembrance of things that are to come by those who will come after. (vv. 4–11)

A phrase Solomon used many times is "under the sun." By using this phrase, Solomon was speaking of a horizontal, strictly human viewpoint of life. He was declaring there was no fulfillment in life under the sun—in other words, in life without God. He'd learned the hard way. Once he began his descent into human excess, Solomon rarely looked above the sun for answers. He proved that the attempt to meet the deepest needs of our lives, while leaving God out of the equation, will leave us empty.

This is ironic when you consider his life story. King David, the man after God's own heart, had raised Solomon in a godly home. When David was on his deathbed, he had called young Solomon in to remind him of what really mattered in life:

> "And Solomon, my son, learn to know the God of your ancestors intimately. Worship and serve him with your whole heart and a willing mind. For the Lord sees every heart and knows every plan and thought. If you seek him, you will find him. But if you forsake him, he will reject you forever." (1 Chronicles 28:9 NLT)

In other words, David had been saying, "Son, you can't live off your father's faith. You need to get your own. You need to serve God with an undivided heart. You need to completely commit yourself to Him. This is the secret I have learned about life."

Remember that David wrote, "One thing I have desired of the Lord, that will I seek: that I may dwell in the house of the Lord all the days of my life, to behold the beauty of the Lord, and to inquire in His temple" (Psalm 27:4).

David had clear focus and purpose in life. He knew what he was living for. And at the end, he tried to pass this legacy on to his son. For a time, Solomon did follow the words that his father gave him. Then he allowed his heart to be divided. He tried to love the Lord *and* the world. According to Scripture, that just won't wash. The Bible reminds us, "Friendship with the world is enmity with God" (James 4:4). If you are going to be the world's friend, then you are going to be God's enemy.

Tried Everything, Gained Nothing

Solomon did what most people only dream of: he personally tried everything that this world had to offer, including sex, drinking, partying, unlimited materialism, lavish entertainment, building huge estates, and more. And Solomon did far more than dabble in these things; he went after them, as they say in the South, "whole hog."

Again, the irony is that he really knew better. Not only did he have David's example and parting words, but in 1 Kings 3 we read,

> The Lord appeared to him in a dream that night and told him to ask for anything he wanted, and it would be given to him!
>
> Solomon replied, "You were wonderfully kind to my father David

because he was honest and true and faithful to you, and obeyed your commands. And you have continued your kindness to him by giving him a son to succeed him. O Lord my God, now you have made me the king instead of my father David, but I am as a little child who doesn't know his way around. And here I am among your own chosen people, a nation so great that there are almost too many people to count! Give me an understanding mind so that I can govern your people well and know the difference between what is right and what is wrong. For who by himself is able to carry such a heavy responsibility?"

So he replied, "Because you have asked for wisdom in governing my people and haven't asked for a long life, or riches for yourself, or the defeat of your enemies—yes, I'll give you what you asked for! I will give you a wiser mind than anyone else has ever had or ever will have! And I will also give you what you didn't ask for—riches and honor! And no one in all the world will be as rich and famous as you for the rest of your life! And I will give you a long life if you follow me and obey my laws as your father David did."
(1 Kings 3:11–14 TLB)

That is such a beautiful story—and a perfect illustration of what prayer is all about. Solomon had figured out that the objective of prayer was to get his will in alignment with God's. That is so important. We sometimes think that through prayer, we are going to somehow cajole God into doing what we want Him to do. I have even heard people say, "I was wrestling with God in prayer." Who won? I hope God did. If you're trying to fight with God, you're going to lose, one way or the other.

As I've pointed out, the purpose of prayer is not to move God our way; it is to move us His way. It is to tap into His will for our lives. Solomon said, "I need wisdom," and that's exactly what God wanted him to request. As a result, the Lord gave him not only what he prayed for, but even more.

What would you say if God came to you tonight in a dream and said, "I will give you whatever you want"? Your answer is a real indication as to where you are spiritually—how you are doing in the spiritual race.

We see that Solomon's heart was right with God because he said,

"Lord, I need wisdom. I'm overwhelmed by my responsibilities."

Have you ever felt that way? Are you overwhelmed by your responsibilities as a father or a mother? Perhaps you're a CEO of a corporation. You're a boss at a worksite. You oversee other people in a ministry. You're a teacher in a classroom.

Everybody comes to you with problems. Often you feel you can't handle it all. You say, "Lord, give me wisdom." He will.

Maybe you're a parent. You're trying to create a godly household while paying the bills and taking care of the children. You feel inadequate for the job. *Lord, give me wisdom.* Again, He will.

The Bible tells us, "If you need wisdom, ask our generous God, and he will give it to you. He will not rebuke you for asking" (James 1:5 NLT).

God told Solomon, "Because you have your priorities in order, I'm about to bless you with a lot of other things as well." He did. Solomon possessed unparalleled wisdom. People came from all around the world to sit at his feet and drink in his words. An authority no less than the Queen of Sheba, after observing Solomon's accomplishments and wisdom firsthand, said, "The half was not told me" (1 Kings 10:7).

That's what made his downfall all the more shocking. Let's take a closer look at his fall from grace.

Compromise Leads to a Painful Tumble

Solomon's fall and disillusionment began with a series of compromises, one of which was marrying the daughter of Pharaoh. He did this because he wanted to establish a political alliance.

It's the sort of thing that happened all the time in that day and age. Other kings were doing it left and right. But it wasn't God's will for *this* king. For all practical purposes, Solomon was "yoking" himself unequally with a nonbeliever.

God had told the Jewish people not to intermarry with the other nations. This wasn't a racial issue; it was a *spiritual* issue. God didn't want the Israelites aligning themselves with people who were worshipers of false gods. He knew their hearts would turn away.

The same is true of us as Christians. You want to run this race with someone who loves the Lord as you do.

If you are a single person, you should pray for and wait on the godly man or woman the Lord will bring into your life. You can be sure He wouldn't want you romantically involved with a person who doesn't believe.

The Bible tells us, "Don't team up with those who are unbelievers. How can righteousness be a partner with wickedness? How can light live with darkness? What harmony can there be between Christ and the devil? How can a believer be a partner with an unbeliever?" (2 Corinthians 6:14–15 NLT).

In the race of life, you want to run with someone who is traveling in the same direction as you are. And if you are Christians, both you and your mate will be running toward the Lord and His plan and purpose for your lives.

Solomon, however, didn't live by that principle. He teamed up with someone—and then a bunch of someones—who didn't share his faith or his God. More problems followed, and they always will.

After a while Solomon said—in spite of the fact that he had great wisdom, wealth, and power, and God had blessed him in every way imaginable—"I want to experience everything this world has to offer." In Ecclesiastes 1:13 he said, "And I set my heart to seek and search out by wisdom concerning all that is done under heaven."

The word that he used for "seek" could be translated "to investigate the roots of a matter." It is as though Solomon were doing a research paper. He didn't want to just read about it; he wanted to actually experience it.

In the process of doing so, Solomon ignored the affairs of state. He neglected his family. He set aside all spiritual principles and truth. Essentially, Solomon was saying, "I don't want to pass judgment and say that a thing is wrong until I've done it myself. I won't just read about getting drunk—I'll do it. A lot! I will commit acts of immorality. I will revel in unlimited possessions. I plan on trying everything that other people do, so I can speak with authority as to whether it's fulfilling or not."

It wasn't. None of it fulfilled his heart.

That's a foolish way to do research, as we will see. Here are some of the things he dabbled in.

1. Knowledge ... for its own sake

He thought, "If I could get the finest education, surely that would satisfy the deepest needs of my soul." But look at the outcome in Ecclesiastes 1:16–17:

> I said to myself, "Look, I am wiser than any of the kings who ruled in Jerusalem before me. I have greater wisdom and knowledge than any of them." So I set out to learn everything from wisdom to madness and folly. But I learned firsthand that pursuing all this is like chasing the wind. (NLT)

Solomon was trying to fill a void that only God could fill. Attaining knowledge is a good thing. *But if you do it without God, it will leave you with an empty space in your soul as wide as the Grand Canyon.*

2. Solomon, the party animal

Then he shifted gears, saying, "Okay, I've had enough of pursuing knowledge for a while. Now I will pursue pleasure." He went from being an academic to being a party animal in a snap of the fingers.

He wrote about it in Ecclesiastes 2:1–2 (NLT), saying, "I said to myself, "Come on, let's try pleasure. Let's look for the 'good things' in life." But I found that this, too, was meaningless. So I said, "Laughter is silly. What good does it do to seek pleasure?"

There are people like that. They want to laugh. They want to have a good time. You can always tell in a restaurant which group is drinking. They get progressively louder and more obnoxious, and they laugh at everything. At some point they don't even know why they're laughing. You can see from their faces that they are trying so desperately to have a good time. It's clear they're thinking, *I want to escape from my problems—whatever it takes.*

These people often live a tragic existence all week long, looking forward to the weekend when they can get inebriated. Then they wake up the next morning with a numbing hangover, and it's back to the routine. Then another week passes. Another month passes. Another year passes. Then you start seeing the effect all this sin brings into their lives, not only spiritually, but physically—their bodies start breaking down prematurely. The "good life" takes its pound of flesh.

Solomon tried that too. He thought maybe getting drunk would satisfy. In Ecclesiastes 2:3 he said, "After much thought, I decided to cheer myself with wine. And while still seeking wisdom, I clutched at foolishness. In this way, I tried to experience the only happiness most people find during their brief life in this world" (NLT).

After a few too many hangovers, and maybe waking up in bed with people he had never seen before, the king saw the emptiness of that as well.

3. Spectacular possessions

Solomon shifted gears again. With unlimited resources at his disposal, he thought he would purchase all the luxurious goods that money could buy. Ecclesiastes 2 describes his further descent:

> Then I tried to find fulfillment by inaugurating a great public works program: homes, vineyards, gardens, parks, and orchards for myself, and reservoirs to hold the water to irrigate my plantations.

> Next I bought slaves, both men and women, and others were born within my household. I also bred great herds and flocks, more than any of the kings before me. I collected silver and gold as taxes from many kings and provinces.

> In the cultural arts, I organized men's and women's choirs and orchestras.

> And then there were my many beautiful concubines. . . .

> But as I looked at everything I had tried, it was all so useless, a chasing of the wind, and there was nothing really worthwhile anywhere. (Ecclesiastes 2:4–8, 11 TLB)

Solomon experienced something over which you often hear lottery winners lament. I've read about it time and time again: Someone wins the lottery. For a while, he enjoys the high life, buying cars, houses, boats, trips, everything he can think of. But after a while, it all begins to overwhelm. He becomes trapped by the very things he thought he wanted. People want to take advantage of him, and he finds himself trapped by the very thing he thought would set him free. How many times have you heard of a lottery winner being quoted as saying, "I wish I'd never won"?

Evelyn Adams, who won the New Jersey lottery—not just once but twice (1985, 1986)—to the tune of $5.4 million, is now penniless and lives in a trailer. "Everybody wanted my money," she now reflects. "Everybody had their hand out. I never learned one simple word in the English language—'No.' I wish I had the chance to do it all over again. I'd be much smarter about it now."

William "Bud" Post won $16.2 million in the Pennsylvania lottery in 1988 but now lives on his Social Security ($450 a month) and food stamps. "I wish it never happened," he says. "It was totally a nightmare."[1]

Solomon was essentially writing about the same nightmare. He had tried to buy the world with money, but in the end, all he bought was misery.

Raging Regret

Solomon was a man who threw his life away. He did it all. He learned that life without God is empty and futile. What can we learn from this? Two principles come to mind.

1. Don't throw your youth away

At the end of Ecclesiastes 12, Solomon summed up his lessons learned in pleasure without godliness. Among other things, we discover Solomon deeply regretted throwing his youth away as he chased after these things. Verse 1 says, "Remember now your Creator in the days of your youth, before the difficult days come, and the years draw near when you say, 'I have no pleasure in them.' "

The New Living Translation puts it like this: "Don't let the excitement of youth cause you to forget your Creator. Honor him in your youth before you grow old and say, 'Life is not pleasant anymore.' "

Youth is such an important time in life. It is there that we lay a foundation and establish our priorities. We set our course. We start the race.

In my thirty-plus years of ministry, I have seen that most people make a commitment to Christ before the age of twenty-one. That is why it is so important to reach people when they are young. As John the apostle wrote, "I have no greater joy than to hear that my children walk in truth" (3 John 1:4). The decisions we make during our youth affect us for the rest of our lives. We sow the seeds of career and marriage, then reap their results in the years ahead.

When we're young, we're more flexible and more open to change, even embracing it. The one thing you hear from kids is, "I'm bored!" (And this while they are watching TV, playing a video game, talking on the phone, and texting—all at the same time.) In contrast, when you get older, you find yourself liking a routine. You become more set in your ways. You go to the same restaurants and order the same things. You actually begin to take comfort in the sameness and repetition of your life.

Now, that's not necessarily a bad thing—if you have established good habits earlier. In the early years, the die is cast. The course charted. The path started. You decide what the evening of your life will be by the choices you make in the morning.

The stand you make today will determine what kind of stand you will make tomorrow. Solomon's conclusion was heartfelt: remember God when you are young. Don't throw your youth away. If you want to heed Solomon's wisdom and run a complete race, start good habits in your youth. Build a healthy foundation. Then you will have established something that will benefit you all of your life—and all of your race.

2. In whatever you do . . . don't leave God behind

Here, in a nutshell, is the lesson learned by a man who ran away from God . . . a man who was raised with a godly heritage and given incredible wisdom from God . . . a man who had more wealth than any person could dream of . . . a man who had experienced everything this world has to offer.

Mark it well:

Now all has been heard; here is the conclusion of the matter: Fear
God and keep his commandments, for this is the duty of all mankind. For God will bring every deed into judgment, including every
hidden thing, whether it is good or evil. (Ecclesiastes 12:13–14 NIV)

Solomon was saying, "Take it from a seasoned pro. I know what
I'm talking about. If you leave God out of the picture, your life will
be empty, meaningless, and futile . . . like a bubble that burst."

Solomon said that if you want to live life to its fullest, "Fear God
and keep his commandments." The phrase "fear God" means to reverence the Lord. It doesn't mean to cower in fear because you think
God will hurt you. Rather, express a sense of awe and worship and
praise to God. It is a healthy desire to want to please him in the way
you live, and it is a healthy dread to turn away from anything that
might displease or grieve Him.

Honor God. Glorify God. Hear God, and do what He tells you
to do. If we would just follow this little piece of wisdom from the
Bible, so hard-won on Solomon's part, how it would change our
lives! How many more people are going to say this doesn't apply to
them and go out to try it all for themselves? How many more lives
will be wasted? How many more marriages will be destroyed? How
many more children will be deprived of a father and a mother to
raise them? How many more people will be destroyed by substance
abuse? How many more people will chase after materialism and living completely selfish lives? God knows.

Don't waste your life the way Solomon did. He was another who
started well but stumbled. You think he would have learned from
the example—both good and bad—of his father. He saw what happened when David followed the Lord and ruled well. He also saw
what happened to David when he sinned against God and the repercussions he experienced. But Solomon had to find out for himself.
He wasted a lot of years.

A Race Is All about the Finish

Let me liken Solomon's race to one I tried when my son Christopher ran track and field in high school. I had heard a rumor that after a certain meet, the dads could race. Just in case this was true, I bought myself the latest and lightest Nike Air shoes available; I had every intention of winning that race. I thought maybe I could relive some of my glory days from high school.

The fact is, I was a pretty good sprinter. I had this burst of energy that kicked in and carried me to the finish line. I usually beat people in a race. I thought I would do it again, even though it had been many years since I had run like that.

Sure enough, after the track meet was over for the kids, the announcement came. All the dads made their way over. Surveying the competition, I thought, *This is going to be good*. I noticed a lot of potbellies. Not only was I going to win, I was going to win big.

They fired the starter pistol. I took off. I was shocked to see almost everybody dash ahead of me. Immediately I was behind. This concerned me. I thought it was time to call on that burst of energy that had always led me to victory. I reached down for that formidable strength. But the burst had gone bust! I was already on empty.

I noticed the pack was even farther ahead of me. I quickly realized that not only was I going to lose the race, I was going to lose big. Not only would I be last, but I probably would be five minutes behind everybody else—if I even finished at all! I would get that courtesy applause that people give when you finish but are pathetic.

I hadn't even finished the first lap, and I was in pain. Let me rephrase that: I was in total agony. I thought, *I have two choices. I can either try to finish this race and come in at the end, or I can quit*.

When I passed a certain tree, I just walked off. Someone said, "Greg, I thought you were running the race."

"No," I assured him, "I was just messing around."

Solomon might have said the same thing. "Sure, I started the race, but I got off-track. I wasn't really in it for the prize; I was just messing around."

The spiritual race of life is nothing to mess around with. *This is the race you must win.*

Just as I got discouraged early and abandoned the race, Solomon got discouraged and quit his. He wasn't satisfied with everything, so he basically pursued nothing. He was a bona fide graduate of the School of Hard Knocks.

It's sad. The wisest man who ever lived, lived like a fool. He started in the race but soon left the track altogether.

Let's face it: the prize is at the end of the race. There's only one way to get it: stay the course—it's the single chance you have of winning!

DRAWING A CROWD

In light of the rampant immorality within, terrorism without, and widespread violence that America is experiencing, it would be easy to say there is no hope for our country today. Life, we suspect, will only get darker. Certainly nothing we could ever do as individuals could turn things around or make any kind of difference.

I want you to know that is definitely not true. If we look at the history of Israel, we see how often our history parallels it. God established the nation of Israel. He ruled over it. Despite the attempts of revisionists to rewrite our history, our founding fathers established our nation on biblical principles, and the Lord has blessed us as the years have gone by.

God intervened in the history of the nation Israel and turned it around. Periodically he brought about a great revival. We can hope and pray He will do the same for us.

As we look at the conditions when Elijah emerged on Israel's scene, we see they were strikingly similar to our own. One man running well in the spiritual race did indeed make a difference.

Elijah: The Lord Is My God

In the midst of Israel's idolatry, wickedness, and immorality—spurred on by the wicked King Ahab and Queen Jezebel—God decided to intervene. The Lord decided to raise up His man, just as He had done so many times before. The man God sent for Israel's release was Elijah. His very name summed up his purpose. It meant "My God is Jehovah" or "The Lord is my God."

In fact, Elijah's very name was a rebuke to the king and queen of Israel. It essentially said, "Your god may be the false gods Baal or Asherah, but *my* God is the Lord, the God of our fathers."

As we read about the life of Elijah, he might seem a little hard to relate to. He seems almost bionic or superhuman. After all, this was the prophet who prayed down fire from heaven. This was the man God used to raise a person from the dead. This was the guy who could get rain to stop and start at his command. It's virtually impossible for us to imagine ourselves anywhere near the league of the wonder-working man of God, Elijah.

Yet, as we will discover, Elijah also had his shortcomings. He had his flaws. In fact, Elijah was just as we are. Why do I bring that up? Because God is still looking for His man for this generation. He is still looking for His woman to make a difference.

Let's read about Elijah and see if we can get a handle on why he was who he was, and why the Lord used him in such a significant way.

In 1 Kings 17:1 we read, "And Elijah the Tishbite . . . said to Ahab, 'As the Lord God of Israel lives, before whom I stand, there shall not be dew nor rain these years, except at my word.'"

What a launch into the public eye that was! What a beginning! Try to see the scene in your mind's eye: Ahab and Jezebel were legendary for their power and cruelty. People normally trembled in their presence, for, with a word, they could end your life. These two had openly rebelled against and defied the true God of Israel.

Enter Elijah. What boldness he had as he stormed into their court. Elijah made no opening statement and dispensed with all formalities. He just announced that between himself and "the Lord God of Israel," the land would enjoy no rain or dew until he said so. Then, as far as we know, he turned around and walked out.

Can't you see the king and queen? *"Who was that guy? How did he get past security? How dare he speak to us in that way?"*

Have You Been to the Brook?

Elijah had delivered his powerful message. Ahab and Jezebel apparently let his lack of reverence pass. Then the Lord told Elijah to go into obscurity—disappear for a while—and God would provide for him there.

What a strange request! Yet we don't see Elijah arguing with God over his odd command or his rather rough provisions. Scripture says, "He went and did according to the word of the Lord, for he went and stayed by the Brook of Cherith. . . . The ravens brought him bread and meat in the morning, and bread and meat in the evening; and he drank from the brook" (1 Kings 17:5–6).

Does Elijah's sudden turnaround sound a little familiar? Maybe things were going reasonably well in your own life, and God redirected you. It didn't necessarily make sense at the moment. Maybe you were a successful businesswoman who married and then got pregnant. You announced to all of your coworkers one day, "I'm going to go home and raise this child that the Lord has given me."

They said, "Don't you know we have day care facilities here?"

You said, "No, I want to be with this child." You turned your back and walked away, and you went to the Brook Cherith. People thought you were nuts, but you knew you had done the right thing.

Maybe you went to the finest university and earned a degree. One day God spoke to you, and you felt called to the mission field.

"Are you crazy?" your friends and family asked. "What about your degree?"

But you've made up your mind. You are going to the Brook Cherith. You obey when God leads you.

That's exactly what Elijah did. But the next thing we know is that the brook dried up.

Maybe that's happened to you too. Things were humming along, then one day your spouse said, "I'm leaving. I don't want to be married to you anymore." They're gone. Your brook dried up.

Maybe your ministry was flourishing. God was blessing it. Suddenly it began to shrink. It didn't make any sense. Your brook dried up.

Maybe you got a call from the place you've worked at for twenty years: "Sorry. We have to downsize." Your brook just dried up. Your world ended. Or so it seemed.

Actually, it might be a whole new beginning. When God closes one door, He opens another. Elijah was about to discover this. In fact, God was preparing him. This is very important: the Lord was getting him ready for what was ahead. We all know about Elijah and his fiery confrontation with the prophets of Baal on Mount Carmel. He wasn't ready for that yet. God first had to whip him into shape.

The Next Assignment

> Then the word of the Lord came to him, saying, "Arise, go to Zarephath . . . and dwell there. See, I have commanded a widow there to provide for you" (1 Kings 17:9).

Once again, Elijah obeyed a command that didn't make much earthly sense.

The Lord directed the great wonder-working prophet to make himself dependent on a poor widow who had a son to raise. This wasn't an easy thing, being a burden to someone like that. But God was teaching Elijah humility—at the same time He was teaching the widow about dependence. That's the way it is with our all-wise, all-powerful God. He is working with many, many people on many, many different levels—all at the very same moment.

Though the widow didn't have enough food for herself and her son, Elijah promised God would meet her needs if she would tend to his: "You take care of me, and God will bless you and multiply what you have. In addition, you will always have enough." Sure enough, the Lord sustained her, her son, and Elijah. It was a beautiful illustration of the importance of Matthew 6:33: "Seek first the kingdom of God and His righteousness, and all these things [the needs of life] shall be added to you."

One day, the worst thing imaginable happened to this poor widow. Her beloved son unexpectedly died. But the Lord stretched her faith even more as God raised him back from the dead through

Elijah the prophet.

You see, God was getting him ready, step by step, challenge by challenge. Really big things were coming—things that would shake a nation and make history. The next phase was about to start. It's the same with you. If you've been told to head for the hills and be fed by birds, so to speak, if your brook has dried up, if a door has closed in your life, don't think God is done with you. You need to just trust Him. He may be getting you ready for phase two. He may be whipping you into shape for something beyond your wildest dreams.

So it was for Elijah. God was going to use him in ways he never thought possible. And after his sojourn by the brook and time with the widow, he was now prepared.

Elijah was ready to rumble.

A New Mission

In 1 Kings 18, we see the prophet's coming-out party.

> And it came to pass after many days that the word of the Lord came to Elijah, in the third year, saying, "Go, present yourself to Ahab, and I will send rain on the earth." So Elijah went to present himself to Ahab; and there was a severe famine in Samaria. And Ahab had called Obadiah, who was in charge of [Ahab's] house. (Now Obadiah feared the Lord greatly. For so it was, while Jezebel massacred the prophets of the Lord, that Obadiah had taken one hundred prophets and hidden them, fifty to a cave, and had fed them with bread and water.) And Ahab had said to Obadiah, "Go into the land to all the springs of water and to all the brooks; perhaps we may find grass to keep the horses and mules alive, so that we will not have to kill any livestock." So they divided the land between them to explore it; Ahab went one way by himself, and Obadiah went another way by himself.
>
> Now as Obadiah was on his way, suddenly Elijah met him; and he recognized him, and fell on his face, and said, "Is that you, my lord Elijah?" And he answered him, "It is I. Go, tell your master, 'Elijah is here.'" (vv. 1–8)

The very next assignment was Elijah's biggest: challenging the prophets of Baal to an old-fashioned shoot-out at the OK Corral.

We will look further at this story in the next chapter, but suffice it now to say that when the prophet encountered the king's servant, Obadiah, after a three-year vacation, Elijah was ready to rock.

An Example of What Not to Do

Obadiah, however, *wasn't* ready to rock.

Let's contrast him with Elijah. He was an interesting character. Scripture tells that us he "feared the Lord greatly" (1 Kings 18:3). We also read that when Jezebel was killing off the prophets, Obadiah hid one hundred of them. But even though he was a believer, he seemed to lack real backbone; otherwise he would not have served in Ahab's court. He was serving the most wicked king in the history of Israel.

Obadiah had heard and seen great atrocities against God's servants, but he had not spoken up for fear of losing his position—or his head. Obadiah's testimony was so diminished and his witness so weak that he in no way deterred Ahab from his evil. In some ways, he was even an accomplice with Ahab and Jezebel in their wicked ways.

Remember, our silence can imply consent and endorsement to actions we actually oppose. If you see something wrong and you don't speak up, others may interpret your silence as approval. Think of how Elijah instantly obeyed and firmly declared God's will. That's the path you need to take.

We need more Elijahs and fewer Obadiahs. Obadiahs may believe and may even fear the Lord, but they don't stand up for what's right. They're afraid of persecution. They don't want to be laughed at. They're afraid of being rejected. So they try to fly under the radar—"stealth Christians." We need more people who will stand for the Lord the way Elijah did.

I think Elijah hit the nail on the head when he said, "Go, tell your master, 'Elijah is here.'" Who was Obadiah's master? Ahab. What did Jesus say? You cannot serve two masters. You will love the one and hate the other. Elijah was saying, "Obadiah, here is your problem: your master is Ahab."

We can see how fear paralyzed Obadiah when he responded, in effect, "No way! I'm not going to tell this to Ahab. I know you too well! You're a strange sort of guy. You show up and say it's not going to rain, and then take off for three years. We've been looking everywhere for you! If I tell Ahab I saw Elijah, you'll suddenly drop off the radar again, and I'll take the punishment."

Obadiah even tried pleading: "How have I sinned, that you are delivering your servant into the hand of Ahab, to kill me?" (1 Kings 18:9).

Elijah essentially said, "Obadiah, it is time to stop being a closet believer. It is time to stand up and be counted. Stop trying to live in two worlds. Go deliver my message."

Like Obadiah, compromising Christians have too much of the Lord to be happy in the world, but too much of the world to be happy in the Lord. Like Obadiah, they know the world doesn't have the answers, yet they don't fully trust God either. It is a miserable no-man's-land. As Elijah made clear then, I say now: It is time to come out. It is time to stand up for what you believe.

I would imagine that Elijah knew Obadiah probably tried to rationalize his position by saying, "It's better that a believer is in the king's house. Perhaps I can have some influence there." Sometimes in our desire to justify ourselves to gain credibility, we lose integrity. Instead of our pulling them up, the nonbelievers pull us down.

Are you compromising your personal integrity right now? Compromise prompts us to be silent for fear of offending when we ought to speak up; to give undeserved praise to keep friends; to tolerate sin, because to fight it might give us enemies; to lower our standards in order to extend our reach. At what cost?

Are you an Elijah, or are you an Obadiah? You are one of the two. Are you someone who is hiding away and not speaking up for your faith in Christ? Are you an Elijah who is standing up and being counted?

The Elijah Choice

This passage in 1 Kings gives us some practical means by which we can be more like faithful Elijah than faithless Obadiah. Where did the prophet get his incredible courage and boldness?

1. Elijah knew God

Elijah served a living God, not a dead one such as Baal. Like Job, Elijah could say, "I know that my Redeemer lives" (Job 19:25).

Elijah realized that he stood in the presence of the most powerful King of all, and it was God himself. This was true also when Elijah stood in the presence of Ahab, because he understood what Psalm 91 meant when it said, "He who dwells in the secret place of the Most High shall abide under the shadow of the Almighty" (v. 1). He wasn't afraid to stand before Ahab.

Have you ever tried to stand in someone's shadow? You have to stay very close. If he moves, you have to mirror his actions. Elijah stood in the shadow of God, no matter where he was. Sometimes we forget that. We think when we leave church, we somehow leave God's presence. The truth is that wherever we go, God is with us.

When you stand in the presence of God, you will not bow before any man. Proverbs 28:1 says, "The righteous are bold as a lion." Elijah was bold because he was aware that he was always standing in God's presence. He seemed to be the only one doing it at the time. Obadiah was standing in the shadow of Ahab.

He was an army of one. Have you heard the U.S. Army's slogan, "An army of one"? That is what Elijah was. Do you feel as if you are an army of one? Perhaps you feel you are the only person in your class, workplace, neighborhood, or family who will speak up for Jesus Christ. You know there are other believers, but they are always fading into the woodwork. You are the single person who will stand up for the Lord.

That's not an easy thing to do. You don't want to come off like a religious nut or a prude. So maybe you compromise a bit. Maybe when someone tells a dirty joke, you laugh along with everybody else. You might wink at an indiscretion for fear of coming off too "holier than thou." You might tell a lie to get that promotion. You might make that compromise to be with the "in" crowd. I ask you today: at what cost?

Elijah was no compromiser. He stood up for what was right, even when he felt he was the only one doing it.

He stood in the gap for Israel. Did you know that God is still looking today for men and women who will stand in the gap for Him? What do I mean by "stand in the gap"? It's a biblical phrase, and it means interceding on someone's behalf. In Ezekiel 22:30, God said, "I sought for a man among them who would make a wall, and stand in the gap before Me on behalf of the land, that I should not destroy it; but I found no one." God was saying, "I am looking for someone right now to be My man, My woman. I am looking for someone to stand in the gap in that family, in that situation, in that sphere of influence. Would you be that man or woman?"

2. Elijah was a man of prayer

James 5:17–18 tells us, "Elijah was a human being, even as we are. He prayed earnestly that it would not rain, and it did not rain on the land for three and a half years. Again he prayed, and the heavens gave rain, and the earth produced its crops" (NIV). It was Elijah's prayer in private that was the source of his power in public.

Another character in the Bible, Daniel, was similar. Every day Daniel bowed before the Lord and prayed. He boldly stood before King Nebuchadnezzar and braved lions before King Darius. Daniel seemed to have no fear. We remember also Daniel's friends, Shadrach, Meshach, and Abednego, who refused to worship the golden image the king had erected. Where did they get this power? Through prayer. Through walking in awareness of the presence of God.

Elijah was a man who knew how to pray. Up on Mount Carmel, with his life at stake and the Lord's mightiness in question, Elijah called on the Lord with passion and complete dependence. We can pray in different ways. If you are sitting down for a meal, you say quietly, "Lord, bless the food." But if you're in an extreme situation—say, one in which your life is in danger—you will cry out to Him.

That is what Elijah did. He prayed with fervency, commitment, and dedication. He prayed as if lives depended on it. They did.

That is the way we all need to pray all the time. One of the reasons we see no power in our prayer is because we put so little heart into it. How can we expect God to put much heart into answering us? You might be thinking, *But come on, things aren't that serious here. Do I really need to pray so fervently?* Yes. Because lives are always at stake, even if only indirectly.

3. Elijah faithfully delivered the message

God gave Elijah a simple message to deliver to King Ahab, which was: "It is not going to rain for three years." It was another way of saying, "Hard times are coming. You will suffer. Your subjects will suffer. Some of them will die." That was his message—not a word of hope in it! Would you have wanted to deliver such a word to the most powerful man in the nation, a man known for his wickedness? It's amazing that Elijah was able to do it.

God calls us to deliver a message as well. It's called the gospel. Fortunately, our message has a good-news aspect attached to it. We can tell people God loves them. We can tell people God offers the hope of heaven beyond the grave. We can tell people God forgives sins.

Sometimes, though, we don't deliver the whole message. We think the listener won't want to hear everything, so we edit out parts. That's a mistake. God has called us to deliver the entire message, just as Elijah did. We have no right to speak of the glories of heaven without warning of the horrors of hell. We shouldn't speak of the promise of forgiveness without telling people about the need for repentance.

We shouldn't tell people about the promise of wearing the crown without telling them also about the importance of taking up the cross. We can't tell them about the prize at the end of the race without telling them about all the laps involved. Sometimes we like to leave those things out for fear of offending.

Our fear should be of offending God by not delivering the whole truth, nothing but the truth. That's why Paul said, "I did not shrink from declaring to you the whole counsel of God" (Acts 20:27 ESV).

Of course, as we share this message, it's important that we do so with grace, love, and compassion. In Colossians 4:6 Paul wrote, "Let your conversation be always full of grace, seasoned with salt, that you may know how to answer everyone" (NIV). If a person rejects the message of God's grace, then you warn him of hell. But don't do it with glee; do it with sadness. The great preacher D. L. Moody said, "You should never preach on the subject of hell without tears in your eyes."

I have seen some people preaching on the topic of future judgment who seem excited about the fact that people are going to burn in hell. That's wrong. It is a serious, life-and-death message that God calls us to deliver. Let's do so with compassion and tenderness.

One of the greatest communicators of this message was the apostle Paul. In the meeting on Mars Hill, he addressed a pagan crowd. He looked at the images they had erected to various gods there in the city of Athens. His opening words to the people were: "Men of Athens, I perceive that in all things you are very religious" (Acts 17:22).

That was tactful. He could have gotten up and said, "Men of Athens, you are a bunch of pagan, idolatrous heathens." Would that have been true? Technically, yes. Would that have built a bridge of communication to his audience? No. He said, "I see that you are religious. I see that you are spiritual. I want to talk to you a little bit about your interest in spiritual things." Paul began to connect with them.

At the close of his message, he said, "Truly, these times of ignorance God overlooked, but now commands all men everywhere to repent" (Acts 17:30). He told them about Christ and what He had done. Paul built the bridge to his audience and then walked over it. He established rapport. He spoke with grace and compassion. But he also gave them the goods.

Sometimes we offend people unnecessarily by being harsh, mean, or short. Sometimes we dwell only on the negative and leave out the positive. Sometimes we give them the positive and don't tell them the ramifications of rejection of Christ. Like Elijah, like Paul, we have to faithfully share the whole message.

4. Elijah was a man of faith and obedience

Maybe Elijah felt apprehensive about his assignment. *I'm going to see the king. I have to tell him a drought is coming. This won't be easy.* But he delivered the message and left with his head still on his shoulders.

Amazingly, nobody said a word. They were probably dumb-founded by it.

We don't read of anybody's trying to stop him or disagree with him. He may have walked out saying, "Lord, you are so good. That went so well. What now, Lord? Let's take on the prophets of Baal tomorrow."

Instead, as we've seen, the Lord said, "I had a different plan in mind. I was thinking of your just going away for about three years and fading into obscurity." As when he delivered the message to Ahab, Elijah obeyed.

He may have wondered, *What in the world is God doing? This is an odd path to send me on.* But God had some prep work to do in the life of the prophet.

Do you know how a mother eagle teaches her little eaglets to fly? When the eaglets are getting to the age where they need to learn independence, the mother unceremoniously kicks them out of the nest. She lets them drop about ninety feet before swooping down and picking them up again, after which she drops them in the nest—then kicks them out again. That might seem cruel to us, but the eaglets quickly learn how to stretch their little wings and fly.

What if the mother eagles didn't do this? If they let the baby eagles stay in the nest, they would turn into teen eagles! They would just sleep and eat and never leave.

Sometimes, when we are comfortable and things have gone well, God kicks us out of the nest. He's not trying to hurt us, but help us. He's teaching us how to fly. He's trying to help us grow up, realize our potential, and turn into Elijahs.

Listen to the apostle James:

> When all kinds of trials and temptations crowd into your lives, my brothers, don't treat them as intruders, but welcome them as friends! Realise [*sic*] that they come to test your faith and to produce in you the quality of endurance. But let the process go on until that endurance is fully developed, and you will find you have become men of mature character, men of integrity with no weak spots. (1:2–4 PHILLIPS)

Later in the book of Kings, Elisha asked, "Where is the Lord God of Elijah?" (2 Kings 2:14). I have another question: Where are the Elijahs of the Lord God? Where are people like this today who will stand up for what is true? Would you be an Elijah to your sphere of influence?

This means you need to know God. You need to walk in a continual awareness of His presence. You need to be a person of fervent prayer. You need to obey God in faith. You need to deliver the whole truth of the Word of God and do so in love. This means you need to be willing to stand in the gap and say, "Lord, I read that you are looking for someone like this. I want to be that person."

If you will volunteer, God will take you up on it. In fact, He's looking for someone just like you—someone whose commitment to the spiritual race supersedes fear. Those who run well serve well.

Now, in the next chapter, let's take a look at how Elijah did after he'd been running a lap or two.

11

RACE TO A CAVE

I've never met a Christian who hasn't been really discouraged at some point. You know, I'm sure, how it feels to be in the depths of despair, a place from which you can see no way out. Has it ever seemed to you that you're the only person doing the hard work of standing up for faith in Jesus Christ?

If so, then you're going to commiserate with the man we've been discussing, God's miracle worker, Elijah the prophet. You might be surprised to know that Elijah, too, knew well feelings of hopelessness, loss, and isolation. Ironically, the depression he experienced came right on the heels of the greatest victory of his life and ministry. This isn't necessarily all that unusual.

Have you ever followed a great celebration with enormous feelings of letdown? That's just how Elijah felt.

Remember James told us "Elijah was a human being, even as we are" (5:17 NIV). He was subject to the same passions we are. Here we will see that Elijah, though he had a temporary setback, was a winner in the race of life. You, too, can shake the track's dirt off, reset your pace, and get back in the race—to win. Watch how God helped Elijah do just that.

Who Is the Real Problem Here?

You'll remember Elijah had declared the coming of a drought, lived on raven food and a widow's mite for three years, then was sent back to face wicked King Ahab. It could not have been a meeting Elijah was eagerly anticipating. First Kings 18 picks up the narrative.

> Then it happened, when Ahab saw Elijah, that Ahab said to him, "Is that you, O troubler of Israel?"
>
> And he answered, "I have not troubled Israel, but you and your father's house have, in that you have forsaken the commandments of the Lord and have followed the Baals. Now therefore, send and gather all Israel to me on Mount Carmel, the four hundred and fifty prophets of Baal, and the four hundred prophets of Asherah, who eat at Jezebel's table." (vv. 17–19)

King Ahab had the gall to call Elijah a "troubler of Israel." The word Ahab used could be translated "viper" or "snake." He may have been saying, "Look who's come back to town! You snake in the grass, Elijah; you are the troubler of Israel."

Elijah refused to let that slander stand. He quickly corrected the king, "You have that all wrong. I'm not the snake in the grass. I'm not the troubler of Israel. *You* are, because of your idolatry and the way you have misled the people."

No one had ever spoken to the king like that and lived to tell about it—that is, until Elijah.

Isn't it interesting how people break God's commandments—disregard what His Word says—and then, when it all comes crashing down on them, blame someone else? They blame God, or they blame the very one who could have helped them avoid the destruction they are reaping. That's exactly what Ahab was doing. He was blaming Elijah for something that was his fault.

How do you think Elijah felt about this? There he was, trying to do God's will, knowing he wasn't exactly bringing good news, and he was stuck trying to defend himself against Ahab's accusations. It was no walk in the park, to be sure. The simple fact is, we will pay a price for standing up for what God says. It may be mockery, it may be slander, or, as was the case with Elijah, it may be outright lies.

I want you to know, if that has happened to you, you shouldn't take it personally. Really it's a backhanded compliment. Those people in the world are seeing you as God's representative. If they share their anger at God with you, it just shows you're a chip off the old Rock! That's a good thing. Jesus said:

> "If the world hates you, remember that it hated me first. The world would love you as one of its own if you belonged to it, but you are no longer part of the world. I chose you to come out of the world, so it hates you. Do you remember what I told you? 'A slave is not greater than the master.' Since they persecuted me, naturally they will persecute you. And if they had listened to me, they would listen to you." (John 15:18–20 NLT)

The Battle of the Gods

Elijah didn't waste time arguing. He challenged, "Let's have a showdown! Let's meet up on Mount Carmel. You bring out the prophets of Baal and the prophets of Asherah [the goddess of sex and violence], assemble all 850 prophets, and we will have a rumble on the mountain."

Understand: this was more than a heavyweight championship between mortal men. This was the battle of the gods. The battle was to determine who was indeed the true ruler of the nation and of the universe—the Lord God of Israel or Baal and Asherah. It wasn't so much a skirmish between Ahab and Elijah as much as it was one between God and Satan.

Amazingly, Ahab agreed to this showdown. Maybe he was desperate. After all, he really needed to see some rain—and he didn't much care how he got it. Israel had been experiencing drought conditions for some three years at that point, and everything had withered into a dingy brown. This was a national crisis, and maybe, somehow, such a confrontation would bring about change.

So Ahab went ahead and assembled all of the false prophets. Basically, he stepped into the trap that God's prophet had set for him.

Elijah determined that the true God would answer by fire. This seemed like a reasonable idea to Ahab, since Baal was known as the sun god. Surely the sun god could send down a stream of fire to demonstrate his mighty power!

Before the battle began, Elijah challenged the people of God: " 'How long will you falter between two opinions? If the Lord is God, follow Him; but if Baal, follow him.' But the people answered him not a word" (1 Kings 18:21). Even the true believers weren't willing to take a position at that point. Nobody wanted to stand up for his faith. They were faltering.

The word translated "falter" also could be translated "totter." It's a term used to describe an intoxicated person. You know how people are when they're drunk. They think they're fine, but they don't think clearly, speak coherently, or walk straight. This was the very idea Elijah was communicating: "You're like a bunch of drunks. You can't even walk a straight line. What side are you on? Are you on the Lord's side or that of the false gods? You have to make a choice."

The problem was that it was unpopular to worship the Lord in that day and age. It wasn't politically correct. The king and queen didn't approve. If you went along with the program, there were benefits. If you worshiped the Lord, you might be executed. Queen Jezebel had, in fact, executed a number of the Lord's prophets. For years the nation had veered back and forth between false gods and the true God, not wanting to be responsible and live fully under God's absolutes.

It sounds like the United States, doesn't it? We were all on our knees in the aftermath of the horrific attack on our nation on 9/11. Members of Congress sang "God Bless America" on the capitol steps. There were prayer vigils on street corners. But now? All of that is gone. It seems that in America, we turn to God only when we feel we need Him. But when things are going all right—or at least they seem like they are—we go back to what we were doing before.

Elijah was saying that the Israelites couldn't live that way. They had to make a choice. And each of us must do the same.

Idols of the Heart

We may not literally follow a false god, bowing down before some carved idol, but we can have idols in our hearts. An idol is anyone or anything that takes the place of the true God in your life. It could be a relationship . . . a possession . . . a pursuit . . . a career . . . a hobby. It is anything you are more passionate about than your faith in God.

If you have an idol in your heart, if you have another god you're bowing before, just understand that it will bring your prayer life to a screeching halt. God said in Ezekiel 14:3, "These leaders have set up idols in their hearts. They have embraced things that will make them fall into sin. Why should I listen to their requests?" (NLT). If you want the ear of the Lord, your heart has to be His.

Imagine how insulting it must have been for the Lord when the Israelites turned their backs on Him. They were worshiping gods that could never, never save them. They had no eyes to see them, no ears to hear them, no mouth to speak to them. Yet the people bowed before them in homage.

Imagine if your spouse left you for someone else. Would that hurt you? What if your spouse left you for a mannequin he or she saw in a store down at the mall? You would say, "I don't get this." Your spouse would respond, "This mannequin understands me. I admit that it doesn't say much, but it doesn't nag either."

Is it any more ridiculous when we leave the true God and worship some other person or thing?

High Noon in Israel

The showdown had finally come. It was time for the duel. Elijah began by declaring that each side should place a bull on their altar, then ask their respective god(s) to send down fire to burn it up. He invited the prophets of Baal to go first.

> So they took the bull which was given them, and they prepared it, and called on the name of Baal from morning even till noon, saying, "O Baal, hear us!" But there was no voice; no one answered. Then they leaped about the altar which they had made. And so it was, at noon, that Elijah mocked them and said, "Cry aloud, for he is a god; either he is meditating, or he is busy, or he is on a journey, or perhaps he is sleeping and must be awakened." So they cried aloud, and cut themselves, as was their custom, with knives and lances, until the blood gushed out on them. And when midday was

past, they prophesied until the time of the offering of the evening sacrifice. But there was no voice; no one answered, no one paid attention. (1 Kings 18:26–29)

Elijah seemed to be having a little fun there. He mocked them. (That's one of the reasons I like this prophet.) "Yell louder," Elijah taunted. "Maybe Baal can't hear you. Maybe he's on a trip. Maybe he's sleeping." The phrase "he is busy" in the original language implies that Baal had taken a trip to the celestial men's room. Or, as The Living Bible so bluntly puts it, Baal may have been "sitting on the toilet" (v. 27). Definitely a derogatory phrase!

The whole thing was absurd. Baal's people were screaming and twirling around, cutting themselves and bleeding. It was a grotesque circus, and everyone could see the futility. That, of course, is why Elijah did it. He was essentially saying, "These prophets have misled you. They have ripped you off. It's time for you to see that worshiping anyone but the true God is phony, empty, and idiotic." He wanted the Israelites to look at the show and think, *Why did we ever follow these people?*

Elijah finally called off the party. Before the people, he rebuilt the altar of the Lord, which the maniacs had destroyed in their raving, and dug a trench around it. He placed twelve stones on it to represent the twelve tribes of Israel. Then he restacked the wood, cut up the bull, and placed it on top. Finally, he ordered that the whole thing be doused with sea water—three times—and he filled the trench with water. He wanted it to be clear that there was no trickery, no illusion. Either God was going to answer by fire, or Elijah would pay the consequences. Like David facing his giant, this was a do-or-die scenario.

The prophet was ready then to pray. He didn't scream. He didn't moan or twirl or cut himself. He spoke with serene confidence in God's power.

When Less Is More

This reminds us that in prayer and worship, we don't have to get worked into a frenzy. Sometimes we feel as though we have to go through spiritual acrobatics to get God's attention. The fact is, when we assemble together as his people, He is already there. Jesus said, "Where two or three are gathered together in My name, I am there in the midst of them" (Matthew 18:20). God said that He inhabits the praises of His people (see Psalm 22:3 KJV). We don't have to rant and rave to bring God down. God is here.

If you have an emotional experience during worship, great! Enjoy it. But if you don't have an emotional experience, don't feel as though you've somehow missed the boat and didn't encounter God. Maybe you were sitting in the second row one week, worshiping, and the Lord's power came on you. You could sense it. So you decide, *Every week I have to sit right here, in the same place!* But what if someone inadvertently occupies your holy seat? "Excuse me. I have to sit there. This is my blessing spot. I had my hands lifted this high when I felt the presence of the Lord. I need to replicate that moment."

Just relax . . . and sit anywhere! Worship God because God is worthy of your praise. Don't worship Him only when you feel like it; come into His presence with that same serene confidence Elijah had.

Serene Confidence

Look at what happened next:

> And it came to pass, at the time of the offering of the evening sacrifice, that Elijah the prophet came near and said, "Lord God of Abraham, Isaac, and Israel, let it be known this day that You are God in Israel and I am Your servant, and that I have done all these things at Your word. Hear me, O Lord, hear me, that this people may know that you are the Lord God, and that You have turned their hearts back to You again." Then the fire of the Lord fell and consumed the burnt sacrifice, and the wood and the stones and the dust, and it licked up the water that was in the trench. Now when all the people saw it, they fell on their faces; and they said, "The Lord, He is God! The Lord, He is God!" (1 Kings 18:36–39)

The people of Israel sure changed their tune.

But the show wasn't over.

Then Elijah commanded them to kill all of the prophets of Baal and Asherah. The people executed all 850 of them. That wasn't a pretty scene, but God meant business.

Finally, Elijah turned to Ahab and said, "There is the sound of abundance of rain" (1 Kings 18:41). He ascended Mount Carmel, bowed before the Lord, and said, "Lord, You have sent the fire. Now it's time for the rain, so people will know I have done these things according to Your word."

Elijah sent his servant to see if the rain was coming. The servant reported there wasn't a cloud in the sky. Elijah kept praying. Six times he prayed and sent his servant. Finally, the seventh trip, the servant returned and said, "There is a cloud, as small as a man's hand, rising out of the sea!" (1 Kings 18:44).

That was all Elijah needed to hear.

Not a Cloud in the Sky

Elijah's example shows the importance of persistence in prayer. Sometimes you pray, and the fire comes immediately. Other times you pray, and nothing happens. Not a cloud in the sky. Not a drop of rain. Not an answer in sight. But Elijah didn't give up.

It may be that the Lord is trying to teach you some lessons of dependence on Him. He is answering, but He is answering in His way, in His timing, and perhaps in increments. Remember the blind man Jesus touched?

> He took the blind man by the hand and led him out of the town. And when He had spit on his eyes and put His hands on him, He asked him if he saw anything. And he looked up and said, "I see men like trees, walking." Then He put His hands on his eyes again and made him look up. And he was restored and saw everyone clearly. (Mark 8:23–25)

Notice that Jesus didn't heal him all at once. That is often how it starts: a little now, a little later. No thunder and lightning, but a cloud the size of a man's hand. Don't give up. Just keep praying.

Elijah the Sprinter

After the rain came, Ahab got in his chariot and left for Jezreel, where his palace was. Oddly, Elijah decided he wanted to run for it. This is an interesting verse: "Then the Lord gave special strength to Elijah. He tucked his cloak into his belt and ran ahead of Ahab's chariot all the way to the entrance of Jezreel" (1 Kings 18:46 NLT).

Elijah the Olympic sprinter! He ran so supernaturally fast that he beat the king in his chariot. Considering what was waiting for him there, it sort of makes you wonder why he did it!

Ahab reached the palace . . . and Jezebel. Remember the dynamics of their relationship: This was a henpecked husband. She was the power behind the throne. She wore the pants in the palace and basically ran the show.

Ahab essentially said to his wife, "There is good news and bad news. First the good news: it's raining again! Now the bad news: all the prophets of Baal and Asherah are dead. And one other piece of bad news: Elijah is back."

Jezebel responded by putting out a contract on the prophet's life. When word of this reached Elijah, how do you think he reacted? You might think he would have just brushed it off or even laughed at such a threat. After all, he had just faced off with most of the idol firepower of Israel. God had answered his prayer with a stream of fire from heaven. Why would he now cower before the threats of this woman?

And yet, that is exactly what he did.

He cowered, and he ran. For whatever reason, Jezebel's threats flattened him like a locomotive. He was devastated and afraid.

In 1 Kings 19:3–4 we read that "He arose and ran for his life, and went to Beersheba, which belongs to Judah, and left his servant there. But he himself went a day's journey into the wilderness, and came and sat down under a broom tree. And he prayed that he might die, and said, 'It is enough! Now, Lord, take my life, for I am no better than my fathers!'"

Only hours before, Elijah had been running for God. Now he was running in panic. Our mighty prophet was giving in to depression. This reminds us of the truth of James' statement: Elijah was indeed a man just like us.

Elijah is not the only biblical figure who felt depression. At one point, the great lawgiver Moses was so despondent that he asked the Lord to take his life. Jonah did much the same after seeing a great revival. It's normal for everyone to have a case of the blues now and then, even if they are great men and women of God.

Have you ever been depressed? Have you ever been down in the dumps? Maybe you are right now. Why? It could be a number of reasons: Problems at work, with your health, in your family, with your spiritual life. Maybe someone has threatened you in some way, or a loved one has recently passed away. It has you down.

Listen to Elijah's prayer: "I have been very zealous for the Lord God of hosts; for the children of Israel have forsaken Your covenant, torn down Your altars, and killed Your prophets with the sword. *I alone am left;* and they seek to take my life" (1 Kings 19:10, emphasis added).

How did Elijah get into this state? We can learn much from his mistakes.

1. Elijah lost perspective

The prophet's emotions had gotten the best of him. Who can rationally explain fear and depression? Sometimes they just hit you and make no sense at all.

Time magazine ran a cover story on the topic of fears and phobias. Some fifty million people in the United States struggle with these, the article said.[1] It listed fears I have never heard of. Some, frankly, seemed kooky to me. Consider *ablutophobia*, which is a fear of bathing, or *cathisophobia*, the fear of sitting. Then there's *cyclephobia*, the fear of bicycles.

Or what about these? *Alektorophobia*, the fear of chickens; *anuptaphobia*, the fear of being single; and *arithmophobia*, the fear of numbers. Finally, we have *automatonophobia*, the fear of ventriloquist dummies. It sounds as though Elijah had a bad case of *Jezebelphobia*.

Whatever the source, fear is a dangerous thing. It can overtake us. It can cause us to worry ourselves into a tizzy.

Elijah was doing just that. He allowed his difficulty to magnify in his mind, and he stopped thinking clearly.

2. Elijah isolated himself

When you are down, you need to be with God's people. Just a few statements and a fresh perspective from a good friend can get you back on course. Elijah needed the encouragement of godly people. But for all practical purposes, he was alone. That is why the Bible says,

> Two are better than one. . . . For if they fall, one will pick up his companion. But woe to him who is alone when he falls, for he has no one to help him up. Again, if two lie down together, they will keep warm. But how can one keep warm alone? Though one may be overpowered by another, two can withstand him.
> (Ecclesiastes 4:9–12)

Don't avoid people when you're depressed, seek them out. Embrace them. They can help you get things back in perspective.

3. Elijah let his guard down

Have you ever noticed that low lows often come after high highs? By that I mean, sometimes after a great victory comes a great attack. For Elijah, the battle of the gods had taken place. The Lord had won. The rainstorm had come, confirming God's word through the prophet. Sounds as though old Elijah had been running on adrenaline.

What happened was that he let his guard down. He questioned his confidence in the Lord.

I know that often after wonderful victories, I find myself feeling down. You would think that after one of my crusades, I'd be on cloud nine. But I have found that once it's over, I am depleted, drained, and tired. I don't feel that great physically or emotionally. After all, preaching to the lost is like doing battle. I once asked Billy Graham what he felt when he was giving the invitation for people to come to Christ. He responded by saying he felt as though "power was going out" of him.

Do you know what I have learned to do about those blues? Ignore them.

They don't mean anything. Lows often follow highs—that's all. We need to realize that the human bodies God gave us need maintenance, rest, and nourishment. Sometimes we overspiritualize. If you are in a depressed state, all that may really be wrong is low blood sugar. When did you sleep last? Have you had a proper, balanced meal lately? Sometimes there is a rational medical explanation.

Look at Elijah, in the depths of despair. The Lord ministered to his need: "As he lay and slept under a broom tree, suddenly an angel touched him, and said to him, 'Arise and eat.' Then he looked, and there by his head was a cake baked on coals, and a jar of water. So he ate and drank, and lay down again" (1 Kings 19:5–6).

All Elijah needed was food and a nap! Might that be your need as well?

4. Elijah forgot God

Look at what the Lord said to him in 1 Kings 19:11–13:

> Then He said, "Go out, and stand on the mountain before the Lord." And behold, the Lord passed by, and a great and strong wind tore into the mountains and broke the rocks in pieces before the Lord, but the Lord was not in the wind; and after the wind an earthquake, but the Lord was not in the earthquake; and after the earthquake a fire, but the Lord was not in the fire; and after the fire a still small voice. So it was, when Elijah heard it, that he wrapped his face in his mantle and went out and stood in the entrance of the cave. Suddenly a voice came to him, and said, "What are you doing here, Elijah?"

What a great question: "What are you doing here?" *How did you get to this place? How did you get yourself into this state? Why have you lost perspective? Have you forgotten that I have brought you this far, and I am going to finish what I have begun? What are you doing here?*

Maybe God would say that to us when we worry ourselves into a frenzy: "What are you doing here? Why have you allowed yourself to end up like this, isolated from your Christian friends, ignoring the perspective of the Word of God, allowing your problems to be magnified beyond comprehension, and forgetting your God?"

On the Road Again

What happened on that windy mountain? The Lord spoke: "I have reserved seven thousand in Israel, all whose knees have not bowed to Baal, and every mouth that has not kissed him" (1 Kings 19:18).

Elijah realized he wasn't alone in worshiping the Lord his God in Israel, and that he had more to do for the Lord. Coming to his senses, the prophet left the cave and got back to serving the Lord.

If you find yourself feeling a little depressed, get things back into perspective. Expect a low after a high. Take care of your body. Spend time with godly friends, and remind yourself that come what may, God is still on the throne.

Remember, races aren't run—or won—in caves. Let the Lord comfort you there, but then lace up those running shoes and jump back on the track. You might even beat a chariot. I'll bet that you run better than ever.

RELAY RACE

After his great victory up on Mount Carmel, facing off with the prophets of Baal and seeing the answer of God come through fire, Elijah got word that Jezebel threatened his life, and he descended into the lowest of the lows. He asked God to take his life. As he hid in the wilderness, the Lord came to him to encourage and restore him.

Elijah's ministry, the Lord said, was coming to a close. But he had one last mission.

The Finishing Touch

The Lord directed Elijah to go and find his successor: "Elisha the son of Shaphat of Abel Meholah you shall anoint as prophet in your place" (1 Kings 19:16). He was saying, "You are to pass your mantle on to a man named Elisha."

Because the names Elijah and Elisha are so similar, sometimes we confuse these two men. Nevertheless, they were two very distinct individuals who spent some time together but had separate ministries. Elijah was passing the torch. It was like a relay race. Elijah was handing the baton back to Elisha to pick up and carry forward and finish the race.

Scripture says that Elijah obeyed: "So he departed from there, and found Elisha the son of Shaphat, who was plowing with twelve yoke of oxen before him, and he was with the twelfth. Then Elijah passed by him and threw his mantle on him" (v. 19).

The next step was to prepare Elisha for the work at hand. How important is this for us, even those of us who aren't prophets, to do? To take all that the Lord has done in our lives and invest it in the lives of others is sometimes called mentoring. The biblical terminology for it is *discipling*.

We find this command in the Great Commission, when Jesus said, "Go into all the world and preach the gospel to every creature" (Mark 16:15). In Matthew, the wording is different: "Go therefore and make disciples of all the nations, . . . teaching them to observe all things that I have commanded you; and lo, I am with you always, even to the end of the age" (Matthew 28:19–20).

We have all heard the part about going into the world and preaching the gospel. Sometimes we miss the part that says we are to make disciples. Just in case you don't understand what that means, Jesus defined it in His challenge and call to us: "teaching them to observe all things that I have commanded you." It means we are to reproduce ourselves spiritually.

A Whole Church—of You

What if the whole church were just like you? What if every Christian behaved exactly as you do? What kind of worship services would we have?

When it's time to worship the Lord, are you one of those people who just sits there and doesn't sing? Then a whole church of people like you would have a silent worship service.

What kind of prayer meetings would we have? Would we have to cancel them for lack of attendance? If all of the church were just like you, how many people in this world would be being reached with the gospel of Jesus Christ? Would people be hearing about Him? If all of the church were just like you, would there be any resources for us to use to get the gospel out? If all of the church were just like you, how knowledgeable would we be of the Bible? Would we be a biblically illiterate church, or would we be a grounded, well-taught body of believers?

We all should be making disciples of Jesus, and people are going to learn by following our example (this is discipling). Paul said in Colossians 1:28, "We warn everyone we meet, and we teach everyone we can, all that we know about [Jesus], so that we may bring every man up to his full maturity in Christ" (PHILLIPS). In other words, our objective as Christians is to try to win people to the Lord and help them reach their full maturity and potential.

Writing to Timothy, Paul said, "You have heard me teach things that have been confirmed by many reliable witnesses. Now teach these truths to other trustworthy people who will be able to pass them on to others" (2 Timothy 2:2 NLT). The idea is to take what God has taught us and teach it to other people. Hopefully, they will repeat the process. This is what we are all called to do: to make disciples for Jesus.

What Does Your Life Teach Others?

Are you doing that today? Have you taken someone young in the faith under your wing, and are you helping him or her to grow spiritually?

Paul discipled Timothy: "But you, Timothy, certainly know what I teach, and how I live, and what my purpose in life is. You know my faith, my patience, my love, and my endurance" (2 Timothy 3:10 NLT). A person should see in you an example he can follow.

This is one of the reasons a lot of us don't want to disciple anyone. We don't want people following our examples. Why? Because we're still working a few kinks out ourselves. We think that maybe when we're "more mature in the faith," we will be better prepared to do it. We wouldn't want young believers to stumble over the way that we live.

What's the solution? Is it that we should continue in our compromise? Well, maybe the presence of a young believer would better enable us to do what we should have been doing all along.

Your life should be something you invest in many other lives. I know sometimes you feel as though it doesn't really matter. You try to import truth that God has given to you to others, but you don't know where it is going to go. Will it bear fruit? Will it fall on deaf ears?

None of us realize the full impact of what we have done in this life. You may reach a person today who will reach her world tomorrow, but you may not live to see it. Who knows? You could take under your wing the next Billy Graham; the next man or woman who will shake a world. Just be diligent in what God has set before you.

We've all heard of such preachers as Billy Graham, Billy Sunday, and D. L. Moody. I'll bet you have never heard of Edward Kimball. The reason you've probably never heard of him is because he never wrote any books or pastored a church. He never conducted evangelistic events or recorded a CD. But Edward Kimball was a faithful Christian. He was a shoe salesman who wanted God to use him more than anything else in life.

Kimball felt burdened for a young man he knew who was working in a shoe store in Chicago. Kimball hemmed and hawed and put it off, but he finally mustered up the courage and told the young salesman about Jesus. Much to Kimball's delight, the boy responded and gave his life to Jesus Christ.

Not long after, that shoe salesman began a preaching ministry. His name was D. L. Moody, and he was one of the greatest evangelists in church history. If that was all that ever happened from Kimball's obedience, that would have been enough. But the story continues.

When D. L. Moody was out preaching one day, a man who was already a believer was listening. Through Moody's preaching, he heard the call to go into full-time ministry. He became a pastor and wrote many wonderful books on the Christian faith. We know him as F. B. Meyer today. Kimball reached Moody. Moody reached Meyer.

That's a great story, but it doesn't stop there.

A young man heard Meyer preaching and gave his life to Christ. God called him to be an evangelist. His name was Wilbur Chapman, and one of the young men he took under his wing was a former pro ball player. The ball player decided instead to preach the gospel, which he did with great success. His name was Billy Sunday.

Then Billy Sunday went to Charlotte, North Carolina, and held a crusade. Many people came to faith. The people were so thrilled, they wanted to have another crusade. Sunday wasn't available. The businesspeople in Charlotte knew of another evangelist named Mordecai Hamm, so they invited him out. They erected a tent in a dairy field. It wasn't all that successful of a campaign, but on one of the final nights a young, lanky farm boy walked the sawdust aisle.

His friends called him Billy Frank. We know him as Billy Graham.

Kimball reached Moody, who touched Meyer, who reached Chapman, who helped Sunday, who reached the businessmen in Charlotte, who invited Hamm, who then reached Billy Graham. Talk about a legacy! You may not be Billy Graham, but you might be Edward Kimball.

Think about Andrew. He once was a disciple of John the Baptist's, but one day the great baptizer knew his work was done and told his disciples to follow Jesus Christ: "Behold! The Lamb of God who takes away the sin of the world!" (John 1:29). Upon discovering Jesus as his Messiah, Andrew wanted his brother, Peter, to come to faith.

Now, Peter was one of those larger-than-life figures. Andrew probably lived in his shadow most of his life, having people ask him things like "Aren't you Simon's brother? Your brother is so wonderful!" How easily Andrew could have decided to keep his newfound knowledge of Jesus as the Messiah to himself. But that thought never seemed to cross his mind.

He went out immediately, found Peter, and brought him to Jesus. Peter, along with James and John, went on to become part of Jesus' inner circle. Andrew could have resented it, but Scripture gives us no hint of anything like that.

Andrew is the model for all Christians who labor quietly where God has called them. We may not know their names as well as others', but they are known by and greatly loved by the Lord.

The fact is, if we didn't have Andrews, we wouldn't have Simon Peters. If we didn't have Kimballs, we wouldn't have Moodys.

You may not be a Simon Peter, but you may be an Andrew.

There is a part for each of us to play in serving the Lord. We need an outlet for what God is doing in our lives. This is what discipling is: as you take truths in, you share them with others and bless them.

Guess what? In the process, you receive a blessing yourself. Do you know what younger believers help us do, besides live the way we ought? They help us rediscover things we have forgotten. They ask hard questions. We have to go find the answers. We get back in the Word. We start studying again. Those we are discipling challenge us, forcing us to grow and explore and remember. We are becoming a part of the process of passing it on.

Lessons for Us

That is what Elijah did with Elisha. Here are some things he wanted Elisha to learn and understand.

1. Untie those apron strings

When Elijah threw his mantle, his outer garment, on that young man, Elisha immediately understood what it meant: "I am asking you to become my successor."

Look at Elisha's response: "And he left the oxen and ran after Elijah, and said, 'Please let me kiss my father and my mother, and then I will follow you.' And [Elijah] said to him, 'Go back again, for what have I done to you?'" (1 Kings 19:20).

Allow me to loosely paraphrase that: "Go home to Mommy if you want to. No one is twisting your arm. You're an adult. You know it's time to do this. Will you?" This was the decisive moment in Elisha's life. Elijah knew that if Elisha were to go back home and say goodbye to his parents, he never would follow. He would get sidetracked.

This is much like the story Jesus told about the man he called to follow him. The man said, " 'Lord, I will follow You, but let me first go and bid them farewell who are at my house.' But Jesus said to him, 'No one, having put his hand to the plow, and looking back, is fit for the kingdom of God' " (Luke 9:61–62).

Why did Jesus say that? For the same reason Elijah did: he knew that if the guy went back to his family, he never would follow.

Have you ever tried to say good-bye at a family reunion? Do you know how long that takes? You haven't seen some members of your family for years. Uncle Harry has come in from Ohio, and Aunt Gertrude flew in from Florida. After a few hours you say, "We have to go."

"No," they plead, "don't go yet. Have another cup of coffee and a piece of pie." A couple more hours pass, and you say you're leaving. You start making the rounds and hugging and kissing everyone. The next thing you know, another two hours have passed. That is what Elijah was warning Elisha about: "This is the time. Let's get on with it. Ministry opportunity has just knocked on your door."

2. When opportunity knocks, answer the door

Maybe it has happened to you. Someone is in need of what you know about the Christian life. You say, "I can't do it right now. My business is taking up my time. Instead, I will put a little more in the offering. My busy schedule has no room for discipling someone. I have too much going on."

Opportunity came, and you missed it. That is too bad.

Sometimes we feel the only "real" ministry is the mission field. Why do you think some supernatural thing is going to happen to you the moment you set foot on foreign soil? You want to cross the sea for Christ, but why don't you start by crossing the street and talking to your neighbor?

I have an idea. I will tell you about a foreign land you can evangelize. The people speak a different language, but you'll catch on. These are people of small stature, indigenous to a certain region. They can be a bit on the wild side. It is called *Sunday school*. The people are called *kids*. They need your help and ministry. Try volunteering at your Sunday school ministry at church.

Ministry is everywhere.

God called Elisha when Elijah threw his mantle on him. Elisha was initially reluctant, but he realized he had to make his move. He accepted and began to follow the great prophet of the Lord.

When opportunity knocked, he answered.

A Last Conflict with Ahab's Family

At that point, Elijah could have said, "My job is done. I have found my successor. I am going to kick back on my front porch and watch the grass grow!" After all, the famine was over. But he still had a few things to do.

The next movement in the life of Elijah the prophet was quite dramatic. By then, Ahab and Jezebel had died brutal deaths, as Elijah had prophesied. Their son, Ahaziah, also rebelled against God. He had failed to learn anything from the lives of his parents.

One day, the Bible tells us in 2 Kings 1, he fell through the latticework of an upper room at his palace and was seriously injured. Instead of asking the Lord for help or calling on the prophet of the Lord for assistance, King Ahaziah sent messengers to inquire in the temple of Baal as to whether he would live. Can you believe this?

After Baal's pathetic showing on Mount Carmel, still there was the son of Ahab and Jezebel calling on this false god.

Meanwhile, the Lord spoke to Elijah the prophet and told him to intercept the messengers the king sent to the temple of Baal. Elijah confronted the men, saying in effect, "Is there no God in Israel? You have to go to the temple of Baal to find out if the king is going to live? Since you sought Baal's counsel, the answer is no. Tell the king he won't survive."

The messengers returned to the king and reported their meeting with Elijah and the message he sent. Not surprisingly, the king was angry. He said that he wanted Elijah brought there immediately.

Ahaziah sent a captain with fifty soldiers to arrest Elijah and bring him back to the palace. When the captain and his men approached Elijah, who was perched atop a hill, they said, "Man of God, the king has said, 'Come down!' " (v. 9).

Elijah responded, "If I am a man of God, then let fire come down from heaven and consume you and your fifty men" (v. 10). He was a man of God. Fire came down and destroyed them.

The king heard about it and sent another captain with fifty soldiers. Ditto—Elijah called, and fire came down.

A third brigade arrived, but this time the captain basically pleaded, "Mr. Elijah, I am just following orders. Give me a break here. I am a family man. Please come." The Lord said to Elijah, "Go down with him; do not be afraid of him" (v. 15). Elijah delivered his message to the king's face: "Therefore, because you have [consulted Baal rather than God], you will never leave the bed you are lying on; you will surely die" (v. 17 NLT). The text continues, "So Ahaziah died" (v. 17 NLT).

This reminds me so much of our own nation. I've mentioned that in the aftermath of 9/11, our churches were packed. People were turning to God. We were having prayer meetings in stadiums around the nation. Now that things have returned to relative calm, the people are gone.

I think that when the next crisis hits, we will see people in church again. Then, if life becomes quiet again, they will go away. Sadly, this is just what Israel did. The people called on God when things were tough, but when things went back to normal, they forgot the Lord.

I pray that we will see a real turning to God and that we will really call upon the Lord. There is no military solution for the problem of terrorism. There is no single enemy we can take out. When the Japanese attacked us at Pearl Harbor, we knew where to find them. Today our enemies hide and plan disaster from afar. We have never faced anything like this before. We need God's help.

Pray for our president. Pray for our congressmen and congresswomen. Pray for our country.

We have seen from the life of Ahaziah that failing to call upon him shows a disrespect that God cannot ignore.

Parting Words

After Ahaziah's death, Elijah realized his time was coming to an end. He put a few challenges in Elisha's path before he went. Three times Elijah asked Elisha to stay put while he took a journey, first to Bethel, then to Jericho, and then to the Jordan River. Each time, Elisha responded, "As the Lord lives, and as your soul lives, I will not leave you!" (2 Kings 2:2).

Each of these requests was a test to see if Elisha really was committed. Each time he passed.

Did you know that God will test us as well to see if our faith is genuine? Many people are excited about following Jesus—at first. Then the tests come. They are persecuted for the gospel. They go through a time of difficulty. They find it is not the most popular thing to be a Christian. They don't feel that emotional high they might have felt right after conversion. They say, "That's it. I am not going to be a Christian anymore."

Elijah might have said to you, "Go home to Mommy."

Real believers stand the test and continue on. Jesus doesn't want fair-weather followers. He wants dedicated men and women— these are the kinds of people He will use to shake the world.

One day He was speaking to a huge group of people (see John 6). The crowds had grown because He had performed his most popular miracle of all: He fed masses of people. They loved that.

Jesus looked at the multitude. They cared nothing for who He was. They cared nothing for His message. He made some radical statements to intentionally thin out the ranks. Hundreds of people left that day. Jesus turned to His own disciples and asked, "Do you also want to go away?" (v. 67). Peter answered for them, "Lord, to whom shall we go? You have the words of eternal life" (v. 68). They passed the test.

Elijah was testing Elisha: Are you sure about this? Are you ready to count the cost? Are you ready to do what God is calling you to do? Apparently he was. Are you?

A Last Request

Now we come to the final movement in the story.

And so it was, when they had crossed over, that Elijah said to Elisha, "Ask! What may I do for you, before I am taken away from you?" Elisha said, "Please let a double portion of your spirit be upon me." So he said, "You have asked a hard thing. Nevertheless, if you see me when I am taken from you, it shall be so for you; but if not, it shall not be so." Then it happened, as they continued on and talked, that suddenly a chariot of fire appeared with horses of fire, and separated the two of them; and Elijah went up by a whirlwind into heaven.

And Elisha saw it, and he cried out, "My father, my father, the chariot of Israel and its horsemen!" So he saw him no more.
(2 Kings 2:9–12)

Elijah said, "Elisha, you have passed the test. What do you want as a reward?" Elisha answered, "I want to follow in your footsteps. I want to do what God has called me to do. I would like twice as much power as you have." I love this. Elijah said, "That is a tall order. If you see me when I am taken away, then you will get what you have requested."

You can be sure that Elisha kept his eyes on Elijah. Suddenly that moment came, and Elijah was caught up into the presence of the Lord. Elisha watched the whole thing. Sure enough, God's anointing came upon him in double strength. You can see that because he did twice as many miracles as Elijah had.

What kind of legacy are you leaving today? Are you discipling anyone? Do you have a life that is worth emulating? Are you just a fair-weather follower? That is the challenge before each of us.

Elijah was one of the two people in the Bible who never died. The other was Enoch, who walked with God and then "was not" (see Genesis 5:24). This reminds us that there is a generation of people who will not see death. They will be caught up immediately into the presence of the Lord in what the Bible calls the "rapture of the church." The Bible says that "in a moment, in the twinkling of an eye," we will meet the Lord in the air (1 Corinthians 15:52). From my understanding of Bible prophecy, this great event could happen at any time.

What are we supposed to be doing in the meantime? The same thing Elijah was doing: proclaiming and discipling. He made sure that before he left this world, he had taught someone to continue

God's work.

What else are we supposed to be doing? The same thing Elisha did with Elijah: he watched him. "If you see me when I am taken from you," his master said, "it shall be so for you."

What does the Bible say to us as believers living in the last days? Are you mentoring others? Are you looking for Jesus? With all of this uncertainty in the air, all of this tension, these threats, with Bible prophecies fulfilled before our very eyes, we need to make every moment count. This is not a time for fooling around. This is not a time for squandering our lives and resources. This is a time to follow the Lord as a true disciple and try to impact others.

We all have a part to play. You might be a Billy Graham. You might be an Edward Kimball. You may be a Simon Peter, or you may be an Andrew. Count on this: you are someone God wants to use. We need to accept the baton, our assignment, as Elijah did—and as Elisha did.

Running well the spiritual race requires that we complete each lap, no matter how hard or easy it is. When the Lord throws you a test, endure—pass it. Every lap brings you nearer to the finish, so finish well.

MARATHON

Falling down doesn't make you a failure; staying down does. The story before us now is probably the ultimate spiritual success story. This is the account of a young man, who, despite dramatic setbacks that would have immobilized most people, kept going back for more. A young man who, against all odds, in the most adverse circumstances imaginable, made it to the end.

We don't ever read of his doubting God or compromising his witness in any way. We find perhaps some minor errors, but no glaring mistakes. For all practical purposes, we cannot uncover a single serious blemish in the life of this young man. God mightily blessed him as a result. His name was Joseph.

A Tuxedo for Field Work

The story of Joseph is really the ultimate rags-to-riches tale, where a person rose from complete obscurity and devastating setbacks to become the second-most-powerful man in the nation of Egypt. Joseph was a young man who started the race of life and finished exceptionally well. He was so amazing that, as you read about him, you might conclude he wasn't a man at all—he was somehow supernatural. No, he was a real man, all flesh and blood just like every one of us. That he started and finished his race dramatically reminds us it can be done.

Initially, Joseph's life showed little promise. He was a simple shepherd boy, the twelfth of thirteen children. As a young man he was apparently given to some visions of grandeur. Like any other teenager, he liked to sleep. This particular young man had some pretty remarkable dreams he believed to be from God himself. In the beginning, Joseph's dreams got him into trouble. Thirteen years later, interpreting other people's dreams got him out of trouble.

Let's read about him in Genesis 37.

> Joseph, being seventeen years old, was feeding the flock with his brothers. And the lad was with the sons of Bilhah and the sons of Zilpah, his father's wives; and Joseph brought a bad report of them to his father. Now Israel [Jacob] loved Joseph more than all of his children, because he was the son of his old age. Also he made him a tunic of many colors. (vv. 2–3)

Jacob was an old man when Joseph was born. Young Joseph was the very apple of his eye. As we see in this passage, Jacob had many wives, but there was only one woman he ever truly loved, and her name was Rachel. The son he and Rachel produced was Joseph. As a result, he doted on the young boy. Naturally, the other brothers didn't like it one bit.

One of the ways Jacob showed his favoritism toward Joseph was by giving him this so-called coat of many colors. Really it was a multicolored tunic or robe. As one translation puts it, "an ornate robe" (NIV).

There is more here than meets the eye. One Old Testament commentator said the tunic was sleeved and extended to the ankles. Obviously Joseph was not going to do manual labor in a garment like that. In Joseph's day, the working garb of the people in the fields would have been a short, sleeveless tunic—a garment that kept your arms and legs free. If you showed up in a long-sleeved, full-length, "ornate" robe, you weren't going to be doing much that day. It would be like showing up for work in the field wearing a tuxedo. It was just not apropos.

By giving this coat to Joseph, Jacob was saying, "Son, you don't have to work the way your other brothers do. Let them tackle all the hard labor. You can sit in the shade and check up on them."

You can imagine this didn't sit well with Joseph's brothers. Day by day, they grew more resentful of him. Verse 2 tells us that Joseph already had taken a bad report about his brothers to his father. This meant that in their eyes, he was a snitch—a tattletale.

The fact of the matter is that Joseph was a godly young man. By just showing up on the scene and being who he was, his very presence convicted his brothers. You need to know that when you are living a godly life, you are going to offend a lot of people. As Jesus said, "Everyone practicing evil hates the light and does not come to the light, lest his deeds should be exposed" (John 3:20).

Maybe Joseph was a bit too harsh. Maybe he came down on his brothers a little too hard. We don't know. But verse 4 says, "His brothers hated Joseph because their father loved him more than the rest of them. They couldn't say a kind word to him" (NLT).

One day, Joseph reported a startling dream: "There we were, binding sheaves in the field. Then behold, my sheaf arose and also stood upright; and indeed your sheaves stood all around and bowed down to my sheaf" (Genesis 37:7).

Joseph probably should have kept this one to himself: "So they hated him even more for his dreams and for his words" (v. 8). I don't know if Joseph was flaunting his position. Some people don't handle authority well. You give them a little power, especially with a uniform and a badge of some kind, and they become little tyrants. Maybe Joseph seemed a bit sanctimonious. The Bible doesn't say. Regardless, he certainly didn't deserve the type of treatment he was about to receive.

A Dream Come True

One fateful day, Jacob sent Joseph out to check up on his brothers:

> When Joseph's brothers saw him coming, they recognized him in the distance. As he approached, they made plans to kill him. "Here comes the dreamer!" they said. "Come on, let's kill him and throw him into one of these cisterns. We can tell our father, 'A wild animal has eaten him.' Then we'll see what becomes of his dreams!"

But when Reuben heard of their scheme, he came to Joseph's rescue. "Let's not kill him," he said. "Why should we shed any blood? Let's just throw him into this empty cistern here in the wilderness. Then he'll die without our laying a hand on him." Reuben was secretly planning to rescue Joseph and return him to his father.

So when Joseph arrived, his brothers ripped off the beautiful robe he was wearing. Then they grabbed him and threw him into the cistern. Now the cistern was empty; there was no water in it. Then, just as they were sitting down to eat, they looked up and saw a caravan of camels in the distance coming toward them. It was a group of Ishmaelite traders taking a load of gum, balm, and aromatic resin from Gilead down to Egypt.

Judah said to his brothers, "What will we gain by killing our brother? His blood would just give us a guilty conscience. Instead of hurting him, let's sell him to those Ishmaelite traders. After all, he is our brother—our own flesh and blood!" And his brothers agreed. So when the Ishmaelites, who were Midianite traders, came by, Joseph's brothers pulled him out of the cistern and sold him to them for twenty pieces of silver. And the traders took him to Egypt. (Genesis 37:18–28 NLT)

Reuben was the firstborn of Jacob, but was not the leader he should have been. The firstborn son was the heir apparent. One day he would become the spiritual leader of his family. Reuben should have been exerting some of this authority when his brothers suggested they kill Joseph. But he didn't. Jacob later described Reuben as "unstable as water" (Genesis 49:4). What an accurate assessment. He was wishy-washy, knowing what was right but unwilling to stand up for it. Ultimately the brothers prevailed.

How afraid Joseph must have felt that first night as he was taken from everything he'd ever known. But even though Joseph had been abandoned by man, he had not been forgotten by God.

Maybe you feel this way right now—that your parents, your spouse, your children, or someone you look up to spiritually has left you behind. No matter what people do to you, God never forgets you. Even when people let you down, the Lord will lift you up.

What looked like a worst-case scenario for Joseph was about to be run through God's framework of providence. This nightmare would become a dream come true. God was going to take the most adverse circumstances imaginable and turn them around for His glory.

The traders took Joseph to Egypt, which then was a pagan country filled with religious superstition. Historians tell us the Egyptian people worshiped over two thousand gods and goddesses, including the Pharaoh himself. The Egyptians also were great builders. The rulers conscripted slaves to help them in their vast building projects.

Joseph was about to go on sale again.

> When Joseph was taken to Egypt by the Ishmaelite traders, he was purchased by Potiphar, an Egyptian officer. Potiphar was captain of the guard for Pharaoh, the king of Egypt.

> The Lord was with Joseph, so he succeeded in everything he did as he served in the home of his Egyptian master. Potiphar noticed this and realized that the Lord was with Joseph, giving him success in everything he did. This pleased Potiphar, so he soon made Joseph his personal attendant. He put him in charge of his entire household and everything he owned. From the day Joseph was put in charge of his master's household and property, the Lord began to bless Potiphar's household for Joseph's sake. All his household affairs ran smoothly, and his crops and livestock flourished. So Potiphar gave Joseph complete administrative responsibility over everything he owned. With Joseph there, he didn't worry about a thing—except what kind of food to eat! (Genesis 39:1–6 NLT)

Specifically, who was Potiphar? We know he was a high-ranking Egyptian official—possibly the head of the military police assigned to be the royal bodyguard. You might say that Potiphar was the head of the Secret Service of his day. He also was responsible for the execution of criminals. Clearly Potiphar was not a man with whom you wanted to trifle. He was one bad dude, and you didn't want to mess with him.

Character Tested ... and Proved

Yet it seems that this man who could have him executed with the snap of a finger did not intimidate Joseph. Verse 2 tells us, "The

Lord was with Joseph" (NLT). Joseph loved and served the Lord with all of his heart. So the Lord just started blessing him, as well as Potiphar's household, because of Joseph's presence.

Proverbs 22:29 says, "Do you see a man who excels in his work? He will stand before kings; he will not stand before unknown men." Though Joseph had been stripped of his coat, he was not stripped of his character.

Here is something we need to remember: When we work hard at what we do, it's a powerful testimony. We need more people like Joseph today who openly express their faith but also demonstrate it through hard work.

Many Christians in the workplace talk about Jesus Christ to their coworkers. They are not embarrassed to say grace over a meal. They are not ashamed to read their Bibles during their breaks. They are not standoffish about telling others about what Christ has done for them. But the problem is sometimes they don't work hard enough. They arrive late. They leave early. They make excuses about why they can't do jobs they are asked to do. That is a bad testimony.

Then we have other Christians who work very hard; they do great work. The problem is, they don't ever talk about their faith. What a testimony it is when your employer comes to you and says, "You are the best person working for me. I want to know why you work so hard." Then you can give the glory—to God.

Had Joseph stayed home with his pampering father, he might not have developed the kind of character that comes from hard work and obeying orders. This was a time of testing in his life.

In time he would become a great leader, but first he had to learn how to be a faithful servant. Maybe you are at such a place in your life right now. You are laboring in obscurity. You feel as though no one notices what you do.

Follow the example of Joseph: Work hard. Flip every burger for the glory of God. Create every PowerPoint presentation as though Jesus Christ himself were going to inspect it. Hammer every nail as though you were building that house for God. Type every letter as if Jesus himself were going to read it. Play every chord with skill and precision as if Jesus were listening. Because He is. What-ever it is you are doing, do it well. Be faithful—even if there are consequences.

Because sometimes there are.

Lust Rears Its Ugly Head

As he often is, Satan was there in the background, carefully watch-ing Joseph handle his experiences. Satan could see that Joseph was a tough nut to crack, so he pulled out what is usually a foolproof strategy: sexual temptation.

Don't forget that Joseph was just seventeen or eighteen. Scrip-ture tells us, "Joseph was a very handsome and well-built young man" (Genesis 39:6 NLT). No doubt he was a typical teenager with raging hormones. He certainly could prove vulnerable to tempta-tion of that kind.

Don't forget that no one less than the man after God's own heart, King David, fell for this sin. Then, of course, there was Samson.

I'm sure that Potiphar's wife was attractive. She probably dressed in a sexually provocative way to get Joseph to notice her. But he just kept on with his work, never taking the bait.

Finally, she decided to cast half-measures aside and just cut to the chase. She approached him and said, "Sleep with me. I want you, and I want you now." Impressively, Joseph refused her advances.

But Mrs. Potiphar didn't give up. If anything, his rejection only spurred her on. She doubled down. She was relentless.

Joseph could have rationalized sin, thinking, *If I give in to her advances, she will speak highly of me to her husband, and I will get a promotion. I will be even more influential. Or if I cross her, she will turn against me. She is very powerful. She could destroy my life. Besides, if I had sex with her, who would ever know?* But deep in his heart, he knew God would know. We need to remember that God is watching us as well.

Genesis 39:8 simply says, "Joseph refused" (NLT). Joseph rec-ognized that temptation is a call to battle. He armed himself and prepared to fight. Verse 10 tells us, "She kept putting pressure on Joseph day after day, but he refused to sleep with her, and he kept out of her way as much as possible" (NLT).

There was a smart boy. I am sure Potiphar's wife used every visual and verbal seductive technique she could. I am sure she tried every trick in the book to excite him and move him in her direction. He wisely kept as much distance from her as possible.

Isn't that an obvious action we all should take? We all have areas of vulnerability, don't we?

A Personal Example

Let me make a little confession.

One night I spoke for a friend of mine who pastors a church. His name is Skip Heitzig. We saw 150 people make commitments to Christ that night, and we were blessed.

How do Christians celebrate? We eat. Skip said, "Do you want to go out for dinner after church?"

I said, "I ate before, Skip. I'd better not eat late."

"How about dessert?"

"I don't want dessert, either."

But Skip wouldn't take no for an answer, so I ended up going. We went to this incredible bakery with unbelievable desserts. Skip said, "What do you want? Greg, get something." I was vacillating between the key lime pie and the apple pie. Skip ordered the apple, and I ordered the key lime.

We sat down. Skip went to get silverware. I took one little bite of his apple pie, and it was so good that I ate all of it before he returned. He said, "What happened to my apple pie?" I said, "I traded. You can have mine." He ate a couple of bites. He didn't want it. And I ended up eating that too!

I never should have gone to that bakery. Quite honestly, if I had returned to my hotel room, I wouldn't have been dreaming about key lime or apple pie. I would have gone to bed, and that would have been the end of it. But I didn't, and I had to accept the consequences.

The best thing to do is to stay away from temptation.

Keys to Overcoming

In Joseph's life, we find a couple of powerful keys to overcoming temptation. These will better enable us to run the spiritual race well and win.

Key 1: Joseph called sin "sin"

Once Potiphar's wife said, "Come and sleep with me," he answered, "How then can I do this great wickedness, and sin against God?" (Genesis 39:9). He was right. He saw sin clearly for what it was. It would have been wrong.

Nowadays, not very many people call sin "sin." People don't seem to say that word anymore. If you lie, you don't admit it; you lie about the lie. Instead of saying, "I lied and got caught," you say, "I misspoke."

Who came up with phrases like that? My favorite one is "Mistakes were made." Not, "I made a mistake," or even, "We made a mistake."

"Mistakes were made" suggests that no one knows who made them. Talk about passing the buck!

These days, if you are an alcoholic or a drug addict, you may call your problem "a disease." Adultery is "having an affair" or "a fling." This soft terminology makes us more comfortable with sin. Shakespeare said, "A rose by any other name would smell as sweet." It also could be said that sin in any other form will smell just as rotten.

Key 2: Joseph realized that all sin was against God

This is the strongest deterrent against sin—not our fear of what will happen if we get caught, though that's not a bad thing to keep in mind. The ultimate deterrent is a love for God. In fact, our response to temptation is an accurate barometer of our love for God. If we want to boast about how much we love the Lord, we have to resist sin.

Someone may counter, "I show my love for the Lord in worship." I'm glad you do. Or, "I show my love for the Lord through giving." That's good too. But one of the most important ways to show your love for God is simply to resist temptation and obey God.

Jesus himself said, "Whoever has my commands and keeps them is the one who loves me . . ." (John 14:21 NIV).

Psalm 97:10 instructs, "Let those who love the Lord hate evil, for he guards the lives of his faithful ones and delivers them from the hand of the wicked" (NIV). Romans 12:9 says, "Hate what is evil; cling to what is good" (NIV). If we really love God, then we should hate evil. If we really love God, then we should seek to resist temptation.

A Strange Transition

How does the story end? Pretty strangely. Potiphar's wife was an attractive woman who probably was used to men falling at her feet. When Joseph avoided or outright rejected her, she finally decided, *I'll have to force him.* When he walked by one day, she tried to literally pull him down on her bed. Joseph escaped her grasp, but he didn't escape her influence.

Potiphar's wife was so angry and humiliated that she cried "Rape!" The fact that she had his garment in her hand was serious evidence. She said as much to her husband. I suspect Potiphar had seen this before. Personally, I don't think Potiphar bought it. I also think he didn't want to mess with his wife. So he did the only "honorable" thing in the eyes of his spouse: he sent Joseph to prison.

At that point, do you think Joseph doubted God? Did he say, "Lord, I don't understand. One day I wake up, I visit my brothers, I tell them about the great dreams You're giving me. They sell me as a slave for twenty pieces of silver. I don't get it. I am taken to this land of pagan idolatry. I honor You. I work hard. Potiphar elevates me. I'm beginning to see what You are doing and give You the glory. Then his wife starts hitting on me. By Your power I resist her. Now she has accused me of rape. Here I am in a prison cell. Why? I thought that by doing good, I would receive Your blessing. Instead, I'm being *punished* for it"?

Yes, he could have said something just like that. And if he had, we would have understood. Maybe in his place we would have said something like that. Maybe in other situations we already have.

Joseph didn't. He just trusted God.

That's not to say Joseph enjoyed himself in prison. But do you think he ever questioned his decisions?

I know there are times when temptations are very tempting. After you resist them, the devil whispers in your ear, "Have you lost your mind? You could have had her [or him]. You could have had that position! You could have had that experience! You said no. What were you thinking?"

Sometimes people who are living in sin appear to be getting away with it. A guy commits adultery. He is married. His family is intact, and he is doing this thing on the side. He tells you what a great time he's having. You wonder how he is keeping this affair a secret.

A person lies on her résumé. Because of that, she gets the job you wanted. Now she's your boss.

Someone steals something, and he never gets caught. He is enjoying the thing he stole—in fact, you wish you had one yourself, but you can't afford it.

It seems sometimes that the wicked are prospering, and we are being punished for doing the right thing. Just hang on. As time passes, you will see the wisdom of God's Word. The guy who has been getting away with the fling will get busted. His little house of cards will come crashing down. It all will catch up with him.

That woman who lied on her résumé will one day prove she doesn't have the skills or experience she claimed to have. Something or someone will blow the whistle on her. She will be publicly humiliated and lose her position.

The guy who stole something will have his dishonesty fall back on him. A jealous person will steal from him. He will not get to enjoy his possession forever.

Not that this is any comfort, but it simply is a reminder that the Bible is true when it tells us, "You will reap what you sow" (see Galatians 6:7). Sin always ends up coming out.

Joseph would see. He was in a prison cell for a little while, but the next thing you know, he was Pharaoh's right-hand man. We'll read about his very satisfying payback in the next chapter.

Maybe you are in one of those in between times right now. You are honoring the Lord, but you have made some sacrifices. Others have progressed by dishonest means. It has been hard. Here is my advice to you: Just hang in there. You are doing the right thing, and you never will regret it. God will give you the strength to resist the temptation you are facing today, no matter how strong it might be.

Apply yourself. Like Joseph, reach down inside for some more perseverance. He kept running, even when the other racers knocked him down on their way down the track. He kept getting up. You need to do the same. It's the only way to be a consistently great runner in the race of life.

And remember, there is a special blessing promised to the person who effectively resists temptation, not only in this life, but in the life to come. "Blessed is the man who endures temptation; for when he has been approved, he will receive the crown of life which the Lord has promised to those who love Him" (James 1:12).

DROPPING DEADWEIGHT

The term "unforgiving Christian" is an oxymoron.

An oxymoron, as you know, is one of those expressions that seems to contradict itself. We hear lots of these: "genuine imitation leather," "found missing," "freezer burn," "fresh frozen," "jumbo shrimp." Here's another one to add to the list: unforgiving Christian. Jesus constantly pressed the issue of forgiving others. His sermons and His parables, so many of the things He said, dealt with our need to forgive each other. As we continue our look at Joseph, we're going to see one of the most dramatic demonstrations of forgiveness to be found in the pages of the Bible.

Once Joseph was second in command to the king of Egypt, he possessed unlimited powers. He was in a position to execute the ultimate payback on anyone who annoyed him. He had the resources to utterly destroy lives, especially those very brothers of his who had heartlessly betrayed and sold him out.

In fact, Joseph faced a prime opportunity to abandon the race of life altogether. Fall out of the competition. Forfeit the prize in favor of revenge. But he made a different choice, one that made him a winner, not a loser.

A Blameless Man

We have discovered in this book that the Bible does not flatter its heroes. Even if a man or a woman of God lived beautifully and suffered only a single lapse, the Bible records it. When we looked at the life of Elijah, for instance, we saw his glorious, powerful, and victorious life and ministry. But when he had a little lapse of faith, a little side trip into self-pity, Scripture recorded it clearly.

Amazingly, we find nothing this damaging in the record of Joseph. This leads me to believe he was truly an upstanding man, an unusually godly individual. We find not a single critical word about him in all of the chapters devoted to him in the Book of Genesis.

You'll remember Joseph endured some serious setbacks: jealous brothers, hateful plots, slavery, false accusations, unjust imprisonment. Joseph had that Midas touch, though, and everywhere he landed, he prospered. One minute a lie threw him in jail; the next thing you know, Joseph was running the prison.

Let's start by taking a look at Genesis 39:

> But the Lord was with Joseph and showed him mercy, and He gave him favor in the sight of the keeper of the prison. And the keeper of the prison committed to Joseph's hand all the prisoners who were in the prison; whatever they did there, it was his doing. The keeper of the prison did not look into anything that was under Joseph's authority, because the Lord was with him; and whatever he did, the Lord made it prosper. (vv. 21–23)

Things were going as well as they could in prison, but Joseph's fortunes were about to take another turn. One day, who arrived in jail but the king's cupbearer and his baker? What they did, we don't know. Whatever it was, they offended the king. One day, the palace, the next, a prison.

The two men had troubling dreams one night. They mentioned it to Joseph, who replied, "Do not interpretations belong to God? Tell me your dreams" (Genesis 40:8 NIV). In other words, "I've been able to interpret a dream or two, by the power of God. Let me have a go."

Well, why not? The cupbearer described his dream to Joseph, which Joseph said meant that he was going to get out of prison, and he would be serving in the king's presence in no time at all. Joseph added, "But remember me when it is well with you, and please show kindness to me; make mention of me to Pharaoh, and get me out of this house. For indeed I was stolen away from the land of the Hebrews; and also I have done nothing here that they should put me into the dungeon" (Genesis 40:14–15).

"Help me out," Joseph pleaded. "Say a kind word for me." The baker, encouraged by this, then described his dream. Joseph had the distasteful job of revealing the devastating interpretation of his dream: "You are going to be dead in a few days."

That's exactly what happened. The baker was executed. The cupbearer returned to serve the king. But, the Bible says, as soon as he was out of jail and out of trouble, he forgot all about Joseph.

Our Timing . . . and God's

Two full years passed while Joseph remained in that prison. That would have been upsetting, right? Joseph could have prayed, "Lord, I thought Your bringing the cupbearer to me and giving me the interpretation of his dream was my deliverance. It was my ticket out. What happened here?"

But he didn't complain. He just waited. God was preparing him for an amazing responsibility.

With God, timing is everything.

Who knows but that God is preparing you for something in your future as well? You might be in a transitional time right now. Maybe you want a certain thing to happen, but the Lord says, "You'd better wait." You want to get married. The Lord says, "You're not ready yet. You need to wait. He isn't the right man. She isn't the right woman. These aren't the right circumstances. That's why I put the brakes on it."

Trust Him—the Lord has to get you into shape first.

Maybe you are retirement age now, and your busiest years seem to be finished. Who knows that they are not just beginning? All of your experiences, all that you have gone through, all that you have learned—who knows what God can do with you still?

God's timing can vary from person to person. One person is

ready for his greatest task at the age of eighteen. Another isn't ready until the age of eighty. Don't assume life is over. Who knows what the Lord has in store?

Maybe you're in a not-so-good transition time right now. Maybe you're in a Joseph-like prison. Maybe . . .

- you've been the victim of false accusations.
- because you are a Christian, people have tried to damage your testimony.
- you, like Joseph, have been separated from a parent you love.
- you've all but lost contact with one or all of your siblings.
- you helped someone out, and he fully took advantage of you.
- you're a husband whose wife violated her marital vows (or vice versa).
- a pastor or a spiritual leader has let you down.

What are you to do? Learn from the life of Joseph: forgive and forget. That is exactly what he did, passing every test that came his way. It's true that the cupbearer forgot about Joseph, but God did not.

From Desperation to His Destiny

One day Pharaoh had a dream. It greatly troubled him. Then he had another dream similar to it. So disturbed was he that he called in all of the astrologers and soothsayers who were supposed to be able to interpret dreams. They were clueless. Then the cupbearer had an epiphany:

> Then the chief cupbearer said to Pharaoh, "Today I am reminded of my shortcomings. Pharaoh was once angry with his servants, and he imprisoned me and the chief baker in the house of the captain of the guard. Each of us had a dream the same night, and each dream had a meaning of its own. Now a young Hebrew was there with us, a servant of the captain of the guard. We told him our dreams, and he interpreted them for us, giving each man the interpretation of his dream. And things turned out exactly as he interpreted them to us: I was restored to my position, and the other man was impaled." (Genesis 41:9–13 NIV)

"Oh, King," he said, "there is this Jewish fellow in prison. . . ." Pharaoh was sufficiently impressed. He said, "I want to talk to him. Bring him up here right now."

Imagine, Joseph got up that morning as he did every day. It was just another day in this stinking prison. Suddenly someone came in and said, "The Pharaoh wants to see you."

Joseph enjoyed a long-overdue shower and shave. He was given new clothes. Then he was brought before the most powerful man in the land. In a matter of minutes, Joseph moved from the prison to the palace, from the worst filth imaginable to the most palatial of surroundings. He went from desperation to his destiny.

He seemed to take it all in stride, much like the apostle Paul, who wrote,

> Not that I was ever in need, for I have learned how to be content with whatever I have. I know how to live on almost nothing or with everything. I have learned the secret of living in every situation, whether it is with a full stomach or empty, with plenty or little. For I can do everything through Christ, who gives me strength. (Philippians 4:11–13 NLT)

Paul was saying, "I know what it's like to be on the bottom and on the top. I am pretty much content wherever I go, because my contentment doesn't come from what I have. It comes from whom I know."

That is a good principle for life. He didn't seem to be affected by where he was. He was a seasoned and prepared young man who trusted in his God.

Pharaoh described his dream to Joseph. Joseph said, "I know what that dream is about: Egypt will have seven years of plenty, where your crops will produce more than they normally would, and you will have more food than you can eat. Immediately following that, you will have to endure seven years of famine."

Notice what Joseph said next: "This will happen just as I have described it, for God has revealed to Pharaoh in advance what he is about to do" (Genesis 41:28 NLT). Joseph remembered his Deliverer, the source of his insight. He made that clear to Pharaoh.

Then he offered a word of advice: "What you need to do is store the extra from the first seven years to prepare for the next seven years. While you're at it, you'd better get somebody who is wise to do this for you. Then you will be able to survive it."

Pharaoh said, "That sounds good to me. I like that. And I think I know just the man for the job: it's *you*."

In a matter of minutes, Joseph was taken from the lowest of the low positions to become the second-most-powerful man in the kingdom. He waited on God's timing and was blessed because of it. He had unlimited financial authority. The Pharaoh gave him a special signet ring that meant he could authorize any expenditure. Joseph had social prestige because he dressed in royal garments and had his own private chariot, which would be the equivalent of a presidential limo. He had his own Secret Service—all of this, mind you, at the age of thirty.

I wonder if Potiphar was standing by while all this happened.

As head of Pharaoh's Secret Service, he most likely was. If so, he was shaking in his sandals, because Joseph was now far more powerful then he was. In fact, Joseph's new authority was second only to Pharaoh's.

What is amazing is that Joseph's change of fortune did not seem to turn his head in any way. He wasn't filled with arrogance or pride. We know what happens to some men when they come into prosperity: it destroys them. Not Joseph. He handled it well.

Mercy Reigns

Notice that Joseph did not misuse his power. How easily he could have said, "I am the second-most-powerful man in the kingdom. I want to see Potiphar and his wife right now. They are now dead people. After that, I want a search party sent out to find my wicked brothers. They are going to be executed."

He didn't do anything of the kind. Once again, he worked hard at his job, and he was a roaring success. We have evidence that he had not only forgiven, but had also forgotten, the pain others caused him. The Bible tells us he had two sons with his wife, Asenath. One he named Manasseh, and the other Ephraim. The meaning of the names is significant. Manasseh means "forgetting." Joseph had forgotten about all of the pain and hardship he had endured. Ephraim means "doubly fruitful." God had blessed Joseph as he had waited upon the Lord.

Then the story took another turn. If Hollywood scripted this, Joseph's brothers would show up, and he would kill them. The scriptwriters would have stretched this out and shown him hunting down each brother and dealing each a dramatic death. The scriptwriters would have saved the most wicked brother of all for the worst possible death. That's how the movies work: Good guy is hurt. Good guy destroys everyone in the end. We cheer good guy. That's entertainment!

But this is the Bible. It's a little different.

Joseph was in a position to do anything he wanted, but he refused the temptation to abuse his authority.

The massive famine he predicted had reached even the family of Jacob, who thought he was dead. Jacob took charge and sent his sons to find provision: "I have heard there is grain in Egypt. Go down there, and buy enough grain to keep us alive. Otherwise we'll die" (Genesis 42:2 NLT).

Off they went to Egypt, where one day someone alerted Joseph, "Some Jewish men want to see you about some food."

Could it possibly be my family? Joseph wondered.

It was. Picture the scene: there was Joseph, sitting regally on his throne, and before him were his brothers. They didn't recognize him. I think maybe he had aged a bit more than normal because of all of the hardship he had endured. Suffering can certainly take its toll, and, truth be told, young Joseph had suffered a lot.

Also, because of where and who he was, he would have had a shaved head, the style the Egyptians wore. I mentioned that he would have been dressed in royal robes. He would have spoken in the Egyptian dialect. Jacob's sons really had no way of knowing that Joseph was before them. They probably thought he was long dead or toiling as a slave somewhere, far from the throne room of Egypt.

But he knew who they were—and at first he didn't tell them. He pretended not to understand their language. He carefully listened to their conversations in Hebrew, but they did not realize he understood every word of what they were saying. He even put them up to a few tasks and tests to make them sweat a little. But finally:

> Joseph could stand it no longer. There were many people in the room, and he said to his attendants, "Out, all of you!" So he was alone with his brothers when he told them who he was. Then he broke down and wept. He wept so loudly the Egyptians could hear him, and word of it quickly carried to Pharaoh's palace.
>
> "I am Joseph!" he said to his brothers. "Is my father still alive?" But his brothers were speechless! They were stunned to realize that Joseph was standing there in front of them. "Please, come closer," he said to them. So they came closer. And he said again, "I am Joseph, your brother, whom you sold into slavery in Egypt. But don't be upset, and don't be angry with yourselves for selling me to this place. It was God who sent me here ahead of you to preserve your lives." (Genesis 45:1–5 NLT)

This was high drama. When the brothers heard this powerful man of Egypt weeping, they had to be thinking, *This can't possibly be good. What did we say? We have to get out of here!* When the royal then ordered, "Everyone leave. I want to be alone with these men," things certainly looked bad. Then he dropped the bombshell: "I am Joseph!"

Their jaws must have dropped to the ground. Now there was no question they were dead.

But look at the improbable words that fall from Joseph's lips: "It was God who sent me here. . . ."

Incredible. Joseph didn't even say, "God allowed it." He simply said, "It was God who sent me here. . . ." He knew God was in control of everything that had happened to him. His brothers couldn't believe their ears.

The rest of the account continues the drama. Jacob found out his sons were a bunch of habitual liars who had covered up their wicked and selfish deception for years, but anger turned to anticipation when he also found out his beloved Joseph was alive. They were reunited. What a joy it was for dear Jacob to reunite with his beloved son after thinking him dead those many years.

The brothers felt none too secure. They thought amongst themselves, *Wait until the old man is dead. Joseph's going to kill us all. It's just a matter of time.*

Jacob did die. The brothers saw their mortality hanging in the balance and sent Joseph an urgent message:

> "Before your father died, he instructed us to say to you: 'Please forgive your brothers for the great wrong they did to you—for their sin in treating you so cruelly.' So we, the servants of the God of your father, beg you to forgive our sin." When Joseph received the message, he broke down and wept. Then his brothers came and threw themselves down before Joseph. "Look, we are your slaves!" they said. But Joseph replied, "Don't be afraid of me. Am I God, that I can punish you? You intended to harm me, but God intended it all for good. He brought me to this position so I could save the lives of many people. No, don't be afraid. I will continue to take care of you and your children." So he reassured them by speaking kindly to them. (Genesis 50:16–21 NLT)

In spite of everything, Joseph still was willing to extend mercy. He was making a variation on his first statement. First he said, "It was God who sent me here. . . ." Then he said, "God intended it all for good." He was saying, "I know you meant it for evil. But God meant it for good to save many people."

Ingredients for a Forgiving Heart

How could Joseph make such a statement? Two reasons we need to remember in our own lives:

1. Joseph knew that God is sovereign

In other words, he knew nothing happens in the life of a child of God that He has not first approved. Did you know that? We forget sometimes.

Remember when Satan wanted to attack God's servant Job? He first had to get permission. Though the Lord did allow hardship and pain in Job's life, the Lord knew what Job could handle.

God knows what you can handle as well. He never will give you more than you can bear. Whenever God allows his children to go through fiery trials, He always keeps an eye on them and a finger on the thermostat.

Remember, the word "oops" is not in God's vocabulary.

2. Joseph knew that God is good

We need to balance the truth of God's sovereignty with this truth: God is good. Therefore, the things that come into our lives by God's sovereignty are for our benefit and others'.

Sometimes we believe God is sovereign, but that He is *mean*. "He is powerful," you acknowledge, "and He won't let anything happen that He doesn't want to happen. But you don't know what He's going to do next. He's not exactly . . . trustworthy." This is wrong. Yes, He is sovereign. Yes, He is all-powerful. Yes, He is all-knowing.

But He is also all-good. God loves you and has a good plan for your life. We've seen this verse earlier in the book, but it's worth repeating: God says,

> "For I know the thoughts that I think toward you, says the Lord, thoughts of peace and not of evil, to give you a future and a hope." (Jeremiah 29:11)

"Good" according to God

There is one New Testament verse that invariably comes to mind when you think about the story of Joseph—and it's a verse every believer should know:

> And we know that all things work together for good to those who love God, to those who are the called according to His purpose. (Romans 8:28)

This is a promise we need to know, to quote, to understand, and to think about through the days and events of our lives.

Some think this verse tells us that everything that happens will always turn into a good thing. Not exactly. Certainly there are times in our lives when something adverse or unexpected happens, and God turns it around so that something great comes of it. But then there are some events that, quite frankly, we don't fully understand. Maybe all things work for good, but it depends on how you define "good." If "good" is what makes us happy now, what makes us experience a certain sense of well-being, then when we experience something difficult or draining, how can we call that "good"?

We need to remember that after Romans 8:28 comes Romans 8:29. Think about what these verses say in context with one another: "All things work together for good to those who love God, and are the called according to His purpose. For whom He foreknew, He also predestined to be conformed to the image of His Son...."

This gives us the big picture. Whatever happens in your life is something that God has allowed. It always will ultimately work for your good, in that it will make you more like Jesus. In other words, although we tend to be interested in and absorbed by what is temporarily good, God is interested in what is eternally good. He is looking at the long term to make us more like the Lord Jesus himself.

How?

Let's say a loved one dies—what we deem as premature. We can't understand why such a thing should have happened, and we struggle to see any "good" in it at all. But maybe at his memorial service, ten people come to Christ. Then, as the years pass, those ten people reach ten more, and so on. Maybe when it is all said and done, a thousand people are in heaven as a result. In the end, even things we can't understand do work for good.

Thinking about this reminds me of when I was a boy. For a number of years I lived with my grandparents, Charles and Stella McDaniel. We all called them Mama Stella and Daddy Charles. They were from Arkansas, so we had a regular diet of good old-fashioned southern cooking: black-eyed peas, collard greens, and fresh mashed potatoes. My grandmother believed in making every meal from scratch. We never had leftovers. When she wanted to cook a chicken, my grandfather often went out into the backyard and killed one. That's how fresh it was. She made incredible food.

Mama Stella's crowning achievement was her biscuits. I have never had a better biscuit made by anyone, anywhere. I used to watch her make them. She used vegetable oil, self-rising flour, and, of course, buttermilk. No ingredient she used was appealing to me on its own. But when she mixed them all together with expert hands and put them into a very hot oven, they made some very good biscuits.

In the same way, when God takes the events of our lives—the good things and the so-called bad things—and puts them into the oven of adversity. When it's all done, we say, "That's good." But it may take time to come to that perspective—even a lifetime.

What We Can Control

You and I can't control our circumstances. But there is something we can control: *how we react to those circumstances*. When people have wronged us (and they will), when people disappoint us (and they will), when people betray us (and they will), and when they turn against us, we can forgive. We can forget.

You may say, "But Greg, they don't deserve it." That's probably true. But do *you* deserve God's forgiveness? Do you? The Bible tells us to forgive as we have been forgiven. Ephesians 4:32 says, Be kind and compassionate to one another, forgiving each other, just as in Christ God forgave you" (NIV). Romans 12:18 says, "Do all that you can to live in peace with everyone" (NLT).

When you carry bitterness and anger toward someone, it eats you up inside. You need to commit it to God and obey His Word. Joseph had done this before his brothers even showed up—that is so clear from his actions. Forgiven people should be forgiving people.

You may say, "Greg, it's easy for you to tell your biscuit stories and say these things to me, but forgiveness isn't easy." I know that. I have been through some hard stuff in my life too. I have been wronged, many times, and not just before my conversion, but afterward. But I know firsthand that all things work together for good to those who love God. I can see how God has turned my life's setbacks around. And He will do the same for you. Again, we can't control our circumstances, but we can control the way we *respond* to them.

Choose to forgive. Choose to forget. You'll never regret it.

We can be certain that Joseph never regretted forgiving his brothers. By doing so, he threw off "everything that hinders and the sin that so easily entangles" (Hebrews 12:1 NIV). That was one of the reasons he ran his whole race well and finished a winner. By dropping all the deadweight, he gained wings.

THE LEAST LIKELY RUNNER

Have you known anyone you just couldn't imagine becoming a Christian?

But then . . . maybe you took him to church and he gave his life to the Lord. And you were stunned! It surpassed all of your expectations of what God could do.

Maybe you know someone who is especially vocal about her opposition to your faith in Jesus Christ. She seems to go out of her way to harass you because you follow the Lord. It's as though she lives for it. You might be surprised to learn that the very person who gives you such a hard time about your faith may be closer to coming to the Lord than anyone else you know.

It has been said, "When you throw a rock into a pack of dogs, the one that barks the loudest is the one that got hit!" In the same way, those who protest (or "bark") the most, those who always have an argument waiting for us about our faith, are probably the ones getting hit. They are under the conviction of the Holy Spirit.

Acts 8 begins the astonishing account of a man who was both the most unlikely candidate for conversion and one who specialized in mocking and harassing Christians. His story is one of the most radical and unexpected turnarounds in the history of the Christian life.

Of course I am speaking of the conversion of the feared Saul of Tarsus. Against all odds, a man whose very name probably sent a shiver down the backbones of most believers became a leader of the early church, Saul of Tarsus was transformed into the beloved apostle Paul.

Paul the Frontrunner

Remember, it was Paul himself who compared the Christian life to running a race. Speaking to the elders in Acts 20, as he realized his life was coming to an end, he said he wanted to "finish [his] race with joy, and the ministry which [he] received from the Lord Jesus, to testify to the gospel of the grace of God." (v. 24). Paul knew that the point was not to start well but to finish well, to learn how to pace himself and make it across the finish line.

It was Paul who wrote, "Do you not know that those who run in a race all run, but one receives the prize?" (1 Corinthians 9:24). It was Paul who wrote in Philippians, "Forgetting those things which are behind and reaching forward to those things which are ahead, I press toward the goal for the prize of the upward call of God in Christ Jesus" (3:13–14).

When you get down to it, if ever there was a winner in the spiritual race . . . a man who had a less-than promising beginning . . . a man you never expected to see following Jesus . . . a man who turned his world upside down . . . it was the apostle Paul. To appreciate how dramatic and unexpected his conversion was, we need to understand the background of the man known as Saul of Tarsus.

Saul was named after the first king of Israel. He was a young man who did everything wholeheartedly. Young Saul grew up in a strict Jewish home where he learned the Scripture from his youth. He also came from the best Jewish soil: the tribe of Benjamin, from which rose Israel's first king. But like Israel's first king, Saul of Tarsus also "played the fool and erred exceedingly" for many years of his life.

Saul opted to become a Pharisee, a part of a very select group of people never numbering more than six thousand. Each Pharisee took a solemn vow before three witnesses that he would devote every moment of his life to obeying the Ten Commandments. Saul was a careful student who studied under the famous Gamaliel. So profound was the influence of this Jewish rabbi that at his death it was said, "Since Rabban Gamaliel died, the glory of the Law has ceased."[1] He was the ultimate teacher, and under his tutelage, this zealous young Jewish man grew by the day, as did his knowledge of Scripture and his grasp of the Law.

You wonder, *How could someone so religious be so wicked?* It was Saul, later to become Paul, who eventually confessed, "I was formerly a blasphemer" (1 Timothy 1:13). He described himself as the chief of all sinners (see 1 Timothy 1:15). How could this happen?

Quite simply, it was religion.

There is a big difference between religion and a relationship with Jesus Christ. It was religion that drove Saul to his wicked state.

Religion That Harms

Some people assert that religion can solve the problems of the world. I would have to disagree with that. If we are quite honest about it, religion is the cause of a lot of the world's problems today. Those wicked suicide bombers who take their lives and the lives of many others do so in the name of their religion. It's clear what a destructive power that is.

In Ireland today, a bloody conflict continues between the Protestants and the Catholics, all in the name of religion. Many people lost their lives in the Dark Ages, all in the name of religion. We must keep in mind that it was religious people, the Pharisees, who ultimately put Christ on the cross.

Let me clarify the fact that none of this religious activity has anything to do with Jesus Christ. When we are proclaiming the gospel, we are not promoting religion; we are promoting a relationship with God. When a person substitutes religion for a relationship with God, trouble inevitably will result. And clearly God would never have us engage in evangelism with threats, but rather with love. Not coercion but conversion. Not with the threat of death but with the promise of life.

Saul was blinded by his own twisted religion. He believed these followers of Jesus were heretics and were to be hunted down, tortured, and executed!

Escalating Conflict

It's quite possible that Saul worked his way up through the religious ranks by becoming a member of the Jewish Sanhedrin, which was the elite ruling group over Israel at that time. Then, Israel's civil and religious lives were closely intertwined. Therefore, the Sanhedrin not only made civil decisions as the Supreme Court does in our country, but it also passed down religious decisions. Needless to say, being a member of the Sanhedrin meant that you were very influential and powerful and, yes, feared.

As Jesus' followers grew in number, they created maddening times for the Sanhedrin. The Sanhedrin's attempt to silence the followers of Christ actually backfired. The members thought that once Jesus was dead, that would be the end of it. But, of course, that was only the beginning. It was the very death of Jesus and His resurrection from the dead that transformed a disorganized bunch of fishermen, tax collectors, and other common folk into powerful preachers of the gospel. Unwittingly the Sanhedrin and religious leaders helped to bring about the purpose and plan of God by executing Jesus.

There it is again: What was meant for evil ultimately produced good. (In this case, you might say the greatest of evils produced the greatest of goods.) That was hard for Jesus' devoted followers to understand as they saw His beaten and bloodied frame hanging on a Roman cross. But the Resurrection would change all of that—and their lives—forever.

The Sanhedrin leaders decided they would start imprisoning the believers. That only made the Christians bolder. It was as though the religious leaders were trying to put out a fire with gasoline—it just grew and grew. The Sanhedrin thought it was time to take it to the next level. Threat of imprisonment was not enough. They decided to execute those who followed Jesus.

And Saul of Tarsus was one of those who took that task to heart.

The First Martyr

The first one to die was a courageous young man whose name was Stephen. It's worth noting that Stephen was not an apostle. He was not even a leader in the church. If anything, he was something of an understudy. When the apostles selected men to handle the more mundane conflicts in the early church, one of the men was Stephen. Stephen faithfully took care of those problems, and he also preached the gospel. God was using him. Miracles were occurring. So he was called before the Sanhedrin and told to cease and desist from all such activity.

If Stephen had played his cards right, he could have gone home to dinner that night with his family. Instead, being a young man with vision, he thought, *Here I am before the Jewish Sanhedrin. God could reach them! I can imagine their influence if they used their office to help people come to faith!*

Stephen began a systematic rehearsal of Israel's history as a nation, showing its pattern of rebellion against the various prophets God had raised up, all of which culminated in the crucifixion of Jesus Christ. Then he looked them right in the eyes and boldly said, in essence, "You are stubborn, and you don't listen to what God is saying." That did not go over well: "When they heard these things they were cut to the heart, and they gnashed at him with their teeth" (Acts 7:54).

Stephen was undeterred. Suddenly he cried out, "Look! I see the heavens opened and the Son of Man standing at the right hand of God!" (v. 56). That was it. They couldn't take any more: "Then they cried out with a loud voice, stopped their ears, and ran at him with one accord; and they cast him out of the city and stoned him" (vv. 57–58).

As life drained from his young body, Stephen's final words were, "Lord Jesus, do not charge them with this sin" (v. 60). A tragic story, but Stephen shined brightly in that dark moment of his life. He forgave.

Why do I tell this story? To remind you what a powerful testimony it is when a Christian forgives someone who has horribly wronged him. Stephen reflected what our Lord did on the cross. As the Roman soldiers crucified him, He said, "Father, forgive them, for they do not know what they do" (Luke 23:34).

The young man of faith might have even reflected back on Joseph's story of forgiving his brothers when he offered that prayer for forgiveness to the Lord that he soon would join. I believe Stephen's very prayer, which was but a reflection of Jesus' prayer, ultimately resulted in the conversion of the feared Saul of Tarsus. Stephen did not live a long life, but he lived a productive one.

By the way, let me remind you that it is the greatest honor imaginable if God allows you to suffer for His name's sake. If a man like Saul is persecuting you, even if it is as subtle as harassment or mockery or ostracism, the Bible says this is an indication that you are living a godly life. Scripture tells us, "All who desire to live godly in Christ Jesus will suffer persecution" (2 Timothy 3:12).

Know that you are in good company. Jesus said, "Blessed are you when they revile and persecute you, and say all kinds of evil against you falsely for My sake. Rejoice and be exceedingly glad, for great is your reward in heaven, for so they persecuted the prophets who were before you" (Matthew 5:11–12).

Blinded by the Light

Let's pick up the story after Stephen's death.

> Now Saul was consenting to his death. At that time a great persecu-tion arose against the church which was at Jerusalem; and they were all scattered throughout the regions of Judea and Samaria, except the apostles. And devout men carried Stephen to his burial, and made great lamentation over him.
>
> As for Saul, he made havoc of the church, entering every house, and dragging off men and women, committing them to prison.
>
> Therefore those who were scattered went everywhere preaching the word. (Acts 8:1–4)

At that point, the persecution of the church was intense. In other parts of the Book of Acts, Paul gave a few details about his actions as an enemy of Christ. In Acts 26 he mentioned that he not only arrested Christians, but he "punished them often in every synagogue and compelled them to blaspheme; . . . I persecuted them even to foreign cities" (v. 11).

This implies that he tortured them. He also mentioned that whenever the chief priests were deciding the fate of a Christian, Paul always voted for execution (v. 10). He was a coldhearted murderer who blindly thought he was doing the will of God.

What drove Saul to have such a hatred for Christians? He was under the intense conviction of the Holy Spirit and did not know it. He was actually quite close to conversion, and no one was aware of it except God himself.

Saul and Stephen had a few things in common, but they had many differences. Stephen was a truly spiritual man; Saul was religious. Stephen was humble, saved by the grace of God; Saul was self-righteous, arrogant, and proud. Stephen defended the gospel; Saul persecuted it. In God's plan, ironically, Saul ultimately carried on Stephen's task. How did that happen?

> Then Saul, still breathing threats and murder against the disciples of the Lord, went to the high priest and asked letters from him to the synagogues of Damascus, so that if he found any who were of the Way, whether men or women, he might bring them bound to Jerusalem. As he journeyed he came near Damascus, and suddenly a light shone around him from heaven. Then he fell to the ground, and heard a voice saying to him, "Saul, Saul, why are you persecuting Me?" And he said, "Who are You, Lord?" Then the Lord said, "I am Jesus, whom you are persecuting. It is hard for you to kick against the goads." So he, trembling and astonished, said, "Lord, what do you want me to do?" Then the Lord said to him, "Arise and go into the city, and you will be told what you must do." And the men who journeyed with him stood speechless, hearing a voice but seeing no one. Then Saul arose from the ground, and when his eyes were opened he saw no one. But they led him by the hand and brought him into Damascus. (Acts 9:1–8)

On his way to hunt down Christians, Saul was "breathing threats." This is an interesting phrase in Greek. It could be translated "to breathe in and out." Just as a wild animal stalks its prey, breathing hard as it is in pursuit, Saul lived on hate. He breathed it like oxygen. His mind was blinded by prejudice, and fury fueled his every act.

I love verse 3: "Suddenly" Saul encountered Jesus. Isn't that just like the Lord? No announcement ahead of time. Without warning, the course of Saul's life changed dramatically and unexpectedly. This is a reminder to us that God always will have the last word.

On the day you became a Christian, did you know that was going to happen? Quite possibly you did. I've heard the stories of many who have come to our evangelistic events intending to make commitments to Christ. They know they will respond to the invitation to come forward and make a public profession to follow Christ, which I always give at the end of each service.

But that's not true of everyone. There are others who had no plan to convert. They reluctantly attended with a friend or a family member. I was one of those people. On the day I gave my life to the Lord, I can assure you the last thing on my mind was conversion to Christianity.

Multiply that a hundred or a thousand times, and you have an idea of how Saul felt. This reminds us that someone can be so set in his ways, so wicked, yet instantaneously God's Holy Spirit can intervene in his life and turn him around. Conversion is the work of the Spirit. It can occur in the most unexpected circumstances and times and ways.

Saul's Encounter with Jesus

Notice what Jesus said first: "Saul, Saul, why are you persecuting Me?" Whenever you see a person's name repeated twice in the Bible, it's because it is a term of endearment. It shows affection. The very Jesus whom Saul had been maligning reached out to him tenderly and asked, "Saul . . . Saul . . . Why are you persecuting Me?" Can you imagine how the word "Me" reverberated through Saul as he realized in a moment what he had actually been doing? "Why are you persecuting *Me*?"

This shows that Jesus closely identifies with us in our afflictions.

Nothing escapes His attention. When a persecutor raises a hand against a follower of Jesus, he is indeed raising his hand against the very Lord himself.

In verse 5 Jesus said, "It is hard for you to kick against the goads." "Kick against the goads" was a common expression in Greek and Latin literature. It described a farmer poking his oxen with a sharpened stick. When his oxen weren't moving, he gave them a poke. Sometimes the oxen resisted and kicked against the goad the farmer was using. That caused them even more pain.

Jesus used the rural expression to describe what Saul had been going through for the previous few months. The Lord had been goading him, poking him, pricking his conscience, and saying, "Saul, you need to believe in Me." Despite the goading, Saul said, "No way." His religion had kept him blind to the truth.

The Enemies of a Twisted Mind

What goads was Saul kicking against?

1. The very life of Jesus

Saul was alive when Jesus had His ministry. It's quite possible that Saul personally heard and saw Jesus speak. Being a leading Pharisee, and possibly a member of the Sanhedrin, Saul probably was in the thick of the conflicts between Jesus and the religious leaders and knew all about the plans to execute Jesus.

Saul also would have been aware of the famed religious leader Nicodemus going to see Jesus by night. That was a goad. It got his attention. Saul probably thought Nicodemus had fallen under Jesus' hypnotic spells, but he knew better.

Perhaps when Jesus appeared to Saul on the Damascus road, Saul recognized the Lord. "Saul, remember Me? I am alive still."

2. The spread of the Christian faith and the commitment of its followers

The Christians Saul tortured probably died calling on God. The more he attacked Jesus' followers, the more their numbers grew. He had never seen anything like that in his own legalistic religion. The

Christians reflected changed lives and persistence, even in the face of death.

3. The peaceful death of Stephen and his forgiveness of his persecutors

The Bible says that Stephen's face looked like that of an angel when he preached to the Sanhedrin. Then, when he gave his life for the faith and prayed, "Lord, do not charge them with this sin," it pierced Saul's hardened heart, but not all the way . . . until his encounter on the Damascus road.

Here is something to remember regarding the three points I just noted: a goad is not comfortable. It's not pleasant to be poked with a stick. Conversion begins with discomfort and results in eternal comfort.

Sometimes we don't want to create conflict with nonbelievers by sharing our faith with them. We don't want to offend. We don't want to get into an argument. So we try to blend into the woodwork.

When we do that, we make a big mistake. The very friction and discomfort a real follower of Jesus provides ultimately produces conversion. I'm not suggesting that we be obnoxious or overly pushy. I'm simply saying we need to be what we are: a bright light in a dark place, and sometimes a pinch of salt in a wound.

Maybe your family, a bunch of nonbelievers, gets together. The whole mood changes the moment you enter the room. Of course, whenever a family gathers, they want to have their token prayer, especially if it's Thanksgiving or Christmas. It usually falls on you as the Christian.

You don't like the tension. You wish they would call on someone else. I'm telling you that this tension, this uncomfortable feeling, can be a very good thing. And remember this: when you are asked to pray, you have the floor! So take full advantage of it for the gospel.

Spiritual Encounter with a Bodybuilder

Once I was getting my cell phone repaired, and, while I was waiting,

I went next door to one of those bodybuilding stores. I quickly scoped it out and couldn't find a thing I needed. As I was walking toward the door, a very muscular guy looked me in the eyes and said, "You're Greg Laurie, aren't you?" Another equally pumped-up guy was behind the counter, watching with great interest.

I replied, "Yes, I am."

He said, "I have a question for you. I'm living with my girlfriend. Why is that a sin?"

I thought for a moment. I don't know if this guy is going to appreciate the answer I have for him here. Yet, I don't really have a choice in the matter.

So I responded, "Because the Bible says it is."

He said, "Let me ask you this: if I died, would I go to hell?"

I said, "You probably would." I thought, *This is crazy. These two guys could put the hurt on me.* There was quite a bit of friction in that room. I tried to be very loving. I didn't scream the truth in his face. I spoke calmly but firmly.

As we talked more, he softened. He admitted that he had made a commitment to Christ but had fallen away. He knew he shouldn't have been living with his girlfriend.

I told him that he needed to recommit his life to the Lord. I said, "Would you like to do that right now?"

"No way."

I said, "I'm going to pray for you."

He took a step back and responded, "Oh, no. Don't do that."

I said, "You know what? I've never been in here before. Obviously I don't frequent this store. This was a divine appointment. The Lord led me in here to tell you these things because He loves you and wants you to get right with Him."

Believe me, there was tension. I tried to diffuse any unnecessary friction without compromising my message. I believe God used this as a goad in this man's life. I am sure he had been using other things and encounters to get his attention as well.

God got Saul's attention through different goads. You might be a goad in someone else's life. You just hang in there and "goad" for it!

Two Questions We All Should Ask

Saul asked two very important questions on the day of his conversion:

"Who are You, Lord?"

And, "What do You want me to do?"

Every follower of Jesus should ask the same things. We need to dedicate our lives to discovering who Jesus is. Certainly Paul did that. He said it best himself in Philippians: "My determined purpose is that I may know Him [that I may progressively become more deeply and intimately acquainted with Him, perceiving and recognizing and understanding the wonders of His Person more strongly and more clearly], and that I may in that same way come to know the power outflowing from His resurrection . . ." (3:10 AMP). That is a good way to live your life: getting to know the Lord.

"What do You want Me to do?" This is a question I think many believers have never asked the Lord. Have you? "Lord, what is Your plan for my life? What do You want me to do with my future? How do You want me to invest my time, my money, my energy?" If you ask, I believe the Lord will give you an answer. He gave one to Saul; He will give one to you too.

Saul's story did not stop at his conversion. That was just the beginning. The man who had dedicated his life to the destruction of the Christian church then dedicated his life to its spread. He who had been controlled by hate was now to be controlled by love.

After his encounter with Christ, Saul blazed a trail, creating countless churches and converts. He fearlessly preached to philosophers, Pharisees, rulers, soldiers, sorcerers, slaves, sailors, and quite possibly Caesar himself.

Saul's conversion was such an unlikely event that a British agnostic of the last century thought it would not be too difficult to disprove. In doing that, he thought he could also show that the rest of the New Testament was not credible—and thus undermine the entire foundation of the Christian faith. George Lloyd Littleton went to work on his book, *Observations on the Conversion and Apostleship of Saint Paul.*

But a funny thing happened to Littleton as he researched Paul's story. He came to a far different conclusion than he had anticipated. At the end of his book, he made this statement: "Paul's conversion and apostleship alone, duly considered, are a demonstration sufficient to prove Christianity to be a divine revelation."[2] As it turned out, Littleton was actually converted in the study of the transformation that took place in Saul's life.

Saul may have done damage to God's people prior to starting the race, but he spent the rest of his life trying to make up for it. He set the pace for all who would follow.

GUN LAP

Just after Saul's conversion, we read in Acts 9 that God directed a man named Ananias to seek out the new convert. The Lord told him to go to a certain place where he would recognize Saul, because he would be praying.

Ananias was understandably reluctant. He reminded God that Saul had been the persecutor of the church:

> "Lord, I have heard from many about this man, how much harm he has done to Your saints in Jerusalem. And here he has authority from the chief priests to bind all who call on Your name." But the Lord said to him, "Go, for he is a chosen vessel of Mine to bear My name before Gentiles, kings, and the children of Israel. For I will show him how many things he must suffer for My name's sake." (Acts 9:13–16)

I find it interesting that when God wanted to raise up someone to minister to Saul, he didn't choose an apostle such as Peter or John, but an ordinary and unknown man. Did Ananias write any book of the New Testament? Did he ever perform a miracle? Did he raise a dead person? Did he give a notable sermon that we know about?

No. Not that we know of.

But at an extremely critical time, he did come into the life of a man who would change his world, and, indeed, world history.

I thank God for the Ananiases of the kingdom. By that, I mean those who faithfully work behind the scenes. We rarely hear their names, yet they faithfully deliver their messages, minister to the sick and the hurting, pray, give, labor away in obscurity on the mission field. We don't know about them. They are unknown to man, but they are beloved of God.

Who knows but that God could not use you in such a way? He could raise you up to be like the apostle Paul or like the humble Ananias.

My Story

A young man did this for me. His name was Mark. Shortly after my unexpected conversion, Mark sought me out and helped me acclimate to this new world of Christianity that I knew nothing about.

First, let me tell you a little about my background. I wasn't raised in the church. For the most part, I didn't read the Bible or pray. I always believed, however, there was a God somewhere, but I never knew He could be known personally.

I grew up in a very dysfunctional home. My mother was married and divorced some seven times and also was a full-blown alcoholic. I spent far too much time in smoky bars, waiting for my mom to tire and be ready to return home. Many times I feared for my life as she drunkenly tried to find her way back to our house in the car. Countless nights I was awakened very late to hear my mother screaming obscenities and throwing things. The next morning she remembered nothing and never made mention of it. Then the pattern repeated the next evening. This went on for years.

As a result of this bizarre upbringing, I quickly developed survival skills and a pretty tough skin. I was known for my quick, biting, sarcastic wit, which got me into quite a bit of trouble in the various schools I attended over the years. The funny thing is, on the inside I was almost a romantic, believing that somewhere in the world was a good, wholesome, and loving life. But on the outside I was hard and bitter.

Despite the horrific example of my mother, I turned to a

partying lifestyle myself. Tiring of that, I got caught up in the drug culture for a few years. This only exacerbated my problems.

I was very unhappy with the course my life was taking and desperately wanted to have some meaning and purpose in my life. I was to find that in an unexpected place.

It all started with a girl on my high school campus who caught my eye. She was attractive, but there was more to her than that. I couldn't quite put my finger on it. I really wanted to meet her and try and discover what made her different from so many of the other girls on campus. One day she was talking to one of my friends, so I thought that would be as good a time as any to make my move.

I walked up to them as they talked and waited for a break in the conversation. I looked down and saw her notebook, a textbook for a class, and something unexpected: a Bible!

I remember thinking, *Oh no! She's one of those Jesus freaks!* At a lull in our conversation, I introduced myself. She didn't jump down my throat with the gospel, as I had expected. She just radiated Jesus Christ. I wondered, *Could there be something to all of this?*

That lunchtime, I went into "enemy territory" and decided to eavesdrop on the Christians as they had their Bible study on the front lawn of Newport Harbor High School in Orange County, California.

I carefully surveyed the group of Christians in attendance that day. I was sitting at a distance but was close enough to hear what was being said. A young man from a local church called Calvary Chapel got up and spoke about who Jesus Christ was and how one could know Him personally. Though, as a very young man, I had prayed at a Christian camp and asked Jesus Christ into my life, I really had no idea then what I was really doing.

But suddenly it was crystal clear.

God loved me. He sent His Son to die on the cross in my place. I needed to believe in and follow Him.

My heart pounded so hard it seemed as though people sitting around me could hear it. I hung my head and thought, *It all sounds so great. It really does. But this would never work for me personally.* I just didn't see myself as "the religious type." I was far too cynical, skeptical, and reluctant to follow the Christian crowd.

But God was working on me that day. The conviction of the Holy Spirit did not let up, and, much to my own amazement, I found myself praying with some others to make a commitment to Jesus Christ. Even as I prayed, I was thinking that God was going to somehow turn me down cold.

But He didn't.

He came into my life and forgave me of my sins that day.

When others I knew on campus found out, they could hardly believe it: "Laurie is a Jesus freak now?" Yes, I was. But I might have quickly fallen through the cracks were it not for a young man named Mark.

A Crucial Role

So, there I was, a brand-new Christian, thinking, *What now?* Frankly, I had no idea what to do next.

No one came to me with a Bible or told me to go to church. No one even explained what had happened to me, and I was perplexed. Despite the fact that I was now a newly minted Christian, I still felt a bit awkward around the other believers. I didn't understand their lingo or lifestyles in many ways. So, I went back to hang out with my old nonbelieving friends for a few days.

But a funny thing had happened. The very things I used to enjoy suddenly had no appeal to me. The jokes weren't funny anymore. The absolute waste of life was evident, so I disconnected from them.

I was in danger of quickly falling through the cracks. That is, until Mark came along. He came up to me out of the blue one day at school and told me he had seen me pray and receive Christ. I was a bit cold and standoffish, thinking, *What does this guy want?*

Mark was patient with me and asked if I had a Bible yet. He then proceeded to get me one and even explained how best to start reading it. I opened this wonderful book for the first time and was absolutely amazed at what I read. It was so relevant to my life!

Mark started having personal Bible studies with me, explaining the basics of the Christian faith. He also took me to church and introduced me to other Christians.

He was my Ananias.

Could you be that for someone else?

Secrets of Paul's Success

Returning to Paul's story: Ananias was understandably hesitant, but in obedience, he did what God told him to do. He found Saul, who had been blinded after his dazzling meeting with Jesus, and prayed that the Lord would restore his sight.

This encounter brings us to a few secrets of Saul-turned-Paul's life that I want to bring to your attention. These principles will help us to understand why God so powerfully used him.

1. Paul was a praying man

God told Ananias to look for Saul, a guy who would be praying. Sure enough, that's exactly what Saul was doing when Ananias came upon him. What was he praying about? I'm sure he was seeking forgiveness of his sins.

Can you imagine how hard it would be to accept God's forgiveness if you were a murderer? And Saul wasn't just someone who took the lives of others, but someone who specifically hunted down the followers of Jesus Christ and brought about their premature deaths.

When Paul later wrote that he was "forgetting those things which are behind and reaching forward to those things which are ahead" (Philippians 3:13), you have to understand that he had a lot to forget. He had a lot of sin to put behind him. So he prayed.

Prayer actually characterized his life of faith. You can't help but notice that. So many of his epistles begin or end with beautiful prayers he offered on behalf of the people to whom he was writing. It was Paul who told us that men ought to pray (1 Timothy 2:8). He told us we should remember to be people of prayer and to "pray without ceasing" (1 Thessalonians 5:17).

Paul practiced what he preached. We read in Acts 16 that Paul and Silas were thrown into a dungeon for preaching the gospel. Their backs had been ripped open by a whip. Their feet were fastened in stocks. There, in that dark, stinking hole, the Bible says that at midnight Paul and Silas prayed and sang praises to God.

Who would want to pray at a time like that? It would make more sense if at midnight Paul and Silas wept or cried out to God or sat in stunned silence. No, the Bible says they prayed and worshiped God. Instead of cursing men, they were blessing God. No wonder the other prisoners were listening to them.

Paul discovered through prayer that he could enjoy an intimate relationship with the God he had known of previously only in a cold, distant way through dead legalism and orthodoxy. He later wrote, "For you did not receive the spirit of bondage again to fear, but you received the Spirit adoption by whom we cry out, 'Abba, Father'" (Romans 8:15).

"Abba" was the affectionate cry of a beloved child. Our modern equivalent would be "Daddy" or "Papa." Paul developed an intimacy with God. This was the transformation that took part in the life of Paul. He was a man of prayer. Are you a man of prayer? Are you a woman of prayer? Does prayer characterize your life? It ought to. If you want to finish well in the spiritual race, then you need to learn how to pray.

2. Paul was a humble man

Now, he wasn't always humble. At one time he was probably the proudest guy around—filled with himself and his accomplishments, knowledge, and skills. Later God transformed him into a man of deep and genuine humility.

Right after his conversion, Paul started preaching the gospel in Damascus (see Acts 9:19–20). He was so powerful and persuasive that the religious leaders wanted him dead right then and there. He was a threat. The believers found out about it and hatched a scheme by which they could get Paul out of the city. They put him into a basket and lowered it over the city walls at nighttime.

Think of the irony of that situation. Just a short time earlier, he had been Saul of Tarsus with his entourage that arrested and executed Christians. Next thing you know, Christians were taking extraordinary precautions to save his life by lowering him over the city wall in a basket.

Even his name gives us an insight into what he was all about at that point. He changed his name from Saul to Paul. Saul was the name of the first king of Israel; it was a respected and powerful name. Then he took the name of Paul, which means "little." I don't know if he took that name because he was small in stature. I think Saul took the name Paul to describe the change that had happened in his life. One name, Saul, denoted power, greatness, influence. The other, Paul, spoke of smallness, insignificance, humility.

This was like having the name "Spike" and changing it to "Squirt." God had transformed him. The hunter had become the hunted. The man who persecuted others was getting a taste of his own medicine. Yet instead of striking out, he practiced humility.

Let's explore the ways in which he did so.

A humble man endures obscurity.
The Lord took Paul away and put him into obscurity in the desert of Arabia for a period of time (see Galatians 1:17). What happened there we are not told. We can only presume that it was then that he drew close to the Lord in fellowship and communion. Most likely it was there that he refined the theology we see in the great epistles that God inspired him to write.

It was typical of how God dealt with many people He prepared for service: he placed them on "pause" for a time. You remember after Elijah made his bold pronouncement to Ahab and Jezebel that God sent him to the Brook Cherith for a couple of years. Moses had forty years of training to get him into shape to deliver the children of Israel.

Even after the young teenager David was anointed to be king, it wasn't until he reached the age of thirty that he actually ascended the throne. Even after Joseph flourished in the house of Potiphar, he lived in prison for two very long years.

God isolated these men only because he was preparing them for his work. God did the same for Paul.

It has been said that it takes a steady hand to hold a full cup. God was going to give a full cup to Paul. He was going to use him powerfully. He had to be prepared and properly equipped to withstand the challenges. The Lord humbled him and made him ready for the tasks that were ahead. Only then did He take Paul back into society.

The Lord may be preparing you today for a greater work He wants to do with you tomorrow.

A humble man prefers worshiping God to being worshiped himself.

An interesting series of events unfolded. According to Acts 14, when Paul was in Lystra, he saw a crippled man. God revealed to Paul that he wanted to heal the man, so Paul, under the inspiration of the Holy Spirit, said, "Stand up straight on your feet!" (v. 10). The man got up and walked. The people in that city, who were largely pagan, were so moved by this demonstration of faith and power that they thought Paul and his companion, Barnabas, were Greek gods come to life. They called them Zeus and Hermes, and they began to offer animal sacrifices to them.

Paul was a humble man, as was Barnabas. Scripture says, "When the apostles Barnabas and Paul heard this, they tore their clothes and ran in among the multitude, crying out and saying, 'Men, why are you doing these things? We also are men with the same nature as you . . .'" (Acts 14:14–15).

Paul proceeded to preach the gospel to them. The leaders were so outraged at Paul's audacity to confront them with the truth that they decided to put him to death. They turned the same multitude that had been ready to sacrifice to him against him.

We read in Acts 14, "Then some Jews arrived from Antioch and Iconium and won the crowds to their side. They stoned Paul and dragged him out of town, thinking he was dead" (v. 19 NLT). It was probably at this point that Paul had his "third heaven" experience. In 2 Corinthians 12, Paul described it this way:

> It is doubtless not profitable for me to boast. I will come to visions and revelations of the Lord: I know a man in Christ who fourteen

years ago—whether in the body I do not know, or whether out of the body I do not know, God knows—such a one was caught up to the third heaven. And I know such a man—whether in the body or out of the body I do not know, God knows—how he was caught up into Paradise and heard inexpressible words, which it is not lawful for a man to utter. Of such a one I will boast; yet of myself I will not boast, except in my infirmities. For though I might desire to boast, I will not be a fool; for I will speak the truth. But I refrain, lest anyone should think of me above what he sees me to be or hears from me. (vv. 1–6)

Paul was saying that he died, went to heaven, and heard things that he could not repeat. He was saying that he didn't even want to boast about hearing these words from God.

It's my opinion that the event we read about in Acts is when this transpired. Paul was preaching. The crowd turned against him, stoned him, and he died. At that point in time, he was immediately ushered into the presence of God Almighty.

This passage reminds us that we should never feel sorrow for people who have died in the Lord. Sure, we miss them desperately. Yes, we wish we could still hear their voices and look into their eyes. *But don't feel sorry for them.* Where they are is far better than where you are right now. They would want you to know that.

That's why Paul basically said, "How can I describe it? It was Paradise! I'm telling you that it's not something I can put into human words."

This shows us the humility of the apostle. If I had died, gone to heaven, and was allowed to come back again, I think I'd talk about it in every conversation. You couldn't shut me up about. In fact, the title of this book would have been something along the lines of *How I Went to Heaven and Came Back to Earth*.

But Paul? He mentioned it once, but we never read of it again. A humble man knows where his strength lies. The Lord knew that this supernatural experience could potentially boost Paul's pride. We read,

And lest I should be exalted above measure by the abundance of the revelations, a thorn in the flesh was given to me, a messenger of Satan to buffet me, lest I be exalted above measure. Concerning this thing I pleaded with the Lord three times that it might depart from me. And He said to me, "My grace is sufficient for you, for My strength is made perfect in weakness." (2 Corinthians 12:7–9)

What this thorn was, we don't know. I will tell you this: in the original language it could be better translated "a stake in the flesh." It was a brutal thing. Some commentators think it was a disability; perhaps he was born with it. Others believe it might have been something that didn't heal after he was stoned. I think that is probably the case. Whatever it was, three times he asked the Lord to take it away.

Understand, God had used Paul to pray for other people to be well, but God didn't heal the apostle himself. Rather, He just extended His grace. Why? Paul said, "I don't know, but I will tell you this much: I rejoice in these things." I love his words in verses 9–10:

> So now I am glad to boast about my weaknesses, so that the power of Christ can work through me. That's why I take pleasure in my weaknesses, and in the insults, hardships, persecutions, and troubles that I suffer for Christ. For when I am weak, then I am strong. (NLT)

Sometimes we want God to take a certain thing away. We pray over and over for Him to remove it. Did you ever stop to think God is using it in your life?

Something else to consider: when you have gone through hardship, you can more effectively minister to others who are going through the same thing. Paul wrote in 2 Corinthians 1:

> He comforts us in all our troubles so that we can comfort others. When they are troubled, we will be able to give them the same comfort God has given us. . . . For when we ourselves are comforted, we will certainly comfort you. Then you can patiently endure the same things we suffer. (vv. 4, 6 NLT)

You have endured tragedies in life that others will endure as well. You can comfort someone else with the comfort you have received from the Lord. Nothing happens by accident in the life of the Christian.

3. Paul was a loving man

Paul had once been so filled with hate. Remember, the Bible says that he was "breathing threats and murder against the disciples of the Lord" (Acts 9:1). It is a vivid picture of a wild animal seething in hostility and anger as it hunts its prey. Paul once lived on hate; then God transformed him into the apostle of love. He wrote the greatest chapter on love in human history in 1 Corinthians 13: "Though I speak with the tongues of men and of angels, but have not love, I have become sounding brass or a clanging cymbal. . . . Love suffers long and is kind . . ." (vv. 1, 4).

These weren't the hollow words of a man who merely liked the sentiment of love. This was a man who lived it.

Paul probably did more to remove barriers between Jews and Gentiles than anybody else in the first-century Christian church. What kept him going through the persecutions and hardships? He loved God, and he loved people. It was Paul who wrote, "For the love of Christ compels us . . ." (2 Corinthians 5:14).

Paul's Obituary

Paul's turbulent life was coming to an end. He had touched thousands of lives. He had fearlessly preached the gospel to great leaders and common people. God had wrought miracles through him. He had written the wonderful epistles we so value today as much of the New Testament.

We read his final words in 2 Timothy 4. When Paul wrote this, he was in the Mamertine Prison in Rome. He had appealed to Caesar. We have good reason to believe that he eventually stood before the Roman Emperor Nero himself. God had somehow revealed to Paul that this was it—his time had come to an end:

> I am already being poured out as a drink offering, and the time of my departure is at hand. I have fought the good fight, I have finished the race, I have kept the faith. Finally, there is laid up for me the crown of righteousness, which the Lord, the righteous Judge, will give to me on that Day, and not to me only but also to all who have loved His appearing. (vv. 6–8)

If I'm preparing to go to some location I don't like, I dread the trip. On the other hand, if I'm going somewhere I like, I look forward to the trip. The trip is relatively painless, even sitting in coach with a person reclined in front of me. It's okay! The destination makes it worthwhile.

Paul had been in pain. Paul had suffered. He had endured hardship. How do you imagine he looked in those moments, as he stood before Caesar? Don't think of a depressed old man—think of a person whose face was radiating with joy: "My departure is at hand. I have fought the good fight, I have finished the race, I have kept the faith."

If you died today, would you be able to say that? I am not suggesting you should be able to say, "I am a perfect person. I never made a mistake." No one could. But could you say, in general, that you have kept the faith and finished the race? We should all be able to say it.

Paul compared himself as a Christian to three different types of people.

A wrestler

"I have fought the good fight." The word translated "fight" points to the Greek wrestling matches in which men struggled against each other with all of their might, sometimes fighting even to the death. It was like a street brawl. Paul was saying, "I have fought this fight to the death."

Make no mistake about it: the Christian life is a fight. The moment you give your life to Jesus, the battle begins. Conversion has made our hearts a battleground. The Spirit wars against the flesh, and the flesh wars against the Spirit. You have the devil, the flesh, and the world as your enemies. The raging fight will not end until the day you are safely in the arms of Jesus. There always will be that dynamic of struggle and conflict because you are in a spiritual war.

It was Paul who wrote, "For we do not wrestle against flesh and blood, but against principalities, against powers, against the rulers of the darkness of this age, against spiritual hosts of wickedness in the heavenly places" (Ephesians 6:12).

A runner

Paul said, "I have finished the race." Notice that he used the word "finished." He didn't say that he merely ran the race. As we have seen, it is possible to run the race poorly, to give up halfway through it. Paul was able to say, "I finished the race." That is the goal: to finish what we have begun.

In Philippians 3:14, you'll remember that Paul wrote, "I press toward the goal for the prize of the upward call of God in Christ Jesus." It gives us a picture of a runner in the last lap of a race. Pain wracks his body. He can see the ribbon. He's almost there.

Are you running for the finish line in the race God has given you—giving it all you've got?

A soldier

Paul said, "I have kept the faith." The word "kept" means having guarded the faith as an armed soldier would guard his post against enemy attack. In other words, Paul was saying that he had not strayed from the truth in his words or in his life.

If your life were to end today, would you be able to say that you had fought the good fight, you had finished the course, and you had kept the faith? Have you been winning in this fight and struggle against Satan and personal sin? Have you guarded and kept the faith in the way you live? Have you kept up the pace in the race of life? If so, then the reward that Paul was looking forward to will be yours as well.

Paul concluded in 2 Timothy 4:8, "Finally, there is laid up for me the crown of righteousness, which the Lord, the righteous Judge, will give to me on that Day, and not to me only but also to all who have loved His appearing."

If you are looking forward to the appearing of Christ, then Christ has a crown of righteousness for you. If you are truly anticipating the Lord's return, then it should affect the way you live.

Life will come to an end. We don't know when. It might be many years from now, or it might not. We all need to give thought to our legacy—to what we are living for and what our lives are all about.

What do you think your last words will be? What will your obituary say? Can you sum up your life the way Paul did?

Don't waste your life. Fight the good fight. Finish that race. Keep the faith. Run this way, and you will win a crown for a prize.

It's the best way we could possibly live . . . with our eyes on the finish line.

NECK AND NECK ...
WITH HIMSELF

A dramatic moment took place in an Olympic competition years ago in Mexico City. It was seven in the evening on October 20, 1968. It was almost dark. The last of the marathon runners were stumbling across the finish line. Finally the very last, a lone runner, wearing the colors of Tanzania, staggered into the stadium. His name was John Stephen Akhwari. His leg had been injured in a fall. It was crudely bandaged. As the crowd looked on, he hobbled the final lap around the track.

When he finally finished, the crowd stood in unison and gave him an ovation. He actually received greater applause than the winner of the race had. Why? Because he had, against all odds, finished this incredible race. Afterward someone asked why he had not quit. This was the response he gave: "My country did not send me seven thousand miles to start the race. They sent me seven thousand miles to finish it."

When I read that, I couldn't help but think of the person in the Bible who, like Okiwari, finished his race . . . but not without some serious injuries. He, too, made a dramatic comeback and crossed the finish line with flying colors. This man's *faux pas* were legendary, his statements priceless, his mistakes public. Of course, I am speaking of Simon Peter.

A Man Like Any Other

You have to love Peter. He was such a classically human character. We can admire a man like the apostle Paul for his great courage, dedication, and commitment. We can stand in awe of a man like the apostle John for the deep love and devotion he had for the Lord. But when we look at Simon Peter, we just step back and say, "That is me." He is a guy we can so easily relate to.

The key to understanding this man is in his name. He was given the name Simon by his parents. He was given the new name of Peter by Jesus.

That tells us who he was, and who he was to become. All of his life, he remained both Simon and Peter. Sometimes Simon prevailed; other times Peter did. If that doesn't make any sense to you, look at John 1:40–42:

> One of the two who heard John speak, and followed Him, was Andrew, Simon Peter's brother. He first found his own brother Simon, and said to him, "We have found the Messiah" (which is translated, the Christ). And he brought him to Jesus. Now when Jesus looked at him, He said, "You are Simon the son of Jonah. You shall be called Cephas" (which is translated, A Stone).

His given name, Simon, means "a listener" or "a hearer." Upon seeing him for the first time, Jesus essentially gave him a nickname—a new title to describe the person he was going to become. He said, "Your name is going to be Peter" (or "Rock," the literal meaning).

I think the others might have done a little snickering at that point. If there was anything Simon was *not*, it was a rock. A rock is stable and solid. Peter was given to the emotion of a moment. He could be hotheaded. But God saw him for what he would become.

A Name to Reflect One's Potential

Maybe your parents gave you a name you don't particularly like. I heard about a mom and dad who decided to give their child the very curious name of Odd.

Poor kid! Obviously that invited ridicule and mockery all

through grade school, high school, and college. But the jibes made him want to achieve, and he became a very successful lawyer.

Because people ribbed him his entire life, he decided that upon his death, he wanted an unmarked tombstone placed at his grave so his name would never be uttered again. His wishes were honored. The problem was when people saw this tombstone without an inscription, they almost always said, "That's odd."

Jesus gave to Simon this new name of Rock. Why? He knew Peter eventually would grow into the name. The phrase that is translated "Jesus looked at [Peter]" means that He looked right through him.

Have you ever had anyone look right through you? Let me restate the question: Do you have a mother? Then you know what it's like to have someone look right through you. You find yourself confessing wrongs that you never even committed!

We know Jesus knew what He was getting. He knew Peter would fail. He knew that Peter would fall short. He even knew that Peter ultimately would deny Him. But Jesus also knew that Peter would make a comeback. He knew that after his early failure, "the Rock" would courageously serve the Lord all the days of his life.

He looked right through him, and He saw potential.

In the same way, Jesus looks at you and doesn't see you just for what you are. He sees you for what you can become. We see a lump of clay; God sees a beautiful vase. We see a blank canvas; God sees a finished painting. We see a lump of coal; God sees a refined diamond. We see problems; God sees solutions. We see failures; God sees potential success. We see a Jacob; God sees an Israel. We see a Simon; God sees an apostle Peter.

Failure Turned to Success

God can take the failures of our lives and use them for His glory. That doesn't mean we should go out and intentionally fail. It means that when we do, we can learn from those mistakes. It has been said that the doorway to success is entered through the hallway of failure. It has also been said that if at first you don't succeed, relax—you're just like the rest of us!

Have you ever tried to do something for God that was a complete failure? Perhaps it was your feeble attempt to share the gospel with some friends. They not only failed to respond in the affirmative, but they became angry with you.

It may have been a prayer for someone to get better physically, who actually got worse. I remember once when a friend was feeling nauseated and asked if I would pray. I did just that, and his nausea increased! He said he would never ask me to pray for him again!

Perhaps you started a home Bible study, and no one showed up. Let me say to you, thank you for your failures! I would far rather try and fail than never do anything at all. Besides, failure isn't always such a bad thing. We learn from our mistakes. Failure can indeed teach success.

Successful people know how to handle failure. Many failed initially only to succeed later. Albert Einstein failed at math before he discovered the theory of relativity. Isaac Newton had to have an apple fall on his head before discovering the theory of gravity. Michael Jordan failed to make his high school basketball team before making the NBA.

You might say, "But I have failed horribly." You can't change your past, but you can choose your response to it. God can take your endings and turn them into beginnings.

Peter's Failures Help Us

We certainly see that in the life of Simon Peter. The gospels are full of his adventures and statements. No disciple spoke as often as he did, and out of necessity, no disciple was corrected as many times as Peter was. Sometimes he opened his mouth merely to change feet! Other times what he said was absolutely profound. Jesus commended him like no other, and, at the same time, sometimes harshly criticized him. (Sometimes both at once.)

You might say that Peter was the patron saint of ordinary people. In short, Peter was a person just like us.

This is important, because sometimes we see the apostles in

stained glass. We imagine them incapable of shortcomings or mistakes. That is simply not true. Again, the Bible is a thoroughly honest book. We will see Peter's victories, but we will also see his vulnerabilities.

The point: God can take an ordinary man or woman and do something extraordinary. Jesus didn't choose the apostles because they were great. Rather, their greatness came as a result of Jesus' choosing them. In the same way, God didn't choose you because you were so great. Here's a news flash: You aren't. Neither am I. Yet in His grace and mercy, He can do something wonderful with both of our lives.

For example, you can take a golf club that you bought at a garage sale, give it to me, and ask me to impress you. You are going to be very disappointed. I have no golfing skills whatsoever. You wouldn't even want me for a partner in miniature golf.

Yet you could take that same club, as flawed and worn as it is, put it in the hands of a master golfer like Tiger Woods, and see a contest won. It all depends on who has the club.

In the same way, you are an instrument in the hands of God. God can make you into someone you were not before to touch this world.

Dual Personalities

It is interesting to note how Jesus said to Simon, "You shall be called Peter [Rock]" in John 1. He didn't say, "You are Peter."

He was only Simon at that point. It was only after Simon's encounter with Jesus at Caesarea Philippi that anyone referred to him as Peter. In Matthew 16, we read,

> When Jesus came into the region of Caesarea Philippi, He asked His disciples, saying, "Who do men say that I, the Son of Man, am?" So they said, "Some say John the Baptist, some Elijah, and others Jeremiah or one of the prophets." He said to them, "But who do you say that I am?" Simon Peter answered and said, "You are the Christ, the Son of the living God." Jesus answered and said to him, "Blessed are you, Simon Bar-Jonah, for flesh and blood has not revealed this to you, but My Father who is in heaven. And I also say

to you that you are Peter, and on this rock I will build My church, and the gates of Hades shall not prevail against it." (vv. 13–18)

The Lord had said previously, "You will be *called* Peter." Then, after Simon had confessed that Jesus was the Christ, He said, "You *are* Peter." He was a new man with a new name.

In the same way, when we put our trust in Jesus Christ, we, too, receive a new name: Christian. With that new name, God gives us a new nature. We have the power to live this life in a way that we never could before. The Holy Spirit of God resides within us, leading us to obey God.

Unfortunately, just as Simon Peter had two natures that constantly battled one another, we, too, have the battle between the old and the new natures. As we read in Galatians 5:17, "The sinful nature wants to do evil, which is just the opposite of what the Spirit wants. And the Spirit gives us desires that are the opposite of what the sinful nature desires. These two forces are constantly fighting each other, so you are not free to carry out your good intentions" (NLT).

You know what this is like. It's not a day-by-day issue; it's a moment-by-moment issue. Every morning when we get up, we face thousands of opportunities to decide: *Am I going to yield to the flesh, or will I yield to the Spirit?* We can go back to our old ways and disobey God, or we can surrender to the leading of the Spirit and do what is right.

Just to show you how quickly this can happen, right after Peter had said, "You are the Christ, the Son of the living God," the Lord went on to describe His future: He was going to be arrested, crucified, and rise again on the third day. Simon, probably feeling that he was on some kind of a roll, protested and said, "Far be it from You, Lord . . ." (Matthew 16:22). He began to rebuke Jesus.

Can you imagine? *Rebuking Jesus?* "Lord, now this is the Rock talking!" Peter blurted out. "You gave me a new name. I have to give You a little career advice. This is a bad move. You don't want to have yourself crucified. This would be a good time for you to establish Your kingdom. There is no way death could be God's plan for You."

Jesus said to him, "Get behind Me, Satan! You are an offense to Me . . ." (Matthew 16:23). One moment the Father in heaven inspired Peter. The next moment the devil from hell told him what to say.

Sadly, it can be that way for you or me as well.

You can do so well spiritually, and then you mess up. You can't believe you did it. You can be driving down the freeway, listening to a worship CD, singing, "Lord, I love you so much." Suddenly, some guy cuts you off, and you explode with anger, screaming and shaking your fist at him.

It's just a little bit shocking, isn't it? How could I be praising God, then do something like that? Answer: It's human nature. I'm not excusing or justifying it. I'm just trying to explain how that nature is always there, just beneath the surface, ready to jump out of its restraints and say or do something that looks and sounds more like hell than heaven. You need to remember that.

How do you deal with it? Jesus gave us a great example when He said to the spirit that inspired Simon Peter, "Get behind Me, Satan." When the devil comes knocking on your door with the temptation, don't give him the time of day.

The Lord had called Simon. He had given him a new name. But right off the bat, just seconds after the name was official, he did something to contradict it. Instead of acting like the apostle Peter, he behaved far more like Simon.

Peter: Humanity 101

That wasn't the only time, either. We learn in Luke 5 that Peter had turned away from following Jesus after a while. The other gospels record that he had already been called by Jesus. He had left his nets and become a disciple. Yet in Luke we see that he, along with his two buddies James and John, had at least temporarily returned to fishing.

Nothing wrong with that. That's what they did for a living. They were hardworking men. Peter still believed in Jesus. He still trusted. The point, however, was that Jesus had called them to be fishers of men. In other words, they had the privilege of being called to serve God, and they had basically gone AWOL.

They were men who knew better. They were men whom God had marked for His service, and they weren't following through. Jesus, however, did something unique to enter into their little universe and bring them to a point of deeper commitment:

> So it was, as the multitude pressed about Him to hear the word of God, that He stood by the Lake of Gennesaret, and saw two boats standing by the lake; but the fishermen had gone from them and were washing their nets. Then He got into one of the boats, which was Simon's, and asked him to put out a little from the land. And He sat down and taught the multitudes from the boat. When He had stopped speaking, He said to Simon, "Launch out into the deep and let down your nets for a catch." But Simon answered and said to Him, "Master, we have toiled all night and caught nothing; nevertheless at Your word I will let down the net." And when they had done this, they caught a great number of fish, and their net was breaking. So they signaled to their partners in the other boat to come and help them. And they came and filled both the boats, so that they began to sink. When Simon Peter saw it, he fell down at Jesus' knees, saying, "Depart from me, for I am a sinful man, O Lord!" For he and all who were with him were astonished at the catch of fish which they had taken; and so also were James and John, the sons of Zebedee, who were partners with Simon. And Jesus said to Simon, "Do not be afraid. From now on you will catch men." So when they had brought their boats to land, they forsook all and followed Him. (vv. 1–11)

When Jesus stepped into Simon's boat and asked him to row out a bit, it may have seemed a little forward on Jesus' part. But He had a work He wanted to do in Simon Peter's life. Note that when the Scripture describes Peter in this passage, it starts by using the name "Simon." It's not until verse 8, when Simon fell down at the feet of Jesus, that Scripture refers to him as Simon Peter. There is that conflict of natures.

He wasn't acting like the Rock. He was acting like Simon again.

He and his friends had gone back to fishing and had caught nothing. They were not realizing the potential that Jesus had for them. They had no idea what their future would be. Jesus desired to mold them into powerful spiritual leaders who would write the very Scripture we hold in our hands today. They were to be the leaders of His church and evangelists to the world. They quite literally would change their world, and that impact would continue for generations and generations.

But they didn't understand or fully appreciate that. He had to whip them into shape first.

When Jesus climbed into the boat and told Peter to row out, Peter was probably waiting for the Lord to wheel around and rebuke him. Jesus didn't. Jesus recognized Peter was a half-hearted follower who needed a personal touch.

I wonder if some of us right now are in the same boat as Peter. By that I mean that you believe in Jesus; you have asked Him to be your Savior and friend. You trust Him for salvation. But are you glorifying Him? Are you really offering your life to God and giving Him control? Are you serving Him as Master and Lord?

Whose Honor and Glory Are You After?

Have you ever thought about dedicating your career to God, saying, "Lord, here is what I do for a living. I want to do it to your glory. I want to find ways in which I can honor you through the skills and abilities you have given me. Lord, here are the talents I have. They may not be a lot, but I'm willing to dedicate them to you. Do with them what you will."

If you were to do that, it could make all the difference in the world. Maybe you're like Peter. You've been fishing all night and have caught nothing. You're working hard, yet barely getting by. You have no opportunities, foresee no successes.

I'm not saying that if you commit your career to Jesus that suddenly you are going to make more money than you can spend. The Lord may prosper you in that way, or you may actually make less for a while. I will say this, though: if you give your work to the Lord, you will be living your life the way God meant you to—to His honor and glory. And when you have done that, you will be your happiest.

Years ago, a movie called *Chariots of Fire* portrayed the life of Eric

Liddell. He was an Olympic runner and one of the fastest men of his time. Eric also was a very committed Christian. It was his desire to go on the mission field and serve the Lord, which he eventually did.

In an early scene in the film, Eric's sister Jenny is concerned that he is still involved in his running when she thought he should already be on the mission field. Eric turned to her and said, "Jenny, I believe God made me for a purpose. . . . But He also made me *fast*. And when I run, I feel His pleasure."

I loved that line. Not all of us are called to the mission field *per se*, but all of us are called with a sense of mission. You may be in business or may be a stay-at-home mom. You may be a construction worker or a musician, a teacher or a computer programmer. Whatever you do, you can do for the glory of God. And when you do so, you, like Eric Liddell, will also "feel His pleasure." That's all that matters in the long run. Leave the results in His hands.

Only a Personal Encounter Will Do

That's what was happening with Peter. He was in an area of non-commitment. He believed, but he wasn't really giving his all to Jesus. Jesus intervened in a personal way for Peter. Jesus produced a miracle that dazzled the seasoned fisherman.

Understand that Simon Peter had seen miracles already. He had seen his own mother-in-law, who was very ill, restored to health. But none of these miracles necessarily appeared to move him much. Jesus' personalized miracle would convince Peter.

Everybody has to have his own personal encounter with Jesus Christ. No one can live off of someone else's faith. You can talk until you're blue in the face to someone about his need for Christ, but you need to pray that God will make himself known to him. It's not your clever arguments that will convince him. Something needs to happen to get his attention, and God will do it.

He did it for Peter. After speaking to the multitudes, Jesus told him, "Launch out into the deep and let down your nets for a catch." Peter said, "At Your word I will let down the net."

Notice that Jesus said "nets," and Peter said "net." Peter had fished those waters since childhood. He knew the most favorable climatic conditions for fishing and when they were most likely to be caught.

In Peter's mind, Jesus was basically a landlubber giving him fishing advice. Peter was saying, "Lord, with all due respect, when You open the Word of God, we hang on Your every word. But when it comes to fishing, we are men who know what we're doing. We're experienced. This isn't something You necessarily know about."

You say, "Greg, how can you read that into the text?" By judging what Peter did next. Jesus said to let down the "nets," and Peter let down a "net." That was not obedience. Partial obedience is disobedience. Of course, then there were so many fish that they were overwhelmed.

We know that because of archeological studies that have found these first-century fishing boats from the time of Christ. They would have been about seven feet wide and about twenty-seven feet long. When Peter and his crew began to pull in the net, two of these boats began to sink. This means they were pulling in tons of fish. It was supernatural, and they knew it.

A boatload of fish may not impress us, but it impressed them because they were fishermen. They knew well this sort of thing didn't just happen. God came to them in a way that they could understand.

Peter was overwhelmed with gratitude and guilt when he saw this. He said in Luke 5:8, "Depart from me, for I am a sinful man, O Lord!" In other words, "Lord, You saw me before. You looked right through me and gave me this new name. I hate to disappoint You, but I haven't been the Rock. I've fallen short. I appreciate Your call in my life, but let's face it. I'm only going to disappoint You. Get someone else. Don't waste Your time on me. I'm just not worth it."

Have you ever felt that way? Have you felt you were totally inadequate for the task of serving God? Good. You're just the man or woman for whom God is looking. He isn't looking for people who are arrogant or self-sufficient, but people who see themselves for what they really are: deficient and in great need of God's help to get anything done.

This reminds me of Job when he came into God's presence and said, "My ears had heard of you but now my eyes have seen you. Therefore I despise myself and repent in dust and ashes" (42:5–6 NIV).

Isaiah said something similar: "I saw the Lord sitting on a throne, high and lifted up, and the train of His robe filled the temple. . . . I said: 'Woe is me, for I am undone! Because I am a man of unclean lips . . .'" (6:1, 5). In the presence of God, Isaiah became immediately aware of his shortcomings. As he saw God for who He was, he saw himself for who he was.

In the same way, Peter saw himself as a sinner, which he was. But this was good because he had come to the end of himself; thus he was coming to the beginning of God.

Have You Left All for Him?

How did Jesus respond to Rock's statement? In Luke 5:10 He said, "Do not be afraid. From now on you will catch men."

Catch men? This is an interesting concept. It appears just two times in the Bible, here and in 2 Timothy 2:26, where the apostle Paul talked about those whom Satan had "taken captive . . . to do his will." That phrase "taken captive" could be translated "caught alive."

It comes down to this: either the devil is going to catch people alive, or we are going to catch people alive. Either they are under the control of Satan or under the control of Jesus Christ. That is why the Lord has called us to go fishing for men.

Luke 5:11 says, "They forsook all and followed Him." Have you done that? Perhaps you're still stuck in one spot. You made an initial commitment to Christ, but your old nature has been prevailing. You need to say, "Lord, I turn it over to you. I ask you to do what you want with my life, my marriage, my career. I ask you to be Lord over everything that I have. Be the Master of my life."

If you have said that, then like Peter you can enjoy a fruitful life.

Yes, you may stumble out of the blocks. You may limp along at times as though you have two left feet. But Jesus sees potential in you, and He knows you can do it . . . all the way to the finish line.

18

DISASTER . . . AND BEYOND

Everyone has taken an unanticipated spill. A number of years ago, I was riding my bicycle to meet my wife at a restaurant for breakfast. Unbeknownst to me, somebody had loosened the little levers that hold the front tire on the bike. When I popped off a curb, crossed a street, and came up to another curb, I pulled up on the handlebars . . . but the wheel kept going straight.

I hit the ground with the forks, flew over the front of the bike, and slammed onto the ground face-first.

I blacked out for a few seconds. When I came to, some man was standing over me, asking, "Are you okay?" I was bloody and bruised. I had lost consciousness.

I thought I was fine, but after a few hours passed, I realized I wasn't. I ached everywhere.

In the same way I didn't see that accident coming, we can fail to see a spiritual fall coming. But when people fall away from the Lord, when they crash and burn, they have already taken steps leading up to that event. Maybe they were not fully aware of the steps, but that doesn't change the fact they were taking them. Nobody falls away from the Lord overnight or immediately. There is always a process that unfolds over a period of time.

That is certainly what happened to Simon Peter. We need to remember the fact that his spiritual crash came as no surprise to

Jesus. In fact, He warned him specifically of the sin he was about to commit. Yet no one was more shocked when it happened than Peter.

A Rock in Progress

We've seen that Simon needed some time to grow into his new name of Peter (the Rock). You will recall that at Caesarea Philippi, Peter had great insight into who Jesus was, declaring, "You are the Christ, the Son of the living God" (Matthew 16:16).

Jesus commended him and said, "Flesh and blood has not revealed this to you, but My Father who is in heaven" (v. 17).

Not all that long after that, Peter denied that he even knew anyone named Jesus.

That was the story of Peter's life: the man of dual natures. We certainly see into his character at the transfiguration of Jesus. What a glorious moment that must have been as Jesus took Peter, James, and John with Him up a mountain. Suddenly they saw Jesus shining like the sun. On one side of Him was the great lawgiver himself, Moses. On the other side was the miracle-working prophet Elijah.

Some people say it was a great miracle that Jesus shone like the sun. The miracle, however, wasn't that Jesus shone on that day, but that He didn't shine that way the rest of the time! Remember, He was God in human form. The Transfiguration showed what He really was: God shrouded in human flesh. As the old Christmas hymn so beautifully states,

> Veiled in flesh the Godhead see,
> Hail the incarnate Deity!
> Pleased as man with men to dwell,
> Jesus, our Emmanuel.

In that blazing moment, Jesus had an in-depth conversation with Moses and Elijah. Were they discussing His impending death, that He was going to the cross to suffer and die?

Most people would be spellbound at such an event. They would stand in awe, speechless. Peter, however, thought it was a great opportunity to make a little speech. He blurted out, "It is good for us to be here; if You wish, let us make here three tabernacles: one for You, one for Moses, and one for Elijah" (Matthew 17:4). Mark's Gospel tells us that Peter didn't know what to say—so that's what came out!

You can relate to that. Have you ever said the wrong thing at the wrong time? The moment you said it, you wished you could have taken your words back.

Peter was excited, and he wanted to throw in his two cents' worth. I think the operative word that Peter used is "here": "It is good for us to be here." In other words, "Lord, it's time for You to forget about this idea of being crucified. It's time for You to stop talking about going to a cross. *This* is where You belong. It's on the mount with Moses and Elijah, shining like the sun. This is where we need to stay. Let's just stay here on the mountain and bask in Your glory!"

In the same way, sometimes we as Christians want to remove ourselves from the secular culture we are living in and just stay in a place of continual bliss. If it were possible, we would never leave church. Yet we must understand that the purpose of the church is to provide a place for believers to grow and learn. It's a place for us to refocus. It's also a place that helps us to go back out into the world, refreshed and equipped to do battle. You might compare it to a gas station—a place to get refilled and recharged.

I don't know about you, but I don't like to go to gas stations. My wife likes it even less than I do. I wait until the tank is just above empty and then reluctantly pull over. Some of us treat church that way: I'll go only when I have to. If we are wise, however, we'll go for constant refills, "topping off our tank." The danger is that we might find ourselves isolating from the world to which God has called us.

But God has not called us to isolate. He has called us to infiltrate.

Jesus didn't say that the whole world should go to church. Rather He said that the church should go to the whole world.

Peter was saying, "It's good for us to be here. We want to stay away from that world. We don't want You to go down there, and we don't want to watch You die." But they had to descend from the mountaintop. They had to go back into the real world.

Almost joining the Lord Jesus in correcting the wayward apostle, God the Father chimed in: "A bright cloud overshadowed them; and suddenly a voice came out of the cloud, saying, 'This is My beloved Son, in whom I am well pleased. Hear Him!' " (Matthew 17:5).

The Father was saying to Peter, "If My Son tells you He must go to Jerusalem to suffer and die, then believe Him. If He tells you to take up your cross and follow Him, that's what you need to do."

Just Like Us

I don't know about you, but I'm sure I would have felt a bit sheepish if God himself had to reprimand me for speaking out of turn. But that's the way Peter was. He just couldn't seem to keep a low profile. You certainly always knew where you stood with him.

Remember his classic moment when Jesus was walking on the water? I can just picture it. The disciples had endured a rough night on the Sea of Galilee. They were frightened; they despaired of life. Who came strolling up to them on the top of the water but the Lord himself. Of course, the disciples were terrified and thought He was a ghost. Jesus said to them, "Take courage! It is I. Don't be afraid" (Matthew 14:27 NIV).

It was another holy moment. It was something to take in. There was the Lord, walking on water. Peter should have savored it. Instead, again he spoke: "Lord, if it's you, tell me to come to you on the water" (v. 28 NIV).

Now, in Peter's defense, he did ask the Lord's permission first. Jesus then gave it, and Peter did the impossible. When the Lord said, "Come," Peter threw one leg over the side of the boat and set it down on the water. It supported him. He put the other leg over the side and stood up. He took his first step and his second. Then, probably seeing how crazy it was, and taking his eyes off the Lord and putting them on his circumstances, he began to sink. He cried out, "Lord, save me!" (v. 30 NIV).

That was Peter—always saying what he thought. He was either knocking it out of the park or he was striking out. There was rarely anything in between. Everything he did, he threw himself into wholeheartedly.

"Satan Is Asking for You"

Unfortunately, this also included his fall. Peter fell big. All of the disciples were in hiding the night Jesus was taken to be crucified. On one hand, Peter wanted to be close to Jesus, but his fear kept him at a distance.

In John 13, we read that the Lord had gathered His disciples in the Upper Room to discuss some very important matters. It would be their final Passover meal together.

Not surprisingly, the atmosphere wasn't joyful or festive, as other Passovers had been. The tension was so thick you could cut it with a knife.

A storm was brewing, but the disciples didn't know exactly what was happening. They could see the burden Jesus was carrying, the pressure closing in on Him. Then the Lord himself did something completely unexpected. He took off His outer garment, wrapped himself in a towel, got down on His hands and knees, and with a basin of water, began to wash the disciples' feet.

Can you imagine this? The Creator of the universe, in human form, washed the dirt of the feet of His disciples. That is nothing short of amazing. But what's even more amazing is the fact that He also included the betrayer himself in that foot washing.

Jesus poured water on and removed the dirt from the feet of Judas Iscariot—the very man, who, in just moments, would cold-heartedly leave to complete his act of betrayal.

Jesus, being God, had complete foreknowledge of this, yet in that act of sacrificial love and compassion, He humbled himself.

As Jesus made His way to each of His boys, the men He had chosen, no doubt a hush filled the room. This was a holy moment, a time to just "be still, and know that He is God" (see Psalm 46:10).

But Peter, true to form, had to offer a bit of commentary. Peter protested and told Jesus that He would never wash his feet. In fairness, Peter felt he was too undeserving of such an act of humility from Jesus. Jesus then looked at the protesting Peter and firmly said, "If I do not wash you, you have no part with Me" (John 13:8).

Then the Lord dropped a bombshell on the disciples:

> And the Lord said, "Simon, Simon! Indeed, Satan has asked for you, that he may sift you as wheat. But I have prayed for you, that your faith should not fail; and when you have returned to Me, strengthen your brethren." But he said to Him, "Lord, I am ready to go with You, both to prison and to death." Then He said, "I tell you, Peter, the rooster shall not crow this day before you will deny three times that you know Me." (Luke 22:31–34)

Can you imagine hearing Jesus say this to you? Put yourself in Peter's sandals for just a moment. Jesus said, "Satan has been asking for you." A literal translation of that phrase would be "Satan has been asking for you specifically by name." Jesus was saying, "Simon, the devil himself, Lucifer, has been personally asking for you."

If this wouldn't make your blood run cold, I don't know what would. Fortunately for Peter, Jesus answered the door. "Peter, don't panic. I have prayed for you!" (see Luke 22:32).

In other words, Jesus was saying to His terrified follower that despite the fact that the very devil of hell was asking for him, he need not be afraid, because Jesus himself would be there to answer him. (I want you to notice that Satan did have to ask God first. He can do nothing in the life of the child of God without our Father's permission. God was watching over Peter.)

You might read this and think, *I wish Jesus was standing for me that way too.* He is! Jesus is interceding for you as well. Romans 8:34 says, "Who then is the one who condemns? No one. Christ Jesus who died—more than that, who was raised to life—is at the right hand of God and is also interceding for us" (NIV) Paul continued, "Who shall separate us from the love of Christ? Shall trouble or hardship or persecution or famine or nakedness or danger or sword?" (v. 35 NIV).

Were it not for the prayers of Jesus, Peter wouldn't have stood a chance. Were it not for the intercession of Jesus, we wouldn't stand a chance either.

What did Jesus pray for Peter? This is a crucial question.

Did He pray that Peter wouldn't be tempted? Did He pray that Peter wouldn't go through a time of trial? No, He prayed that Peter's faith would not fail. Peter was about to take a graduate-level course in the School of Hard Knocks. He would be a better man for it.

Why did the devil set his sights on the salty fisherman? Simply because he was a mighty instrument in the hand of God. The devil targets leaders today as well—that is why we must pray for them. It's easy to play armchair quarterback and second-guess every decision a leader makes: "If I were the pastor, I never would have done that. If I'd been in charge, I never would have made that decision."

Everyone is entitled to his opinion, but you may not be privy to all of the information that went into the decision-making process. Not that every decision every leader makes is right. That's why you ought to pray for each one and understand that they come under attack.

For that matter, any man or woman who is making a difference for the kingdom of God is going to be a candidate for the onslaught of Satan. If God is using you to bring people into the kingdom, to touch people for Jesus Christ, to bring His Word to people, then the devil is going to try to bring you down. But remember that Jesus, God's Son, intercedes for you as He did for Peter.

Steps to a Fall

Yes, Peter did deny the Lord, just as Jesus said he would. But the steps—actually *missteps*—that led to that denial were subtle and very significant.

Let's look at the missteps that led to Peter's fall so that we may try to avoid them in our own spiritual race.

Misstep 1: Peter was overconfident

According to Matthew's gospel, Peter made this statement: "Even if all are made to stumble because of You, I will never be made to stumble" (26:33). Why did Peter say that? Because Jesus pointed out that one of them was going to be a traitor. Peter thought it was a great opportunity to boast of his love for the Lord. "Judas may betray You, but I will never do anything like that. I will never let You down."

Jesus was basically saying, "Well, Peter, since you brought it up, you are going to deny Me three times.'"

You should never boast of your love for the Lord. Rather, boast of His love for you. Sometimes I hear people say, "I just love the Lord so much." That's good. But I would rather boast of how much the Lord loves me. My love can be so fickle, so hot or cold, depending upon my mood. In contrast, God's love is consistent.

I love the way the apostle John described himself in his Gospel: "the disciple whom Jesus loved "(see John 13:23). Some might critique John for saying that, because it implies Jesus loved him more than the others. I disagree. Would you rather he said that he was the apostle that loved Jesus? Instead of boasting of his love for the Lord, he boasted of the Lord's love for him. That's a smart thing to do.

You know what? You, too, are a disciple Jesus loves.

Peter was boasting of his dedication, of his commitment, of his tenacity. His first step down was overconfidence. In speaking those words, Peter not only was revealing an unfounded faith in himself, but he also was directly contradicting the Lord's prediction that he would deny him. What he should have said was, "Lord, I have a hard time believing I am capable of such a thing, but You said it, therefore it is true."

Instead he said, "Jesus, You are wrong. No way. Even though You are the Creator and Truth incarnate and know all things, You are wrong on this thing. I know me. I know that I would never deny You. The rest of these guys? Well, maybe. But not *me*."

But no, Peter didn't know himself as well as he thought. Nor do you or I. Nobody knows you better than Jesus.

Mark's Gospel records that Peter repeatedly insisted on his loyalty. At first blush, this could almost seem commendable, but in fact it was sinful. He was full of himself. When you see somebody fall into a sin like lust or greed, at the foundation of that sin was overconfidence. By that I mean the one who fell was probably a person who said, "I would never do such a thing. No matter what, I would never cave in to such a temptation. I am above that."

Be careful! Know that you have this vulnerability, even a propensity toward doing the wrong thing.

In Scripture, many men who were known for one trait were also known for its opposite. For instance, when you think of Elijah the prophet, what comes to mind? Courage. Bravery. We remember his facing off with the prophets of Baal on Mount Carmel. We also recall that Elijah fled in panic and sank into depression when he heard a threat from Queen Jezebel. This man who was known for courage also was filled with fear.

What comes to mind when you think of the great patriarch Abraham? Faith. But we know that Abraham had lapses. On one occasion he asked his wife Sarah to say she was his sister because he was afraid the strangers whose land they were visiting would kill him to get her. Then he had sexual relations with Sarah's handmaid, Hagar, instead of waiting on the Lord for the fulfillment of his promise to give a child to Abraham and Sarah.

We need to realize that any great strength we have also can be an area of weakness. We all need a good dose of reality when it comes to our vulnerability for doing the wrong thing—regardless of how many years we have known the Lord.

Misstep 2: Peter was prayerless

Coming out, He went to the Mount of Olives, as He was accustomed, and His disciples also followed Him. When He came to the place, He said to them, "Pray that you may not enter into temptation." And He was withdrawn from them about a stone's throw, and He knelt down and prayed, saying, "Father, if it is Your will, take this cup away from Me; nevertheless not My will, but Yours, be done." Then an angel appeared to Him from heaven, strengthening Him. And being in agony, He prayed more earnestly. Then His sweat became like great drops of blood falling down to the ground. When He rose up from prayer, and had come to His disciples, He found them sleeping from sorrow. Then He said to them, "Why do you sleep? Rise and pray, lest you enter into temptation." (Luke 22:39–46)

This was a direct result of the first sin of overconfidence. Even after Jesus had specifically instructed Peter, James, and John to pray, they decided to sleep instead. Granted, they were emotionally and spiritually drained from the events of the day. They were sleeping "from sorrow," the Bible tells us. This probably means they cried themselves to sleep. But our Lord had specifically told them to pray so as not to enter into temptation, and that the flesh was weak. Peter, James, and John should have been on high alert. Clearly the Lord was warning that something significant was coming.

In the same way, we often pray when we think we need to, but we don't when things seem to be stable and secure. That is human nature for you. We need to pray in the good times as well as the bad. Paul said we should pray at all times (see 1 Thessalonians 5:17).

While the three disciples were sawing logs and counting sheep, Judas, the temple guard, and Roman soldiers apprehended the Lord. Judas Iscariot betrayed him with a kiss. When Peter awoke, he was outraged. How dare Judas do this to Jesus! "Don't worry, Lord, I will defend You! Rock is here!"

He started swinging his sword and cut off a bystander's ear in the process. Soldiers led the Lord away, and Peter's world came crashing down.

Because of prayerlessness, Peter was unprepared for the very temptation of which Jesus spoke.

Misstep 3: Peter followed at a distance

Luke 22:54: "Having arrested Him, they led Him, and brought Him into the high priest's house. But Peter followed at a distance."

This distance from the Lord in closeness and fellowship is always at the foundation of all spiritual regression. Granted, Peter was following, but not closely.

Here is Simon Peter's dual nature once again. On one hand, he was terrified of what others would say about him. On the other hand, he wanted to be close to Jesus—just not as close as he had been before. At best, at that moment, Peter's was a halfhearted commitment.

Many people like Peter go to church. Granted, they are there, but they are following at a distance. This kind of person often sits at the very back of the church and is the last one in and the first one out. During the time of worship, he doesn't sing. When the offering plate is passed, he keeps his hands in his pockets. He doesn't want to engage. He wouldn't even think of going to a midweek Bible study. He gives only his bare minimum to the Lord. His is a half-hearted commitment.

It's so sad when people do that. They miss out on what God wants to do in their lives. They miss out on all that church could be to them and all they could be to the church. Yes, they are following, but they do so from a distance.

Have you ever noticed in nature-type programs on TV that the animal that ends up being picked off is usually the animal that has strayed from the rest of the pack? He's vulnerable. Weak. An easy target. In short, he's *lunch*.

Whom do you think the devil is going to pounce on? It's easiest to bring down someone who is following at a distance—someone who is separated from fellow believers.

Misstep 4: Peter warmed himself by the enemy's fire

At the courtyard of Caiaphas, the Lord was being falsely charged in a kangaroo court of gross injustice. People were gathered around, warming themselves by a fire in the courtyard.

The chill of sin is strong, and the warmth of trust Peter had known before was shattered by his denial. Peter was hoping to go unnoticed in the large crowd. He stepped near the fire.

At that point, he was worn down, weak, and vulnerable. He was a train wreck waiting to happen. To Peter's eternal credit, at least he was there, but only at a distance, and, frankly, he had run out of ideas. He was just waiting for the end of this nightmare to finally come.

Matthew's Gospel says that Peter sat down with the servants at Caiaphas's house to watch the proceedings. Peter was at the wrong place with the wrong people, about to do the wrong thing. It wasn't the fire itself that was bad. It was the people around the fire. He was in a place where he shouldn't have been.

Misstep 5: Peter tried to escape reality

Luke 22:56–57: "And a certain servant girl, seeing him as he sat by the fire, looked intently at him and said, 'This man was also with Him.' But he denied Him, saying, 'Woman, I do not know Him.'"

Peter was already busted. He couldn't escape recognition, but he tried to take refuge in a lie.

Misstep 6. Peter remained with the enemy

Luke 22:58: "And after a little while another saw him and said, 'You also are of them.' But Peter said, 'Man, I am not!'" Note that a little time had passed. Peter had had some minutes, or perhaps even an hour or two, to think about his first denial and the spiritual danger he was in. Yet he stayed put with the enemy. Not only had he denied knowing Jesus, but then he denied being one of His disciples.

Misstep 7: Peter lost all awareness of God

Luke 22:59–60: "Then after about an hour had passed, another confidently affirmed, saying, 'Surely this fellow also was with Him, for he is a Galilean.' But Peter said, 'Man, I do not know what you are saying!'"

Galileans didn't normally hang around near Jerusalem, especially in the courtyard of Caiaphas. To those in the sophisticated city, a Galilean was akin to what we might refer to as a "country bumpkin." That is what the person said to Peter: "You are a Galilean." If we were to put it in our modern vernacular, it would be like calling someone "trailer trash" or worse. There was disdain in the person's voice.

According to Matthew's Gospel, at that point Peter "began to curse and swear" (Matthew 26:74). This doesn't mean he swore like a sailor (though he was one). Peter was taking an oath. It's an interesting phrase that means "to pronounce death on oneself by the hand of God if he is lying." Peter essentially said, "May God kill me if I am not speaking the truth." That is taking the Lord's name in vain.

Peter had lost all sense of reality and awareness of God.

Luke 22:60–62: "Immediately, while he was still speaking, the rooster crowed. And the Lord turned and looked at Peter. Then

Peter remembered the word of the Lord, how He had said to him, 'Before the rooster crows, you will deny Me three times.' So Peter went out and wept bitterly."

Jesus looked at him.

Can you imagine this scene? Put yourself there if you can. Peter has denied the Lord three times. Now he has called down God's judgment on himself if he has been lying. The rooster crows. He spins around, and there stands Jesus, looking right into his eyes. Can you feel the intensity of that gaze—the feelings it ignited in Peter?

Did the denial come as a shock or a surprise to Jesus? Absolutely not. Did this denial come as a shock and surprise to Simon Peter? Absolutely. But the Lord knew he would fail. He predicted it.

Did Peter let the Lord down? Yes. Did Peter deny the Lord? Yes. Was he still a believer? Was he still loved by Jesus? Yes and yes. Peter needed to remember what else the Lord said to him: "And when you have returned to Me, strengthen your brethren" (Luke 22:32). In other words, "The setback is going to be temporary, and you will be back."

Praise God, He gives second chances! He gives third, fourth, and fifth ones. Remember, nobody is above falling into sin.

Peter Is All Too Familiar

Maybe some of us can identify with the failings of this great follower of Jesus. Maybe right now you are where he was. In some way, you have denied the Lord. Maybe you have fallen into some gross sin, and you need God's forgiveness today.

Then again, maybe you're somewhere along the road that Peter traveled. You're not quite at the bottom, but you're headed there. Overconfident, prayerless, following Jesus only at a distance, drawing near and camping out by the enemy's fire. . . . You are flirting with disaster. You are walking along a precipice. The race no longer seems as enticing as the sin that is calling your name.

Don't mistake Peter's restoration to Jesus as an excuse to sin. Remember the agony he felt in catching Jesus' gaze at the courtyard. His was an intensely painful fall, and it took a miracle to restore him to his Savior. Don't let that happen to you.

Run the race. Stay on the right track. If you crash, recover. Jump up, and get back in the race.

Go for the prize.

Head straight for the finish line.

A COMPASSIONATE COACH

Have you ever failed miserably in life? You wanted your marriage to thrive, and it has ended in divorce. You had hoped that one day you would get a degree from a leading university, but you had to drop out for some reason. You were hoping you would be very successful in business at this point in life, but you are fighting for survival.

Maybe you set goals in your spiritual life as well. You hoped to be at a certain place right now spiritually—stable, invested in others' lives, full of purpose—that you have not reached. You have faced failure after failure, so many that you've even begun to wonder if you are truly a child of God. You have questioned whether you really love the Lord or not.

If this is the case, you're in good company. As we've seen, one of Jesus' closest followers felt this way after he denied the Lord. Yet we know Peter went on to preach the gospel to thousands, to author two books of the Bible, to become a powerful apostle of the Lord. Something had to happen between those disastrous denials and his eventual glory.

What happened for Peter also can happen for you.

It's Raining Regrets

The last sight Simon Peter had of his Lord was of Him hanging on a cross, beaten and bloodied beyond recognition. Poor Peter. All that he held dear was placed in a tomb. He had so many regrets. He wanted to say that he was sorry.

You know what this is like if you have experienced the sudden death of a loved one. You think about your last conversation and encounter with him or her; maybe you had a disagreement, or you just didn't leave on the best terms. You deeply regret that. You wish you could tell that person how much you loved him, how much you treasured her. Imagine how Simon felt—not only had he blown it big with Jesus, but he couldn't even sustain the thought of forgiveness. It seemed impossible.

Of course, three days later our Lord rose from the dead. An angel outside His tomb told Mary Magdalene, "Go, tell His disciples— and Peter—that He is going before you into Galilee; there you will see Him . . ." (Mark 16:7). One could interpret that statement two ways—as a promise of coming revenge or one of hope and encouragement. Clearly it was the latter.

Peter did indeed encounter the Lord, and they spent time together that we don't know much about, because Scripture doesn't address it. We can be confident that it was there that the Lord forgave Peter and pardoned him for all of his sin.

As the story begins, we read, "Simon Peter said to them, 'I am going fishing.' They said to him, 'We are going with you also.' They went out and immediately got into the boat, and that night they caught nothing" (John 21:3).

The disciples had fished all night. Why?

Probably because they didn't know what else to do at that point. The Lord had risen. He had been making appearances to various disciples. But He had delivered no clear marching orders, so they went back to what they knew how to do: fish. But once again, they were pulling up nothing but empty nets.

It was a picture the Lord was going to draw on: the futility and uselessness of living without His direction and blessing. Sometimes God won't allow you to get what you want. You'll try to achieve something, and the Lord will simply say no. Other times, God will allow you to accomplish your goals to teach you a lesson. As the

Scripture says of the nation Israel, "He gave them their request, but sent leanness into their soul" (Psalm 106:15).

As it has been said, "There are two sources of unhappiness in life. One is not getting what you want, and the other is getting it."

Sometimes success can be a form of failure. What cost did you pay to achieve it? Deception? Betrayal? Abandoning your principles? Sacrificing your integrity? Neglecting your family and friends? Forgetting—or perhaps even denying—Christ? If so, your so-called success is a glaring failure. This is what was happening with the disciples and especially with Peter. They had failed, in a sense, by abandoning Jesus at the cross. But remember, failure often can be the doorway that leads to real success.

What is success, anyway? How would you classify successful people? We probably would say they are wealthy, powerful, popular, and have others' respect.

If we applied those standards to Jesus Christ, would we say He was a success? Was Jesus popular? For a time He was. But the fickle multitudes soon turned against Him. Was Jesus a person who had a lot of friends? For a time He did. When trouble came, most of them ran for cover. Did Jesus have money and possessions? We know He didn't have a home or a place to hang His hat (so to speak). We know He had a single garment that people gambled over at His crucifixion.

Did Jesus' peers respect Him? If you classify His peers as the religious leaders of the day, the answer would have to be no.

Despite these apparent failures, Jesus Christ has changed millions of lives over the centuries. In the world's eyes, maybe He was a failure, but in God's eyes He was the ultimate success. He accomplished the Father's goals.

Now He was saying to His own disciples, to Peter, "You have had some failures. Let Me teach you through them."

The Other Side of Failure

An interesting scenario unfolded that early morning. John 21:4: "But when the morning had now come, Jesus stood on the shore;

yet the disciples did not know that it was Jesus." A figure stood on the beach, which was not uncommon. Often those who sold the fish in the market waited there for the fishermen to bring in the catch.

"Then Jesus said to them, 'Children, have you any food?' They answered him, 'No'" (John 21:5). A better translation would be, "Boys, did you catch anything?"

I like the word *boys*. It is a word you would use only with someone you knew well. It implies a parental role. You can imagine the disciples bristling. "Who's He calling 'boys'? We are adult men." I wonder what Peter was thinking—perhaps that he deserved to be called a child?

Why did Jesus ask this question? He wanted the disciples to answer it. He wanted them to admit their failure. But why?

So He could bring them to the other side of failure.

God often asks probing questions. After Adam's sin, what did the Lord ask? "Have you eaten from the tree of which I commanded you that you should not eat?" (Genesis 3:11). Was God ignorant of what Adam had done? No. Why did God ask the question? He wanted confession.

In the same way, Jesus asked Peter and the disciples, "Did you catch anything? Have you been successful? Have things gone the way you had hoped? Are you satisfied?"

They needed to say, "No, Lord. We're not satisfied. We haven't been successful." Then He could say, "Then do it My way."

> And He said to them, "Cast the net on the right side of the boat, and you will find some." So they cast, and now they were not able to draw it in because of the multitude of fish" (John 21:6).

John, the spiritually perceptive one, exclaimed, "It is the Lord!" (v. 7). Peter was so excited that he jumped out of the boat and swam to shore. He couldn't wait to get close to Jesus.

> Then, as soon as they had come to land, they saw a fire of coals there, and fish laid on it, and bread. Jesus said to them, "Bring some of the fish which you have just caught." (vv. 9–10)

This amazes me. The Lord who had been crucified and had risen again was making breakfast for His boys. You would think He had better things to do. Certainly He didn't need their fish. He could have spoken that breakfast into existence.

But instead He said, "Bring Me the fish you have caught." What do we learn from this? God doesn't need us, but He wants our participation in the work He is doing. Jesus had fish already, but He said, "Bring yours too. Let Me prepare it. Let Me serve you."

That must have been an interesting moment. No one knew quite what to say. There probably was an awkward silence as they slowly chewed their food. There in the fire's flicker, Peter may have been flashing back to his earlier denial and the moment when he and Jesus met each other's glance. Peter most likely felt a searing shame. His heart was broken for what he had done, but it was so good to be near Jesus again.

Steps Leading Back to Success

Finally the Lord broke the silence with this probing question: "Simon, son of Jonah, do you love Me . . . ?" (v. 15). Notice that He didn't say, "Simon Peter." Remember, Jesus used the names Simon and Peter interchangeably, depending on how the fisherman was behaving. Simon had not been behaving like a rock lately. So Jesus asked, "Simon, do you love Me?"

This is interesting. If we were going to try to determine a person's spirituality, we probably would want to know about his theology. What are his views on this or that topic? We would want to know if he had been obedient to God. These are valid issues, and we should look for them in another believer's life.

But Jesus didn't say, "Simon, are you theologically correct?" Nor did He ask Peter, "Are you full of faith?" or "Have you been obedient?" Rather, the Lord said, "Do you love Me?"

Why is that significant? If you really love the Lord, you will *want* to be doctrinally correct. You will *want* to study His Word. If you really love the Lord, you really will grow in your faith. If you love the Lord, it will be your delight to obey Him. Love for God is at the basis of everything else.

If you don't love God, nothing else much matters. That's why the Lord said,

> "'You must love the Lord your God with all your heart, all your soul, and all your mind.' This is the first and greatest commandment. A second is equally important: 'Love your neighbor as yourself.' The entire law and all the demands of the prophets are based on these two commandments." (Matthew 22:37–40 NLT)

Three Questions, Three Tests

There are three tests in the questions Jesus asked Peter.

Test 1: Have you learned anything?

The first question, "Do you love Me more than these?" meant "Are you still the same boastful Simon of a few days ago?" I think the old Peter would have said, "Do I love You more than these? Are You kidding? Do fish swim? Of course I do! I'm Your most devoted disciple on the face of the earth."

But the new, improved, repentant Simon Peter, who had gotten a glimpse of how weak he was, simply said, "Lord, I love You."

Jesus accepted that answer. He said in response, "Feed My lambs" (v. 15). Allow me to loosely paraphrase: "Very good. You got that right. Feed My sheep."

What does it mean to feed sheep? Jesus was saying, "I am commissioning you to service. I am calling you to tend the flock. Up to this point you've been a fisher of men, but now I'm calling you to be a tender of sheep." This was an investment in Peter's life. It was an acknowledgment that Jesus was recommissioning Peter to service.

Test 2: Do you love Me with a sacrificial love?

Again, Jesus asked Peter, "Do you love Me?" (v. 16). In the original language, different words for love were used. Jesus was using the Greek word *agape*. Peter was using the Greek word *phileo*.

Agape is a very important word in the New Testament. Paul's definition of the word "love" in 1 Corinthians 13 is the Greek word *agape*. When you read, "Greater love has no one than this, than to lay down one's life for his friends" (John 15:13), that is *agape*. "For God so loved [or *agaped*] the world that He gave His only begotten Son . . ." (John 3:16). *Agape* love speaks of an all-consuming, sacrificial, 100-percent love. It is the highest of all loves, because it is utterly unselfish.

Jesus asked, "Peter do you *agape* Me? Do you have a sacrificial, all-consuming, dedicated love?" Peter answered, "Lord, I *phileo* You."

Phileo refers to brotherly love. It's the kind you have for a close friend or companion. It's not unconditional. You basically *phileo*-love people with whom you like to spend time. It's a give-and-take love.

So when Jesus asked, "Do you have this *agape,* all-consuming love?" Peter answered, "Lord, I love You like a brother."

In our English vernacular, the conversation would be this: "Do you love Me?"

"Lord, I like You."

In high school, if a girl you loved said to you, "I love you like a friend," she was really saying, "Forget about it." That was her nice way of trying to let you down easily.

You must be thinking, *Peter should have said he agape-loved the Lord.* But I think Peter's answer was just right. He was saying, "Lord, all I can commit to is this. I can't trust myself with more right now." If Jesus was dissatisfied with the answer, He would have said so. Rather, He accepted Peter's answer. We know this because He responded by saying, "Tend my sheep" (verse 16). *That's good enough, Peter.*

Test 3: Is your love for Me real or just words?

Jesus questioned Peter a third time. This time Jesus used the same word Peter used: "Do you *phileo* Me?" (v. 17). *Do you love Me like a friend? Are you sure about this? Have you thought this through?*

This pierced Peter's heart. It grieved him. He answered, "Lord, You know all things; You know that I love You." In other words, "Lord, You know. You know what's in my heart. To the best of my ability, I love You."

Are you disappointed in Peter's response? I would rather see this than someone boast about a nonexistent love for God. The proof is in the pudding. We can talk all day long about how much we love God, but the Lord is looking for action. He's looking for reality, not boastful words.

Peter had learned a lesson. He said, "I'm not going to boast about my love for you anymore. How could I, after what I've done? I will just say that I like you a lot."

The bottom line? Peter did love the Lord. Peter did indeed *agape* the Lord Jesus. His courageous preaching on the Day of Pentecost in the Book of Acts proves this. The suffering he endured for preaching the gospel proves this. Peter was martyred for his faith, and this proves he loved the Lord.

But that day, face to face with Jesus, he was communicating, "Lord, I want to try to *demonstrate* it to you from this point on. I'm tired of talking about it. Let me show it to you."

How to Know If Your Love Is Real

Let's bring it to our world. Let's say that Jesus Christ is sitting next to you right now. He turns to you and asks, "Do you love Me?"

What do you say? "Yes, Lord, I love You."

That's a good answer . . . if you mean it.

How can you tell if you really love the Lord? Let me give you five litmus tests to determine whether or not you love God.

1. You long for personal communion with God

King David wrote,

> O God, my God! How I search for you! How I thirst for you in this parched and weary land where there is no water. How I long to find you! How I wish I could go into your sanctuary to see your strength and glory, for your love and kindness are better to me than life itself. How I praise you! I will bless you as long as I live, lifting up my hands to you in prayer. At last I shall be fully satisfied; I will praise you with great joy. (Psalm 63:1–5 TLB)

This is a man who was in love with God. A person who loves the

Lord will delight in communion with God.

How do we commune with God? If you really love the Lord, you will have an active prayer life. If you really love the Lord, you will open up His Word and see what it has to say to you. This isn't some oppressive Christian "duty"—it's a delight! It shouldn't be a drudgery; it should be your heartfelt desire. In church, it will be your joy, not your burden, to worship God.

This is so important. The last time you went to church, were you looking forward to a time of worship? Were you anticipating hearing a message from the Word of God? Were you looking forward to having fellowship with your Christian friends? Were you anticipating the offering as your opportunity to contribute to God's work?

All of these are acts of worship, of personal communion with God.

2. You love the things the Lord loves

The psalmist wrote, "Oh, how I love Your law! It is my meditation all the day" (119:97). If you love God, you will love the Word of God. You will love the church.

I've heard people say, "I love the Lord, but I can't stand Christians." I know the church has its flaws. We're just sinners saved by grace. Don't expect perfection from everyone.

You need to love the church. The church is God's people. If you really love the Lord, then you will love His people as He does.

If you really love the Lord, then you also will love lost people. The Lord's heart aches for them as well.

3. You hate the things He hates

Did you know there is a place for hatred in the Christian life? What are we to hate? Psalm 97:10 says, "You who love the Lord, hate evil! He protects the lives of his godly people and rescues them from the power of the wicked" (NLT). Paul wrote in Romans 12:9, "Abhor what is evil. Cling to what is good." God hates sin, and we should do the same.

The truth is, however, we are often fascinated by evil. It's not that we want to participate in it, but we kind of like to look at it. When you're stopped in backed-up traffic on the freeway because there has been an accident, do you take a long look at it as you drive by?

Sometimes we do that with sin. We think, *I would never do such a thing. That is horrible.* But we get pretty interested, don't we? We like to hear some of the juicy details about what happened and what so-and-so did. Romans 1:32 says that it's not only wrong to do these things, but it's also wrong to take any kind of pleasure in those who do them.

4. You long for the return of Jesus Christ

Paul said in 2 Timothy 4:8, "There is laid up for me a crown of righteousness, which the Lord, the righteous Judge, will give to me on that Day, and not to me only but also to all who have loved His appearing."

If you are a true Christian, you will love His appearing. You should look forward to the day when Christ comes back. When you are reminded that Jesus is coming soon, it should send joy to your heart. If you find instead that you have a sense of dread, remorse, or fear, then something isn't right with you spiritually. A man or woman who is walking with the Lord will look forward to the Lord's return.

5. You keep His commandments

Jesus said in John 14:21, "He who has My commandments and keeps them, it is he who loves Me. And he who loves Me will be loved by My Father, and I will love him and manifest Myself to Him." Those who love the Lord do what God tells them to do.

How About You?

Peter, I believe, passed all five tests with flying colors. As a result, Jesus recommissioned him for service.

Do you need to be recommissioned today? Do you need to be restored? Maybe you have failed the Lord recently. You've done things of which you are ashamed. You know what Peter must have felt. You've been reluctant to look at Jesus. You are hesitant to go to church because of the shame in your life.

You need to get right with God . . . and get back into the race.

Jesus is asking you and me, "Do you love Me?" If you do, then you need to get on with the business of walking with and obeying Him. These things can't take the place of love, but if you love Him, you should certainly do them. God will restore and forgive you if you will come to Him.

What did Peter have to do first? He had to admit his condition. You need to admit your failure. Then you need to say, "Lord, I want to do it Your way. I'm not going to pledge some great love that I'm not sure I have. I'm coming to You with what I have, admitting all that I lack and all that I need. Here I am."

If you will go to God like that, He will forgive you. Perhaps you once received a distinct call of God on your life—a specific goal to race toward. Maybe the path has been much rougher than you expected, and you are off course. God's Holy Spirit is bringing it to the forefront of your mind as you read this.

God would like to recommission you today—put you back on the track with fresh energy and renewed hope. Come back.

Give what love you have to Him, and watch Him multiply it. Yes, Simon grew into that name Peter in time. He stumbled in the race of life, but he got back up again, and he was a winner in the race of life.

If you are down, it's time to get up. It's time to grow into your new name: Christian.

And carry it all the way to the finish line.

GOD'S STOPWATCH

Have you ever misused your time? Maybe you bought a car or house on impulse. Maybe you signed a contract you did not carefully read. Maybe you entered a business deal with someone you didn't know well enough. Maybe you got married without seeking the Lord about it first. Whatever the case, you are sorry you did it now.

Ecclesiastes 3:1 says, "For everything there is a season, a time for every activity under heaven" (NLT). Timing is important in the race of life as well. The fastest runner wins—the one who finishes as well as he started gets the prize. I have come to discover that just as important as the will of God is the timing of God.

This is something a certain person in the Bible had to learn. This guy had really bad timing. If he were in a race, he would have come out of nowhere to take the lead—and then suddenly fall hard. So hard, in fact, you would never have expected him to get up again. But he did. His name was Moses.

More than a Movie

If you were to draw up a short list of men God has used in a powerful way, Moses would be at the top: Moses the great lawgiver; Moses, the man who, through his personal godliness and integrity, kept three million people from turning to idolatry. Perhaps the best description of all: Moses the man of God.

It's hard for us to take Moses off his pedestal. We see him engraved in stone by a great artist like Michelangelo with light emanating from him. We see him in *The Prince of Egypt* as a powerful youth. We see him portrayed by Charlton Heston in *The Ten Commandments,* parting the Red Sea. It's difficult to separate fact from fiction.

Yes, Moses was one of the greatest men of God—one who ran to win the prize—but he also was a man who endured devastating setbacks and committed a serious sin or two. It's worth noting that, along with Saul of Tarsus, Moses is one of the men God used who was guilty of the very sin of murder.

Moses was born during hard times for the Jewish people. As you recall, they were living as slaves in Egypt. They were about three million strong, so naturally the pharaoh thought of them as a potential threat. He did his best to quell the people's growing power. He told the midwives that when a Jewish woman gave birth to a son, they were to kill the baby and declare it stillborn. The midwives feared the Lord and wouldn't do it. In frustration, the pharaoh decreed that all Jewish baby boys were to be drowned in the Nile River. That's how bad things had gotten.

God once made a promise that still stands today. Years before He had said to Abraham, speaking of the Jews:

> "I will make you a great nation; I will bless you and make your name great; and you shall be a blessing. I will bless those who bless you, and I will curse him who curses you. . . ." (Genesis 12:2–3)

Satan has been busy over the years, attacking and seeking to exterminate the Jewish race, because they are God's chosen people. There was another reason why Satan hated the Jews: he knew that through them the Messiah would come. The battle lines were drawn clear back in the Book of Genesis. After the serpent deceived Adam and Eve, the Lord told Satan one was coming who "will strike your head, and you will strike his heel" (Genesis 3:15 NLT).

The devil knew a Deliverer was coming for Israel. Pharaoh's plan to kill all the Jewish baby boys was Satan's attempt to stop the

Messiah, who eventually arose from the Jews.

The Jewish people were suffering, crying out to God day and night for deliverance. Enter Moses, the man of God.

Beautiful Boy

As soon as Moses was born, his parents knew he was special. The Bible says he was "beautiful" and that his mother, Jochebed, hid him successfully for three months. She knew she couldn't hide him forever, so she came up with a plan: waterproof a basket, place Moses in it, and put it in the river. She trusted in the providence of God to protect him.

Sometimes in the retelling of the story, the facts get changed. Some say that Jochebed sent Moses downstream in his basket. The Bible says, however, that she placed the little basket in the reeds by the edge of the Nile. She knew that would be a good place for him, because she knew what happened in that particular spot on a regular basis.

Timing was everything—even a matter of life or death.

> Then the daughter of Pharaoh came down to bathe at the river. And her maidens walked along the riverside; and when she saw the ark among the reeds, she sent her maid to get it. And when she opened it, she saw the child, and behold, the baby wept. So she had compassion on him, and said, "This is one of the Hebrews' children." Then his sister said to Pharaoh's daughter, "Shall I go and call a nurse for you from the Hebrew women, that she may nurse the child for you?" And Pharaoh's daughter said to her, "Go." So the maiden went and called the child's mother. Then Pharaoh's daughter said to her, "Take this child away and nurse him for me, and I will give you your wages." So the woman took the child and nursed him. And the child grew, and she brought him to Pharaoh's daughter, and he became her son. So she called his name Moses, saying, "Because I drew him out of the water." (Exodus 2: 5–10)

You have to love Jochebed, the mother of Moses. She apparently was aware of the fact that the pharaoh's daughter bathed every day at that particular bank of the Nile. I think she intentionally positioned that little basket there, hoping this royal woman would rescue her son. She couldn't be certain of what would happen, but she certainly took practical steps to save her child.

Sometimes we say, "Lord, I need you to provide for me. I need money to pay the rent. I need food. I am praying you will provide it." We say this as we are kicked back in the reclined position in our La-Z-Boys, watching television. What we ought to be doing is looking through the want ads for employment. Then, as we are handing out our résumés to prospective employers, *that* is when we should pray. Sometimes we pray, but we don't take practical steps.

I think Jochebed knew that her son's fate was ultimately in the hands of God, but she wanted to do her best to save him as well. Her plan went smoothly. She even got paid for nursing her own son! Everything worked out beautifully.

An Inauspicious Beginning

In Acts 7:22 we learn that "Moses was taught all the wisdom of the Egyptians, and he was powerful in both speech and action" (NLT).

The Jewish historian Josephus tells us the pharaoh had no son or heir; therefore, Moses was groomed to become the next king of Egypt. He was raised as a royal person and schooled in all that Egypt had to offer.

At that time in history, Egypt was a marvel. It was highly developed. The people had extensive knowledge in engineering, mathematics, and astronomy. That very knowledge of astronomy helped them develop an amazingly accurate calendar. Their engineers planned and supervised the construction of edifices that still stand today, such as the pyramids and the Sphinx. As we look at Egyptian antiquities, we marvel at the skill and craftsmanship. They also were experts in embalming. Their sophistication was impressive.

Moses learned the way of Egyptian military tactics, art, music, painting, philosophy, law, and even their religion. He learned about the thousands of gods that the Egyptians worshiped. They believed that the Nile River was a god. They believed animals were gods. They even believed Pharaoh was a god. It was pretty much you name it, they worshiped it.

In the midst of all this, Moses knew who he was. He was a true believer in the Lord God. Underneath those Egyptian robes of royalty beat the heart of a passionate Jew. Something had to give!

Should he have played it cool? In racing terms, should he have hung back until the final turn and then put on a blaze of speed from the outside, overtaking the competition? If he'd timed it right, couldn't he have become Pharaoh of Egypt and released the Jews, his countrymen?

Possibly. But for Moses, that would have been a compromise of what he so deeply knew and believed. Deep inside, he knew that living compromised in the very lap of Egyptian luxury and comfort was bringing him down spiritually. He saw the mistreatment of his fellow Jews while he was living in wealth and extravagance. He had to do something. Hebrews 11 tells us,

> It was by faith that Moses, when he grew up, refused to be called the son of Pharaoh's daughter. He chose to share the oppression of God's people instead of enjoying the fleeting pleasures of sin. He thought it was better to suffer for the sake of Christ than to own the treasures of Egypt, for he was looking ahead to his great reward. (vv. 24–26 NLT)

Moses' heart was in the right place, but his choices were foolhardy, to say the least. When he took action, it was one of the worst mistakes of his life.

> Now it came to pass in those days, when Moses was grown, that he went out to his brethren and looked at their burdens. And he saw an Egyptian beating a Hebrew, one of his brethren. So he looked this way and that way, and when he saw no one, he killed the Egyptian and hid him in the sand. (Exodus 2:11–12)

Clearly the Lord had not told Moses to do this. Notice how the passage says, "He looked this way and that way." He should have looked up. If he had done that, the Lord would have said no. God wants us to do His will in His way in His time. Sometimes we want the will of God, but we will go about it in our own way, according to our own timetable.

I read about a guy who decided to rob a Baptist church. He grabbed the loot and tried to escape through a bathroom window. At six feet and 235 pounds, he required four police officers' pushing and pulling to get him out. That's about how subtle Moses was when he tried to bury the guy in the sand.

It was Moses who later said in Numbers 32:23, "Your sin will find you out."

Are you trying to cover up something? Is there a secret sin in your life? May I make a suggestion? Just confess it. Otherwise, sooner or later, it will be exposed. Nothing is hidden from God.

A Leader in Training

Moses probably thought his fellow Jews would applaud his act of courage. He was hoping they would say, "That Moses is something. Here he is, the son of the pharaoh, but he risks everything to help us. He is our hero." Things didn't go as he had hoped.

The next day he saw a couple of fellow Hebrews arguing. When he tried to settle the argument, they said, "Who made you a prince and a judge over us? Are you going to kill us the way you did that Egyptian yesterday?" (see Genesis 2:13–14). Moses realized that everybody knew. He thought he had hidden his sin, but it was on the front page of the Egyptian *National Inquirer*. He realized he was in trouble.

He was right. When the pharaoh heard about it, he said, "Moses is a dead man." Moses had to flee for his life, and he escaped to the desert.

Now it could have looked as though Moses' chance at leadership was over—that he'd blown it. Not true. It wasn't that Moses wasn't leadership material; it was just that he needed time. Moses was a leader-in-training. He wasn't ready yet.

People often ask, "How can I become a leader in the church?" The best course of action is to serve wherever you can. A good leader needs to learn how to be a good servant first. You should also try leading to see if anyone follows you. If not, maybe you aren't a leader. At least not yet. You may, however, be a leader-in-training.

Moses was gifted to be a leader, but he wasn't quite ready. He had to flee for his life. He had lost everything: his position, his people, his reputation. But he hadn't lost God! Moses made a huge mess for himself, but God had not turned against him. What looked like the end of his life was actually the beginning of his training for a new life.

Wait Training

There are lessons we can learn from Moses' failure.

First, Moses did the wrong thing in the wrong way at the wrong time. His heart was in the right place, but he went about it all wrong. There was no need to kill the Egyptian who was mistreating the Hebrew. I'm sure there was a lot of pent-up anger in Moses' heart after seeing the Jews so miserably mistreated, but it was a serious sin and crime that would haunt him for years.

Moses' timing was horribly off—by about forty years, to be exact. Moses' life can be divided into three, forty-year increments. Moses spent forty years in Pharaoh's court finding out he was a somebody. He spent forty years in the wilderness finding out he was a nobody. Then he spent forty years finding out what God can do with a somebody who realizes he is a nobody!

After he murdered the Egyptian, Moses entered the "nobody" phase where he would live in a desert. There he found a family who befriended him. He married one of the daughters and ended up a shepherd for his father-in-law. That is probably where he thought he was going to die: in obscurity, in the desert, far from his people, watching his sheep. You might say he had taken an early retirement. He was sure he was disqualified in the race of life and never expected to run again.

God, however, had other plans:

> Now Moses was tending the flock of Jethro his father-in- law, the priest of Midian. And he led the flock to the back of the desert, and came to Horeb, the mountain of God. And the Angel of the Lord appeared to him in a flame of fire from the midst of a bush. So he looked, and behold, the bush was burning with fire, but the bush was not consumed. Then Moses said, "I will now turn aside and see this great sight, why the bush does not burn." So when the Lord saw

that he turned aside to look, God called to him from the midst of the bush and said, "Moses, Moses!" And he said, "Here I am." Then He said, "Do not draw near this place. Take your sandals off your feet, for the place where you stand is holy ground." (Exodus 3:1–5)

God told Moses he had seen the suffering of His people. God appointed Moses to go to the pharaoh and lead the Jews to freedom. Moses was stunned, to say the least. He'd thought he was done.

What Moses didn't realize was that God had been preparing him during all of that time he spent watching sheep. The Lord was getting him ready to lead a human flock, numbering more than three million, to freedom. God was seasoning him. When he woke up that day, Moses had no idea that his life would forever change. It came unexpectedly.

Look for the Lord in the Unusual

Moses encountered God in a burning bush. Now, Moses had spent a lot of time in the desert; he'd seen plenty of tumbleweeds. He'd seen bushes catch fire and burn out. This bush was different. It continued to burn, but it didn't *burn up*. It was an ordinary bush doing an extraordinary thing—something God used to get Moses' attention. Then the Lord spoke.

I've discovered that when something out of the ordinary happens in my life, it may signal that the Lord is trying to speak to me. When you have an unexpected change of plans, you may think it's a disaster. Look again. It might be the hand of God trying to direct you a certain way. What may seem like a coincidence may actually be Providence. Disappointment is His appointment.

Note that this was an ordinary bush that God touched—just like Moses at that point in his life. He was an older man, his skin weathered and tanned from the sun. He was seasoned, wiser. But, unbeknownst to himself, old Moses was ready to rumble.

God was saying, "Look at that old bush. See how it keeps burning? That is what I am going to do with you. I can take an old bush like you and set you on fire. And you'll keep burning until My purpose is accomplished. Are you up for that?"

Listen to what God said in Exodus 3:6: "I am the God of your father—the God of Abraham, the God of Isaac, and the God of Jacob." What was God really saying? Though we often look at these men through rose-colored glasses, Abraham and Jacob both had lapses of faith. God was telling Moses, "I am the God of men who have failed. I am the God of ordinary men who have accomplished extraordinary things. There is hope for you. I'm not just the God of Abraham, Isaac, and Jacob; I am the God of Moses. I am calling you. I am giving you a second chance."

In verse 7, God further explained Moses' mission: "I have surely seen the oppression of My people who are in Egypt, and have heard their cry because of their taskmasters, for I know their sorrows." God had seen. He had heard. He was aware.

"I have come to deliver," He said. "You are My man. Moses, just as this old bush burns, so you will burn with My message. Are you ready for this?"

Moses Fumbles His First Play

What Moses should have said was, "Absolutely. Thank you for calling me." Instead he offered up a plethora of excuses. People offer the same ones today as to why they think God can't possibly use them.

Excuse 1: "I don't have all the answers"

> Then Moses said to God, "Indeed, when I come to the children of Israel and say to them, 'The God of your fathers has sent me to you,' and they say to me, 'What is His name?' what shall I say to them?" And God said to Moses, "I AM WHO I AM." And He said, "Thus you shall say to the children of Israel, 'I AM has sent me to you.'" (Exodus 3:13–14)

We say the same thing: "I can't do that. I can't share the gospel. What if that person asks a question I can't answer?" Or maybe, "I can't teach a Bible study. I just don't know enough."

Don't misunderstand. There is definitely a place for preparation and study. But God can use you in some capacity wherever you are in your Christian life.

I began preaching at nineteen and pastoring at twenty. I had been a Christian for three years. My knowledge of the Bible was limited, to say the least. Prior to my conversion, I had no background in the Scriptures or in the church. It all was relatively new to me.

So I taught everything I had learned to that point, and then I continued to study and prepare myself with on-the-job training from that day to the present. My point is that I took what little I had and offered it to the Lord. You can do the same.

You have much more information in your head than you may realize. You don't know that because you have never tapped it. You have surrounded yourself with people who have the same level of knowledge as you do. If you were to speak to a nonbeliever, he or she might fire some questions at you. In that case, you might be surprised at what you have to say under the inspiration of the Holy Spirit.

That is why God reassured Moses, "Don't sweat it. I will be with you. Nothing will overwhelm you."

Excuse 2: "I'm not a good speaker"

> But Moses pleaded with the Lord, "O Lord, I'm not very good with words. I never have been, and I'm not now, even though you have spoken to me. I get tongue-tied, and my words get tangled." (Exodus 4:10 NLT)

Maybe you are afraid to speak publicly. That may be an advantage. Sometimes people who lack self-confidence are better communicators than those who have it. Some people can talk you into anything. They can sell ice to an Eskimo. Such people can sometimes be manipulative.

A person who isn't overconfident may be the very person who should be a preacher. A person who isn't even comfortable standing up in front of people, who is a little embarrassed or shy, is a person who will depend totally on God. Then when he speaks, his message and persuasion will be from heaven instead of being manipulative techniques.

You may know me as a pastor and evangelist, but I have to

remind you that this isn't anything I aspired to. When I was in school, I didn't like to be in front of crowds. I didn't like to study. Frankly, I was a bit of a goof-off. But then God called me—and I had to become dedicated to study and public proclamation. Frankly, it was the very opposite of what I felt prepared for.

In fact, after I gave my life to the Lord, I had a secret fear that God would call me to preach—and I recoiled from the idea. I wanted to serve the Lord in some other capacity. I was a graphic designer, so I wanted to do artwork.

One day when I was a brand-new believer, I went to Big Corona Beach in Newport Beach, Orange County, to attend a baptism. I arrived late, though, and the baptism was over. I saw a group of Christians gathered, singing songs. I sat down with them and joined in the singing.

As we sang, I kept waiting for somebody to say something. And then I realized that this group had no leader, and no one was going to speak. Suddenly my heart started to burn within me, as if the Lord wanted me to say something. I finally said (with a very shaky voice), "I would like to share what the Lord showed me in the Bible this week."

As I spoke, I saw people nodding in agreement. When I was done, I offered up a silent prayer of thanks to God for allowing me that opportunity. But I was so glad it was done!

God wasn't finished. I was feeling good about having the courage to speak when two girls said, "We missed the baptism. Pastor, can you baptize us?"

Pastor? I assured them I was nothing but a very new Christian. They didn't care. "Could you baptize us?"

Everyone else said, "Yeah, you should baptize them!" So, I reluctantly stood and led my newly acquired flock down toward the water. I felt like Moses Junior!

I didn't even really know how to technically baptize a person. I had been baptized myself but had never noticed the technique itself. Do I hold the person's nose? What exactly do I say?

I did the best I could and baptized those girls that day. Once again, I was thankful but very relieved it was all over.

But I noticed that a rather large crowd had gathered as they observed these baptisms. Then it came to me as clear as day. The Lord spoke to my heart: "Proclaim My gospel to them!"

It was the moment I dreaded. It was what I'd had nightmares about. But now that I was doing it by the leading of God's Holy Spirit, it wasn't a nightmare at all, but a dream come true. At the end of my mini-message, I even offered an opportunity for those listening to come to Christ, and, as I recall, a few did. I baptized them as well. What a day that was!

God will give you the words when He wants you to speak. We may not all be called to be preachers, but we are all called to communicate His Word. You just take that step of faith.

Excuse 3: "I Can't"

"Moses again pleaded, 'Lord, please! Send anyone else'" (Exodus 4:13 NLT). In other words, "I'm the wrong person for this. I stumble over my words. I just can't do it."

The Lord grew angry. He agreed to let Moses' brother Aaron do the talking. Moses liked that, but it was a big mistake. Aaron turned out to be a real albatross around Moses' neck. Don't forget that it was Aaron who had the bright idea of making a golden calf while Moses was away, receiving the Ten Commandments. Moses should have left Aaron at home and done what God had called him to do.

Don't tell the Lord, "I can't" when He knows you can—with His help. Paul reminds us that we "can do *all things* through Christ who strengthens [us]" (Philippians 4:13, emphasis added).

The bottom line is that God can use anyone He wants to, even people who have made mistakes, even people who have sinned. It's all about His timing.

It's a fact that every runner in the race of life has sinned, has blown it in some way. Don't let appearances fool you: sin is an equal-opportunity sport. Run the track God assigns to you. Keep your excuses to yourself. If God is the one providing the power, how can you lose?

And if you're trying to run ahead of God's plan, slow down. Let Him start and stop the stopwatch. You'll never lose by letting the right one control your pace. Let's see how Moses fared with the God of Abraham as his coach.

RUN WITH ALL YOU'VE GOT

Prior to knowing Jesus Christ, we perhaps thought we were the captains of our own ships, that we ran our own lives. But for all practical purposes, we were under the power of the Prince of Darkness. It was a big rip-off. He offered us life but gave us death. He promised us pleasure but gave us guilt. He promised us fun but brought us misery.

Then we discovered there was a God who loved us and had a plan for our lives. We took the plunge and gave our hearts to Jesus Christ. He forgave us of our sins and changed our eternal address from a place called hell to a place called heaven. It was a wonderful day that every Christian remembers vividly.

I hope that having done that, you weren't expecting a standing ovation in hell. You need to know that the devil was not happy about it—and still isn't. He lost one of his own. Consequently, the devil wants to bring you down. Satan knows that he cannot overpower God; therefore his objective is to draw you out through compromise.

Compromise has brought down more believers than has any other ploy the devil has in his toolbox. Through it he takes you down a bite at a time. It is so subtle you don't even realize that it's happening.

In a race, compromise might mean skipping a lap, then saying you ran it . . . claiming to have run every day when you slept in instead . . . saying you were running to the end, but quitting halfway there.

In our study of individuals from the Bible and how they ran the race of life, we return now to our flawed hero, Moses. Compromise might have been a poison in his life that slowly ate away his purpose and power. Was it? Read on.

Nobody Said It Would Be Easy

We pick up the story where God had given Moses and Aaron their assignment, and they set off for Egypt:

> Moses and Aaron went in and told Pharaoh, "Thus says the Lord God of Israel: 'Let My people go, that they may hold a feast to Me in the wilderness.'" And Pharaoh said, "Who is the Lord, that I should obey His voice to let Israel go? I do not know the Lord, nor will I let Israel go." So they said, "The God of the Hebrews has met with us. Please, let us go three days' journey into the desert and sacrifice to the Lord our God, lest He fall upon us with pestilence or with the sword." (Exodus 5:1–3)

Moses and Aaron probably were hoping Pharaoh would say, "No problem. God has been speaking to me about that as well. Go forth, and God bless you."

But it didn't exactly work out that way, did it?

You need to know that Moses and Aaron journeyed to Pharaoh with the support of Israel's elders. God had given Moses the power to perform certain wonders, to show Pharaoh he was on the side of the Israelites. Moses and Aaron showed these signs to the elders, and the elders believed their mission was from God.

But Pharaoh's response was less than enthusiastic: "Are you kidding? There is no way I'm going to let that happen."

What does this show us? It reminds us that being in the will of God doesn't mean we will always have green lights and blue skies. Sometimes we think if the Lord has shown us to do something, then it will be easy to do. Not necessarily. The devil will oppose you.

What did Moses and Aaron do? Did they say, "Forget it" and go back home? No. I love their tenacity and commitment. They refused to renege on their mission and went back for more.

> Moses and Aaron went in to Pharaoh, and they did so, just as the Lord commanded. And Aaron cast down his rod before Pharaoh and before his servants, and it became a serpent. But Pharaoh also called the wise men and the sorcerers; so the magicians of Egypt, they also did in like manner with their enchantments. For every man threw down his rod, and they became serpents. But Aaron's rod swallowed up their rods.
>
> And Pharaoh's heart grew hard, and he did not heed them, as the Lord had said. (Exodus 7:10–13)

You may know that the serpent, specifically the cobra, was a respected symbol among the Egyptians. What was the first miracle Aaron did? He threw down his staff, and it turned into a serpent, which was probably a cobra. The pharaoh's magicians said, "We can do that too." Sure enough, their stick transformed into a snake as well. But the snake that God produced through Aaron consumed the snakes of the magicians. Still Pharaoh refused to believe.

Imitation and Infiltration

Who were Pharaoh's magicians? In 2 Timothy 3:8, Paul gives us a little more information.

> Just as Jannes and Jambres opposed Moses, so also these teachers oppose the truth. They are men of depraved minds, who, as far as the faith is concerned, are rejected. (NIV)

These two sorcerers opposed and resisted Moses just as people oppose and resist the truth today; they were men with depraved minds.

We find in Jannes and Jambres one of Satan's most effective strategies: imitation and infiltration. He will try to stop a work altogether, but if that doesn't work, he will imitate it. In these ways he seeks to minimize the power and glory of God and neutralize the impact of someone's life and testimony.

Let me illustrate. You know the story Jesus told of the wheat and the tares. A farmer sowed a field of wheat and, in the darkness of night, his enemy sowed tares in the field. The tare is a plant almost identical to wheat in its initial stages of growth. To the undiscerning eye, it looks exactly like wheat. You can't tell the tare is there until it actually grows up and chokes out the wheat.

In the same way, the devil floods—infiltrates—the market with cheap imitations. How many times have you heard someone say, "The reason I'm not a Christian is because there are so many hypocrites in the church"? That puts us in the very uncomfortable position of trying to defend people that don't practice what they preach.

But maybe they aren't believers at all. Maybe they are tares among the wheat.

Can you see how effective that ploy could be? Maybe Satan has placed those imitations there for the very purpose of keeping the nonbeliever from coming to faith.

Only the uncompromised life, such as the one Moses was then leading, can reveal God's glory and draw people to the Savior. The fakes can only do damage.

Pharaoh's Strategy

Pharaoh was fooled by his fake magicians' trickery—or, at least, he chose to be. The result? Ten disastrous plagues sent from God.

He and his people faced nothing less than a river of blood, an abundance of frogs, dust turning to lice, relentless flies, wiped-out livestock, boils, hail, locusts, unending darkness, and finally, the death of every family's firstborn. During his weakest moments, Pharaoh actually began to relent—but only a little.

In moments when the pharaoh realized he was outgunned, he tried to trick Moses through a series of compromises. As we watch Pharaoh try to manipulate Moses and drain him of his power, we see a picture of how the devil attempts to do the same to us.

Compromise 1: Go, but stay

Scripture shows us that after the plague of flies, Pharaoh was beginning to soften.

Then Pharaoh called for Moses and Aaron, and said, "Go, sacrifice
to your God in the land." And Moses said, "It is not right to do so,
for we would be sacrificing the abomination of the Egyptians to
the Lord our God. If we sacrifice the abomination of the Egyptians
before their eyes, then will they not stone us? We will go three days'
journey into the wilderness and sacrifice to the Lord our God as He
will command us." So Pharaoh said, "I will let you go, that you may
sacrifice to the Lord your God in the wilderness; only you shall not
go very far away. Intercede for me." (Exodus 8:25-28 NLT)

Pay careful attention. This is the anatomy of a compromise.
What did God tell Moses and Aaron to do? Take the Jews three
days' journey into the wilderness. Put three days' distance between
them and Egypt, then sacrifice to the Lord. Pharaoh said, "Go sacrifice. Go call on your God—only do so here in Egypt."

Pharaoh was trying to get Moses to make some concessions.
"Go ahead. If you don't want to worship the gods of Egypt and have
to worship your God, go do it. But don't go far. Stay around."

Then he added a little twist: "Pray for me." That sounded promising. Moses might have said, "Look, Aaron, the Lord is opening
Pharaoh's heart. He wants us to remember him in prayer. Maybe we
should agree to his demands. After all, it's close enough to what God
commanded."

No, Moses knew very well what the Lord had said—and meant.
God had told him to put significant distance between Egypt and
Israel before making a sacrifice. Pharaoh's compromise was nothing
but a trick.

Have you ever seen this trick before? Perhaps after you gave your
life to Christ, the devil whispered in your ear, "I didn't want you to
do that, but I will concede that you have gone to the other side. Let's
strike a deal. Don't be too fanatical here. Can we still have a little
fun together? You don't have to give up all of your old friends or lifestyle. You can still believe in God, but be practical."

Essentially Satan says, "Go ahead and go, but don't go too far.
You don't have to believe all of this stuff. You don't have to do everything the Bible says."

Some people have never fully repented. They have believed in

Jesus but haven't moved very far from the old life. They stayed close enough that the enemy still has a foothold. Ungodly friends still influence them. Persistent sins still drag them down.

Maybe that is what the devil is trying to pull off when he initiates a romantic relationship between a believer and a nonbeliever. I know sometimes Christians think they can reach the unsaved if they operate on their level: I'll just lay low and be cool with them. No one has ever been won to Christ by so-called coolness. They are won by godly living. They are won by a person's living a genuine, uncompromised life before God. And they are won as we lovingly and faithfully proclaim the gospel to them.

Sometimes we are trying so hard to be cool and relate that we forget about living a righteous life. We forget about standing up for what is right.

This is what the pharaoh was trying to do: "Sure, take a journey. But stay within the borders. Sure, offer a sacrifice. Just do it here. And while you're at it, pray for me." The pharaoh knew that if he could keep the Israelites near Egypt, he could keep them under his influence and reel them back again.

Compromise 2: Leave the kids here

After the plagues of boils and hail, Pharaoh again showed signs of cracking. Look at Exodus 10:

> So Moses and Aaron were brought again to Pharaoh, and he said to them, "Go, serve the Lord your God. Who are the ones that are going?" And Moses said, "We will go with our young and our old; with our sons and our daughters, with our flocks and our herds we will go, for we must hold a feast to the Lord." Then he said to them, "The Lord had better be with you when I let you and your little ones go! Beware, for evil is ahead of you." (vv. 8–10 NLT)

Pharaoh retorted "You think I'm going to let you go with your kids? Forget about it. Go on and leave if you want. But leave your children here. I want them."

As a result of Pharaoh's continued resistance to release the Jews, God's judgment once again came on Egypt (see Exodus 10:12).

The devil wants you distracted. Do you see a spiritual lesson here? Do you think the devil wants your kids? How many generations of young people have been destroyed by drugs, sex, and rock and roll? It's amazing how each successive generation acts as though this is a new phenomenon. Kids get into the same things we got into when we were their age.

One of the ways the devil tries to get your children is by distracting you as a parent. How many children have been neglected as parents chased after success? Do any of these excuses sound familiar?

- "We do all this so we can give them a better life than we had."
- "We have to work the two jobs and put the kids in day care so they will have nicer toys at Christmas."
- "We focus on quality time with them instead of quantity of time."

No! You would be better off living in a smaller house and being home with your kids. *The best thing you can spend on your children is time, and lots of it.*

Face it: chasing success up the ladder rather than chasing your kids around the yard is a compromise of your job as parent. Now, I know that some parents, especially if they're single, don't have the luxury of staying home full-time to raise their children. But do whatever you can to spend as much time as possible with your little ones. Those days will pass so quickly.

The devil wants to divide and conquer you. Think of how many children have been destroyed as selfish husbands and wives have dissolved their marriages because of so called irreconcilable differences.

What are irreconcilable differences, anyway? I've had irreconcilable differences with my wife for thirty-two years. She's neat, and I'm messy. She's often late, and I'm usually early. She is more kicked-back and relaxed, and I'm more rushed all the time. I don't think we will ever completely agree. *So what?* Welcome to the real world.

If you want to spend life with someone who always agrees with you, then marry yourself. Or better yet, stay single. Why were you initially attracted to your spouse? Because he or she was different from you. He or she had qualities that you admired or aspired to. That person balanced you, and you balanced him or her. You complemented one another.

Now those differences have turned into a wide chasm. Maybe you think that by dissolving your marriage and moving on to another, you won't have any more problems. In your mind, your mate is the source of all evil, and you are all good—is that it? Wake up and think about the children!

"Oh, they'll be fine. Children are resilient. They will bounce back."

How I hate those words! Who says that children are "resilient" when their home and their hearts are being torn in two? Who says kids bounce back quickly after their parents split up?

That's a lie. I know this as a child of divorce. I have experienced it firsthand. And I have seen it with so many others over thirty-one years of being a pastor.

Roland Warren, president of the National Fatherhood Initiative, said, "Fatherless kids have a hole in their soul in the shape of their father, and it leaves a wound that is not easily healed."[1]

Granted, there are other reasons marriages fall apart. There are even biblical allowances for divorce. But my experience is that many, if not most, of the marriages that have dissolved could have been saved if the husband and wife had made a greater effort to forgive and forget.

Parents, listen to me. Don't let the devil have your kids. Draw the line. You say to the enemy, "They belong to the Lord, and you can't have them."

Moses was digging in here. There would be no compromise.

Compromise 3: Leave a little livestock

Pharaoh had yet one more compromise up his sleeve. In Exodus 10:24, he said to Moses: "Go, serve the Lord; only let your flocks and your herds be kept back. Let your little ones also go with you."

The devil was fighting tooth and nail for Moses' character. Why did Pharaoh care about their animals? Because it would have been a victory, albeit a small one, to get something of the Israelites.

Imagine how tempting this must have been for Moses. "You want our animals? You'll let the rest of us go? Good deal!" Aaron might have said, "Moses, this sounds doable!"

I love what Moses said: "Not a hoof shall be left behind" (v. 26). In other words, "Pharaoh, read my lips: You get zero, zip, nothing, *nada*. You don't even get an inch. You don't even get a sick animal. We're taking everyone and everything, and we are leaving, whether you like it or not."

That is what we need to say to the devil. The devil says, "If I can't have all of your life, then let me have this one area. How about your fantasy life—a little fun with pornography? It won't go any further. How about this area? Just skim a little off the top."

Do you know why he wants something? Because little things will lead to big things. That's why you can't make deals with the devil. That's why you can't negotiate with Satan. That's why there can be no compromise.

If you aren't prepared to go far away from him, you're never going to make it to what God has for you. If you want to stay close to the enemy and give him pieces of your life, he will manipulate you and kill your influence. It's time to break free.

Is there an area that you know you need to deal with? Is there a situation in which you've been compromising? If something just jumped to the forefront of your mind—it feels like a raw nerve— the Lord brought that to your attention for a reason. It isn't to drive you away in despair and guilt. It is a problem and a potential weakness. The Lord brought it to your mind so you can deal with it.

Take action. Right now, make a decision to dedicate that area of your life to God. Give it to Him. It's not too late. God can free you from it. He is still in the miracle-working business, but He needs your cooperation. Make a decision today that in giving your life to the Lord, not a hoof will be left behind.

Living an uncompromised life is how you get all your energies back in the race. Remember Moses and how he unflinchingly remained faithful to the task God set before him. He put his all into the race before him. You can do the same.

RUNNING WITH CHARACTER

Character counts.

In fact, it may be the most important thing in a person's life. And it's not just what you say, but what you *are*. In fact, if you want to know who you really are, here is what it comes down to: when you are all alone, when no one is watching, when there is no one to impress—*that* is who you really are.

The measure of a man's real character is what he would do if he knew he never would be found out. A poll was taken of Americans asking, "Why do you not steal?" Here are the results:

• Reason 1: "I might get caught."
• Reason 2: "The other person might try to get even."
• Reason 3: "I might not need the item."

That strikes me as really missing the point. What about not stealing because it's *wrong*? More specifically, because God himself has told us, "You shall not steal" (Exodus 20:15)?

If you were to take this flawed reasoning to other areas of life, you could say, "The reason I don't commit adultery or lie or whatever is fear of being caught." If that's the situation with you, then it only will be a matter of time before you do one of things. Why? Because, in all likelihood, a situation will arise in which you think you can get away with one of these sins. And if there's nothing else to hold you back, then you'll go ahead and do it.

There is a better deterrent. It's called *integrity*.

Who Are You When No One Is Watching?

I read an article in the paper about three men who stole some items from a home, including a DVD player, computer, TV, and other electronic gear. One of them realized that the owner of that house had a pet parrot, and he might have heard one of the thieves refer to the name of one of the others.

So they decided to go back and get the bird, who, they feared, might turn out to be a stool pigeon! When they were loading the bird into their getaway car, the police showed up. This ended up in a chase with the burglars and bird thieves being arrested.

This reminds me of a statement by humorist Will Rogers: "So live that you would not mind selling your pet parrot to the town gossip."

Again, character or integrity is all about what you are when you are alone:

- What do you think about the most?
- What do you like to watch on TV?
- What websites do you visit?
- What saddens you?
- What makes you angry?
- What makes you laugh?

That is your character. As one German proverb says, "A man shows his character by what he laughs at."

Everyone has character of some kind, either good or bad. This personal integrity or character is something you develop on a daily basis. With every thought you think and deed you do, you are either building it up or tearing it down. It comes down to this: if you cheat in practice, you'll cheat in the game. If you cheat in your head, you'll cheat on the test. You'll cheat on the girl. You'll cheat in business. You'll cheat on your mate.

It's been said: Sow a thought, and you reap an act. Sow an act, and you reap a habit. Sow a habit, and you reap a character. Sow a character, and you reap a destiny.

I heard the story of a pastor who boarded a bus one Monday

morning. He paid his fare and the bus driver gave him too much change. Even though he could have used the money, the pastor went up to the driver and said, "You must have made a mistake. You gave me too much change!"

The driver responded, "It was no mistake. I was in your church last night, and you spoke on honesty. I thought I would put you to the test!"

That's character.

The Imperfect Moses

Moses was a man who had integrity—so much so that his personal godliness kept literally millions of Israelites from falling into idolatry. As long as Moses was around, his influence was so profound and significant that it kept a massive number of people from doing the wrong thing. He was such a good runner in the race that he inspired others to run as well as he did.

But even Moses wasn't perfect. Although he almost daily mirrored the personal character God desired in the Israelites, he had his moments of failure. And he paid for them. What's important is that he was constantly striving to be a man of integrity, in spite of his human shortcomings. He might have been temporarily barred from the track, but in the end, he finished strong.

Let's pick up his story where we left off.

Shallow Faith

You'll remember that ten successive plagues fell on Egypt, each growing in intensity, until finally and reluctantly the pharaoh relented and released the Israelites to Moses' care. Off they went from the bondage they had suffered for so many years.

God continued to look after the Israelites. As they were making their way out of Egypt, they came to an apparent impasse. Before them was the Red Sea. To the right and left was treacherous territory they could not enter. Behind them was Egypt. To make matters worse, Pharaoh had second thoughts about releasing the Israelites, and his armies were in hot pursuit.

God's people cried out, "What is going to happen to us?" They went from being wildly ecstatic and thankful to Moses and God for their release to being wildly panicked.

Moses told the people, "Stand still, and see the salvation of the Lord . . ." (Exodus. 14:13). He opened up the Red Sea, and Moses led the Israelites through to dry ground. Then God released the waters, and the sea crashed down on and drowned the pursuing Egyptian army.

The Israelites sang a song of praise to God. Then the Lord began to lead the Israelites in a very obvious way. In the daytime, a big cloud served as their guide; when the cloud moved, they were to move. When the cloud stopped, they were to stop. At night it was a pillar of fire. It was better than GPS! (What a great way to get around. For someone like me, who is clearly navigationally dysfunctional, this would be wonderful!)

The Lord provided for their physical needs as well. Every morning when they emerged from their tents, fresh manna was waiting for them. God faithfully provided this supernatural foodstuff. All they had to do was gather it up and enjoy it. You can imagine how the Israelites must have revered Moses at this point.

Then Moses went away to receive the Ten Commandments . . . and everything fell apart. Bickering, confusion, and idol worshiping became the rule of the day. Think about this: the Israelites literally were surrounded by miracles and the supernatural, yet in a relatively short period of time, they turned to full-tilt idolatry. How could such a thing happen?

Because miracles don't necessarily guarantee godly living. You might think if only there were miracles in your life or more supernatural phenomena taking place, you would be stronger spiritually. Not always. Not if you're misplacing your thankfulness.

The Israelites' problem came down to one thing: the shallowness and superficiality of their faith. As we will discover, they bowed before a manmade golden calf. That clearly was idolatry. But their first idol wasn't the golden calf; it was Moses. They never seemed to develop their own relationship with God. It is as though their relationship with God was dependent on Moses' presence. That's a wonderful tribute to the influence of a godly man, but it is also a criticism of their lack of personal faith.

Let me illustrate. When you travel overseas, you need to take electrical adapters with you. Your American plugs won't fit foreign outlets, and your electrical currency needs might not match what is available.

A number of years ago when I was in Israel, I plugged my hair dryer into the wall and noticed that my hair was drying a little more quickly than usual. I discovered that 220 volts of electricity were pumping into that little hair dryer, which was designed for 110. I also noticed that my hair dryer was on fire. The nozzle was literally melting. I needed an adapter.

Without an adapter, you can't utilize the electricity that is available to you. In the same way, the Israelites needed an adapter. They couldn't relate to God on their own. If Moses wasn't there, whatever connection they had with the Lord seemed to fall apart. Their relationship with God depended on Moses' relationship with God. This is never a healthy thing spiritually.

Case in point: God called Moses up to Mount Sinai to receive the Ten Commandments. Look at what happened:

> Now when the people saw that Moses delayed coming down from the mountain, the people gathered together to Aaron, and said to him, "Come, make us gods that shall go before us; for as for this Moses, the man who brought us up out of the land of Egypt, we do not know what has become of him." (Exodus 32:1)

Moses was gone, and Israel needed something or someone to worship. Instead of recognizing it was the Lord, through Moses, who had led them out of Egypt, they credited Moses himself. As soon as Moses was gone, they wanted something to take his place.

Basically the Israelites were saying, "We need something tangible. It's hard for us to relate to an invisible, supernatural God. We want something we can reach out and take hold of."

So began the plans for the golden calf. This ultimately led to a pathetic scene of sexual immorality and idol worship. Moses was

Israel's first idol, and the golden calf was their second.

A Little Integrity Goes a Long Way

We can't blame Moses for this, because it was his personal godliness and integrity that had kept Israel in line up to that point. Consider this: one man had kept three million people from turning away to worship false gods.

It reminds us that God can do a lot with a little. Jesus said that we as His church are "the salt of the earth" (Matthew 5:13). As you know, a little salt goes a long way. Just a pinch of salt in some oatmeal can enhance its flavor. Too much, and it's ruined.

In life, one "salty" person can go a long way. One Christian in a family, in a neighborhood, or in a workplace can influence many, many people. Often, though, we try to get out of those uncomfortable situations.

Perhaps at your worksite, all of the other guys are nonbelievers. They laugh at you. You are the brunt of their jokes. You want to get a new job.

Maybe in your classroom, you are the one Christian who will disagree with the professor when he is promoting evolution or some other secular worldview. It's hard. You're definitely in the minority, and it makes you uncomfortable.

Perhaps you have some neighbors that like to stay up late and drink and party the night away.

You want to be in a Christian school, a Christian neighborhood, a Christian job. Life would then be easier. But did you ever stop to think that maybe God put you where you are to be an influence?

That is what Moses was. Imagine how hard it was for him. Those people were so full of unbelief and whining and complaining. But through his integrity and personal holiness, Moses influenced them for the good. Oh, how we need more people like this who will make a difference in this world! You think things are bad in this country now—and they are—with our terrorism, immorality, epidemics of divorce, and suicide.

These are crazy times. But think: it is the presence of the church in the world today that is keeping it from getting even worse. Just wait until the Lord calls His church home. Imagine what will happen when we who are the salt of the earth are no longer here. We are God's representatives.

Moses was God's representative. In contrast to this man of integrity, there was Aaron his brother. Aaron made a mess of things. In the absence of Moses, the people sought a new leader, and, unfortunately, Aaron complied. When they demanded something to worship, Aaron told them to give him all their gold earrings. He took the gold, melted it, and fashioned it into a golden calf (see Exodus 32:4). They stripped off their clothes and danced naked before it.

Let's look at some of the characteristics of integrity and how Moses and Aaron did or didn't represent it well.

A man of integrity is an intercessor

Down in the valley, Aaron had allowed the Israelites to worship a golden idol. Up on Sinai, God alerted Moses to what was happening. What did Moses do when God told him?

> And the Lord said to Moses, "Go, Get down! For your people whom you brought out of the land of Egypt have corrupted themselves. They have turned aside quickly out of the way which I commanded them. They have made themselves a molded calf, and worshiped it and sacrificed to it, and said, 'This is your god, O Israel, that brought you out of the land of Egypt!'" And the Lord said to Moses, "I have seen this people, and indeed it is a stiff-necked people! Now therefore, let Me alone, that My wrath may burn hot against them and I may consume them. And I will make of you a great nation."

> Then Moses pleaded with the Lord his God, and said, "Lord, why does Your wrath burn hot against Your people whom You have brought out of the land of Egypt with great power and with a mighty hand? Why should the Egyptians speak, and say, 'He brought them out to harm them, to kill them in the mountains, and to consume them from the face of the earth'? Turn from Your fierce wrath, and relent from this harm to Your people. Remember Abraham, Isaac, and Israel, Your servants, to whom You swore by Your own self, and said to them, 'I will multiply your descendents

as the stars of heaven; and all this land that I have spoken of I give to your descendants, and they will inherit it forever.'" So the Lord relented from the harm which He said He would do to His people. (Exodus 32:7–14)

You might read these passages and think the Lord was really in the wrong, and Moses brought him around. That's not true at all. God wanted to see if Moses was learning anything.

Remember Jesus tested His disciples. We read of the multitudes that gathered. Jesus turned to His disciple Philip and asked, "Where are we going to find food to feed all of these people?" The Bible says, "This He said to test him" (John 6:6). He wanted to see if they had learned anything.

Moses faced such a test. When the Lord said, "I am going to destroy these people," Moses said, "Hold on now, Lord. These are Your people that You brought out of Egypt, and You made a covenant with Abraham, Isaac, and Jacob that You would multiply their descendants. If You kill them, then the Egyptians will say, 'Look at this God who delivers His people to death.' This is a bad move. Spare Your people."

The Lord answered, "I will spare them." God was always going to spare them. But he wanted Moses to be an intercessor.

That's what prayer is all about: It's seeing things the way God sees them and praying accordingly. It's standing in the gap. God wants you to care about lost people as He does, see them as sheep without a Shepherd, and pray for them.

We see how much Moses cared when in Exodus 32:32 he prayed, "But now, if you will only forgive their sin—but if not, erase my name from the record you have written!" (NLT). Do you understand what Moses was saying? "Lord, if this is what it takes, I'm willing to go to hell so they could go to heaven."

Fortunately God required no such thing, but it shows the heart of a true intercessor, one who really cares.

Paul said something similar when he wrote, "My heart is filled with bitter sorrow and unending grief for my people, my Jewish brothers and sisters. I would be willing to be forever cursed—cut off from Christ!—if that would save them" (Romans 9:2–3 NLT). That is the heart for people we need to have.

A man of integrity is responsible for his actions

Moses descended from the mountain, holding the commandments God gave him in his arms. When he encountered Aaron, he heard perhaps the lamest excuse found in the pages of the Bible. Aaron's rationale for the Israelites' behavior was so absurd that it should be permanently enshrined in the Excuse Hall of Fame, along with "My alarm didn't go off," "The dog ate my homework," and "The check is in the mail."

Upon seeing the people dancing before the golden calf,

> Moses said to Aaron, "What did this people do to you that you have brought so great a sin upon them?" So Aaron said, "Do not let the anger of my lord become hot. You know the people, that they are set on evil. For they said to me, 'Make us gods that shall go before us; as for this Moses, the man who brought us out of the land of Egypt, we do not know what has become of him.' And I said to them 'If you have any gold, let them break it off.' So they gave it to me, and I cast it into the fire, and this calf came out." (Exodus 32:21–24)

How lame was that? He refused to take responsibility for his actions. Aaron should have drawn the line when Israel said, "Moses is gone, and we need something to worship." He should have said, "You just worship God, and wait until Moses gets back." Instead he caved in. Then when Moses confronted him, he passed the buck.

It reminds me of a substitute teacher. God bless you if that's what you do for a living. We used to abuse them horribly when I was in school. We knew we could get away with anything. They didn't know all of the rules, so we made them up. The substitute lacked the authority and knowledge of the teacher, so we tormented him or her to no end.

Aaron was sort of like a substitute teacher. He was the polar opposite of Moses. Moses had backbone. He thought clearly. He was decisive. He had integrity. Aaron had no backbone. His thinking was muddled. He had no integrity. He wanted to be popular. He didn't want to offend anyone. Not only did he go along with Israel's plan, he even facilitated it. He lacked the authority and steadfastness of Moses, Israel's true leader.

Many people are like Aaron today. When they are around committed Christians, they are temporarily strong. But when they get away from Christians, they blend into the woodwork. The story of Aaron's spiritual demise serves as a warning to the vacillating, compromising person who always wants to go along with public opinion and is more concerned with what people think than with what God thinks.

Don't be an Aaron. Aarons reach no one. Be a Moses. Be a man or a woman who stands up for what is right. One person can make a big difference.

Even the Best Runner Sometimes Stumbles

Fast-forward to the time when Moses and the Israelites had traveled through the wilderness for thirty-nine years. They were on the brink of entering the Promised Land. Moses had put up with years of whining, sniveling, complaining, ingratitude, and outright sin. Finally, he was just about to blow his lid.

Numbers 20 records the incident:

> Now there was no water for the congregation; so they gathered together against Moses and Aaron. And the people contended with Moses and spoke, saying: "If only we had died when our brethren died before the Lord! Why have you brought up the assembly of the Lord into this wilderness, that we and our animals should die here? And why have you made us come up out of Egypt, to bring us to this evil place? It is not a place of grain or figs or vines or pomegranates; nor is there any water to drink." (vv. 2–5)

Moses and Aaron entered the tabernacle and prayed. God was gracious and told Moses, "Take the rod; you and your brother Aaron gather the congregation together. Speak to the rock before their eyes, and it will yield its water; thus you shall bring water for them out of the rock, and give drink to the congregation and their animals" (v. 8).

Notice that God said only to *speak* to the rock. When God tells us to do something, we need to do it. The problem is that sometimes we selectively hear and obey God. If God says to do something we like, we respond, "Yes, Lord." Then He tells us to stop doing something we personally enjoy, and the reception suddenly grows fuzzy: "God? . . . You're breaking up!"

Jesus said, "You are My friends if you do whatever I command you" (John 15:14). He didn't say, "You are My friends if you do the things with which you personally agree."

God has told us how to live in His Word. It's not for us to pick and choose the parts of the Bible we like and throw the others aside. This is a package deal.

Back to Moses and the rock. Earlier in his travels with Israel, they also had run out of water. In that case, God told Moses to "strike the rock, and water will come out of it, that the people may drink" (Exodus 17:6). This time He said, "Speak to the rock."

It may seem like a small thing to us, but it was a big thing to God. He had His reasons for saying what He said. One may be that the rock is used in Scripture as a picture of God. How many times do we read of God being compared to a rock? Psalm 31:3 says, "You are my rock and my fortress; therefore, for Your name's sake, lead me and guide me." In the New Testament we read in 1 Corinthians 10:4 that the Israelites "drank of that spiritual Rock that followed them, and that Rock was Christ."

When God told Moses to strike the first rock, it was a symbol of what happened to Jesus. The Rock was struck—He was crucified. Because of His death on the cross, we can be forgiven. From that time forward, then, all Moses had to do was speak to the rock.

The second time, though, Moses disobeyed the Lord's specific command:

> Moses and Aaron gathered the assembly together before the rock; and he said to them, "Hear now, you rebels! Must we bring water for you out of this rock?" Then Moses lifted his hand and struck the rock twice with his rod; and water came out abundantly. . . .
> (Numbers 20:10–11)

Whoops. God said, "Son, I want to speak with you. What did I tell you to do? I told you to speak to the rock. You struck it. Come back behind My woodshed for a moment."

> Then the Lord spoke to Moses and Aaron, "Because you did not believe Me, to hallow Me in the eyes of the children of Israel, therefore you shall not bring this assembly into the land which I have given them." (v. 12)

How Moses Blew It

Think of how close they were to the Promised Land. For thirty-nine years, Moses had, with integrity, led, tolerated, and interceded for God's stubborn people, and yet now . . . he would not enjoy their reward. Why?

1. Moses stole the limelight

First of all, Moses took personal credit for what God had done. That isn't a smart thing to do. What did he say? "You rebels! Must *we* bring water for you out of this rock?" (emphasis added). Moses never got water out of any rock for Israel. Not a single drop. It was God who caused the water to come out abundantly.

It sounds as if Moses, instead of giving the glory to God, had begun to believe his own press clippings. That is always a danger. When God uses you, you may start thinking you are indispensable. *It won't happen without me. I am God's man [or woman] of faith and power for this hour.* When God does something through your life, always be very, very careful give Him the glory.

2. Moses disobeyed

Mistake number two was that Moses went against God's wishes. God told him to speak to the rock, and he struck it instead.

Have you ever done something in a rage that you were sure was right? But when the adrenaline wore off, you realized you had acted like a fool. That's what happened to Moses. He was so angry, he snarled at the people and beat on the rock. He was out of control. He disobeyed God.

Leaders have an awesome responsibility. James reminds us, "Let not many of you become teachers, knowing that we shall receive a stricter judgment" (3:1). One day God will hold leaders accountable for what they have done. So we want to be very careful that everything we say and do is based on God's truth. When we stand to speak for God, we need to treat it as a serious responsibility.

We should prepare ourselves. We should make sure it is the real work of God. God does not like misrepresentation. Remember that Jesus saved His most scathing words for the religious hypocrites of the day, the Pharisees, because they misrepresented God to the people.

Moses misrepresented God and failed to honor Him. He lost entrance to the Promised Land. What a price to pay!

Even If You Trip, Finish the Lap

"Isn't that overkill?" you say. "Poor Moses. Look at all of the things he put up with!"

Yes, he was sort of like a runner who tripped in his final lap. In the end, however, he did do well. Moses was a winner in the spiritual race. How so? He eventually entered the Promised Land. Remember when Jesus was transfigured? Who stood on each side of him? Moses and Elijah (see Matthew 17:3).

In the end, Moses still was the man of God, the man of integrity.

How do you measure up? What if we were to interview people whom know you well—your spouse, your children, your coworkers? What would they say about you? "He is a man of God"? "She lacks integrity"?

Are you seeking to be an influence on those around you? Are you living a life of integrity? Are you an intercessor, caring enough to pray for those who are separated from God?

Let's remember to give God the glory for everything He does in our lives. Let's be careful that we do things the way the Lord tells us to. If we remember to do these things, who we are in private and who we are in public will be one and the same. We will finish the race well, whatever our stumbles along the way.

We will hit the finish line as winners.

FOOD FOR AN
ULTRAMARATHON

There are runners and there are runners.

In the Introduction of this book, I called myself a runner, because I occasionally do some jogging (though I've almost transitioned into walking only these days.)

What qualifies you to call yourself a runner?

It really depends on whom you talk to. You have people who run around the block in the morning and modestly refer to themselves as runners. Then you have people who have worked their way up to a 5K, and they tend to look down on the people who just run around the block: "They're not really runners." Funny thing is, people who graduated to running a 10K look down on people who run a 5K: "After all," they might say, "a 5K is just a 'fun run.' It's not the real deal."

Then there are the marathoners, the men and women who run 26-plus miles at a time over the course of long, agonizing hours. They might very well imagine themselves to be the *true* runners. Everyone else, in their view, is just playing at it and aren't real runners at all.

When you think about it, I guess the marathoners have a pretty good case. But have you heard about ultramarathoners? These are folks who routinely run, 30-, 50-, or even 100-mile races. And many of these "ultras" take place on mountain trails, where participants must navigate fallen logs, streams, rocks, and roots in the trail, hostile wildlife, extreme temperatures, and thousands of feet of elevation gain.

How in the world does a person run for fifty miles in one day, let alone a hundred? I couldn't even ride my bike that far on a dare!

Even so, I think the ultramarathon is really one of the best word pictures for the Christian life that I can think of. If you think following Christ is a sprint, you'll soon find out differently. The race we have been given to run, "the race that is set before us," as it says in Hebrews 12:1, lasts for a lifetime. We don't cross the finish line until that day when we break the tape of this life and enter heaven. Before we arrive, however, there are many, many miles, innumerable obstacles, and countless ups and downs that will mark our journey.

Since I never go very long without thinking about food, it makes me wonder what an ultramarathoner eats to keep himself or herself going mile after endless mile. I'm not sure you'd make it a hundred miles on Twinkies and Dr Pepper.

Food for the Long Haul

What do people eat in the course of an ultra-marathon? Peanut butter and jelly sandwiches, for one thing. Others nibble on nuts and cranberries, crackers, Fig Newtons, pudding cups, and even brownies. In one aid station up in the mountains of North Carolina, one runner I heard about was surprised to encounter gummy bears and whiskey. He wisely steered away from that "aid" and actually finished his race. Others swear by high-tech gels, powders, protein bars, and sports drinks.

Eat too much, and you'll be sluggish—or sick.

Eat too little, and you'll fade out before you finish.

Eat the wrong stuff, and your body will rebel, cutting short your race.

If you're ever going to run an ultramarathon, you have to eat the right things in the right amounts.

In this chapter, we'll look at a lesson the Lord's disciples learned about food for the longest journey of all—the journey of life.

Jesus Enjoys His Meals

One of the things I so love about Jesus as I read the Gospels is the priority He gave to meals. Even though His time on earth was brief, the biblical record gives us a number of examples of His enjoying meals with His disciples. Even after He rose from the dead—to prove the fact He was a real flesh-and-blood person and not a ghost—He asked them to bring Him a piece of fish, which He ate in their presence. (An excellent menu choice, by the way.)

In another encounter, the risen Lord met His disciples on the shore of the Sea of Galilee early one morning. He had some coals burning on the shore with some fresh fish sizzling away on the fire. Remember this beautiful verse in the gospel of John?

Jesus said to them, "Come and eat breakfast." (John 21:12)

Do you even have any doubt about how good those fish must have tasted? Wow! Grilled fish from the Inventor of fish! In the Book of Revelation, Jesus even used the analogy of eating to illustrate what it means to have fellowship with Him. In Revelation 3:20, He said, "Behold, I stand at the door and knock. If anyone hears My voice and opens the door, I will come in to him and dine with him, and he with Me."

When Jesus issued this invitation, He wasn't talking about a TV dinner in the microwave.

It's pretty typical in our culture today for people to eat *quickly*. This is especially true when we're eating lunch at work. We maybe have an hour at most—and often less than that. So we'll go to a take-out restaurant and grab a bag of something to take back to work.

But they didn't have takeout food in the first century. You couldn't just hop into your chariot and hit the drive-through at the local McDavid's. No, in that day and time, meals were leisurely, drawn-out affairs, where people would take time to really enjoy each other's company.

In John 6, we have the story of a huge crowd that had gathered to hear Jesus. But while they were there, lunchtime arrived, and their stomachs were growling. And we read about how the Lord stepped in to meet that need in a stunning way.

Lunch is on Jesus

The "feeding of the five thousand" is the only miracle found in all four of the Gospels. Evidently the Lord thought what happened that day was so important that He wanted us to have it in quadraphonic.

Let's take a minute to read the story in the text:

After these things Jesus went over the Sea of Galilee, which is the Sea of Tiberias. Then a great multitude followed Him, because they saw His signs which He performed on those who were diseased. And Jesus went up on the mountain, and there He sat with His disciples. Now the Passover, a feast of the Jews, was near. Then Jesus lifted up His eyes, and seeing a great multitude coming toward Him, He said to Philip, "Where shall we buy bread, that these may eat?" But this He said to test him, for He Himself knew what He would do. Philip answered Him, "Two hundred denarii worth of bread is not sufficient for them, that every one of them may have a little." One of His disciples, Andrew, Simon Peter's brother, said to Him, "There is a lad here who has five barley loaves and two small fish, but what are they among so many?" Then Jesus said, "Make the people sit down." Now there was much grass in the place. So the men sat down, in number about five thousand. And Jesus took the loaves, and when He had given thanks He distributed them to the disciples, and the disciples to those sitting down; and likewise of the fish, as much as they wanted. (John 6:1–11)

A Teachable Moment

I heard about a little boy who was asked the question, "What is your favorite Bible study?" He responded, "I like that story where everyone loafs and fishes!"

Well, that's not exactly what happened here. But it's one of my favorite Bibles stories too.

Leading up to this miracle, you'd have to say that Jesus had been on a roll. His popularity was growing. His fame was swelling. The crowds were getting bigger and bigger. But why were all these people *really* following Him? Were they doing so because He was their long-awaited Messiah and they wanted to submit themselves to His rule and reign in their lives?

No. John gives us the blunt answer in verse 2: "A huge crowd kept following him wherever he went, because they saw his miracles as he healed the sick" (NLT).

For the most part, these followers were nothing more than thrill seekers. This is demonstrated by their reaction to His words at the end of John 6, where He challenged them to a deeper commitment . . . and most of them turned around and walked away.

When we speak of the "feeding of the five thousand," we need to realize there were more than five thousand there. The text says there were five thousand men present that day—*plus women and children*. That means there were as many as ten thousand people present to witness this dramatic miracle.

As amazing as the teaching certainly was that day, when lunch-time rolled around, the crowd started getting hungry. But as far as we know, there weren't any food vendors selling Hebrew National hotdogs or any grocery stores where people could load up on snacks. There was literally nothing to eat, and the Bible says that Jesus had compassion on these hungry people. Now Jesus, being God, knew very well that these same people were going to reject Him and turn away from Him. He knew they were following Him for all the wrong reasons.

If I had been in the Lord's sandals (scary thought), I don't think I would have responded in quite the way that He did. If I had been in that circumstance, knowing what Jesus knew in that moment, I never would have fed those ungrateful hangers-on (even if I could have). I would have said, "I know why you guys are following me, and I'm not going to give you lunch. In fact, I'm going to eat lunch right in front of you! How do you like that?" (Aren't you glad I'm not the Messiah?)

Jesus, however, had compassion on these people and wanted to feed them and meet their needs. But He also used the miracle as an unforgettable teaching moment for His own followers.

Three primary characters emerge in this story, apart from Jesus himself, and you might find yourself relating to one of them. The Bible records the Lord's encounters with Philip, then Andrew, and finally with a nameless little boy with his lunch bag.

Philip's Big Test

Surrounded by the massive crowds, and seeing they are hungry, Jesus turns to His disciple Philip and gives His first test. And by the way, this is the only recorded time in the Gospels where Jesus ever asked anyone for advice.

> When Jesus looked out and saw that a large crowd had arrived, he said to Philip, "Where can we buy bread to feed these people?" He said this to stretch Philip's faith. He already knew what he was going to do. (vv. 5–6 MSG)

In the course of His ministry, Jesus asked people some deep and searching questions. This wasn't one of them! *"Hey, Philip, how are we going to deal with this problem?"* It shouldn't have been a difficult question at all. For Philip, it was like standing in front of Niagara Falls and wondering where you're going to get a drink of water.

Philip *could* have said, "Well, let's see. . . . Considering the fact that You are God in human form, and . . . considering that You created the heavens and the Earth, I'm sure You could come up with a solution to feed all of these people."

But that's not how Philip replied. In fact, if he had been graded on this little pop quiz, he would have received an F. Philip effectively said, "It would take a small fortune to feed them all, Lord. There's just no way."

How could Philip have responded this way after walking with Jesus for over two years, hearing His teaching, and seeing Him perform miracle after miracle? The fact is, Philip may have had the awesome privilege of walking with Jesus, but he still was spiritually dull to the obvious. He was looking at this situation through human eyes and evaluating it on the basis of human resources.

How pathetic is this? Let me restate that. *How like us is this? How like* me *is this?*

I can think of times when I have come up to what seemed like impossible situations and have thought to myself, *How in the world are we going to handle this? What are we going to do? What's the answer for this?*

And I actually have to come to my senses, and say, "Wait a minute. The Lord knows exactly what I'm facing here, and He has the answer! I need to commit this to Him in prayer right now."

But we forget that sometimes, don't we? And we find ourselves overwhelmed by our situations and circumstances.

Do you ever find yourself (like me) having to relearn the same life lessons over and over again? Maybe when you were younger, the Lord taught you to trust Him for His provision, and you did. But now, as you've gotten older and have enjoyed a stable income for a number of years, maybe it's time to relearn that lesson.

Or maybe there was a time in your life when you didn't know the will of God, and you sought after Him with all your heart and waited on Him for direction. But some time has passed since those days, and you find that you're not relying on Him as you once did. Days slip by, and you realize that you haven't been opening the Bible or seeking Him in prayer as you used to. And God has to reteach you—perhaps through some trying circumstances—what it means to be completely dependent on Him once again.

I'm reminded of the words of Hebrews 5:

> You have been believers so long now that you ought to be teaching others. Instead, you need someone to teach you again the basic things about God's Word. You are like babies who need milk and cannot eat solid food. For someone who lives on milk is still an infant and doesn't know how to do what is right. (vv. 12–13 NLT)

I know people like this, and most likely, so do you. They have known the Lord for years and years, and yet they're still like little spiritual babies who have never learned to fend for themselves or feed themselves spiritually. They need everything simplified for them, given to them in prechewed, bite-sized portions. They don't know how to just open up the Bible and read it and let God speak to their own heart.

We need to learn how to feed ourselves!

One of my great privileges is to take my little granddaughter, Stella, out for lunch. I've done that since she was about fourteen months old! Even at that age, she could feed herself. No, not with a fork or chop sticks of course. She just picked the food up off her little plate or tray and popped it into her mouth. Since that time, of course, she's learned how to eat with utensils, and she's doing a great job.

You and I need to do the same thing with the Word of God.

On the other hand . . . it's easy to tell someone else to trust the Lord for provision until *you* have to. It's easy to tell someone else to trust the Lord for healing, until *you* find yourself needing to trust Him as well.

Philip didn't do so well on this particular test. "Well, Lord, we really don't have enough money to handle it."

So then it was Andrew's turn.

Andrew Comes Close

Andrew, of course, had been listening to this whole exchange with Philip. And even though Jesus hadn't asked him for advice, he was ready to offer up an opinion.

We don't know a lot about Andrew, overshadowed as he was by his brother, Simon Peter. He didn't write any books of the Bible, and—as far as we know—he performed no miracles. But what little we do know is quite impressive.

Andrew was originally one of the followers of John the Baptizer. And it was John who pointed to Jesus and said to Andrew and some others, saying, "Behold! The Lamb of God . . ." (John 1:29).

And so Andrew became a follower of Jesus, and the first thing he did was bring his brother Simon Peter to the Lord. In fact, every time we read about Andrew, he was always bringing someone to Jesus! If that's all that we ever learned about Andrew, what a great pedigree that would be.

In this particular story in John 6, Andrew brings a little boy to Jesus—a boy with a sack lunch: "There's a young boy here with five barley loaves and two fish. But what good is that with this huge crowd?" (v. 9 NLT).

Give Andrew credit. He at least came close! He knew enough to bring this small provision to Jesus . . . but then seems to second-guess himself, saying, "But what am I thinking? What good will this do when the need is so great?"

If only he had followed his first instinct! Right out of the box, the first thing Andrew did was to bring this boy and his small supply of food to Jesus. That was the best and wisest course he could have taken, and Andrew came close to taking a step in faith . . . but not close enough.

Neither Philip nor Andrew were the heroes of this story. The real hero was a little boy . . . and we don't even know his name.

The Little Boy with the Lunch

We may not know this boy's name, but we do know this much: he was poor. How do we know that? Because he brought barley bread with him—the cheapest of all breads at that time. Actually, this was a bread that was held in contempt by many people of that day—the kind of food you would feed to an animal, not to a person.

And then he had a couple of small fish—no doubt little, dried-up things. It's almost as though he was bringing his stale crackers and sardines to Jesus or his Wonder Bread and cold Spam. Whatever it was, it wasn't much. It wasn't a gourmet feast, and it certainly wasn't impressive. *But he brought it to the Lord.*

The lunch was as insignificant as it could be. The boy was as insignificant as he could be. But here's the point of the whole story: *that which was insufficient from the hands of the insignificant became sufficient and significant when placed in the hands of Jesus.*

Don't make the mistake of thinking you have so little to offer that you might as well not even bring it to the Lord.

God can do a lot—more than you could envision in your wildest dreams—with a little.

And that has to be the understatement of the century.

So I can take my life—my talents, my time, my resources, my abilities, such as they are—and lay them down as an offering before God. Then just watch what He does! It's no longer me doing these things; it is Almighty God working in and through me.

Too Big . . . or Too Small?

Getting back to our story . . . why was it that no one seemed to get the idea that Jesus could feed these people? Was it because it seemed like too big of a task for Him? Yes, that might have been part of it.

But maybe some of them didn't think it was too big of a task, but rather too *small* of a task for the Lord. In other words, what does God care about something as insignificant as lunch? God cares about great, dramatic, and newsworthy things like raising the dead, restoring sight to the blind, casting out demons, and healing leprosy.

But lunch? Does He really concern himself with what we eat?

Actually, He does.

In His Sermon on the Mount, Jesus spoke of some basic human needs and said, "For your heavenly Father knows that you need all these things" (Matthew 6:32). He is concerned about what concerns you. And the fact of the matter is, we do think about what we're going to eat. And we do think about what we're going to wear . . . or where we're going to live. We do think about the necessities of life.

That's not evil. That's not even carnal or fleshly. It's just *human*.

In Psalm 103:14, the Bible reminds us that "He knows our frame; He remembers that we are dust." Jesus said, "Seek first the kingdom of God and His righteousness, and all these things shall be added to you" (Matthew 6:33).

He knows and cares about little details—things you might not imagine God would concern himself with. He knows your name, your address, your phone number, and your fondest dreams that you've never shared with anyone. He knows everything about you. In fact, the Bible tells us that the very hairs of our head are numbered. Now experts tell us that the average person has one hundred thousand to two hundred thousand hairs on their head. (I have about a hundred, give or take.) But the point is, God knows about every one of those hairs. He knows about every sparrow that falls to the ground.

Listen . . . the psalmist says He knows about every tear that falls from your eyes. In Psalm 56:8 (TLB) we read, "You have collected all my tears and preserved them in your bottle! You have recorded every one in your book." Jesus shows that nothing is too big for Him to handle and nothing is too small for Him to care about.

The story goes on:

> Then Jesus said, "Make the people sit down." Now there was much grass in the place. So the men sat down, in number about five thousand. And Jesus took the loaves, and when He had given thanks He distributed them to the disciples, and the disciples to those sitting down; and likewise of the fish, as much as they wanted. (vv. 10-11)

Did you catch that phrase? "As much as they wanted."

This wasn't a limited-portion arrangement. No one had to order off the light-eater or senior menu. As the disciples were passing around the food, they weren't required to say, "Please just take one piece of bread and one piece of fish. Let's make sure there's enough for everyone." No, there *was* enough for everyone. Jesus made sure of that.

Have you ever been to one of those restaurants that serve the so-called "gourmet portions"? You know what I mean—a little pile of half-cooked food in the middle of a plate with some decorative sauce drizzled around the edges. Two bites and you're done.

No thank you! I like food that fills a plate. I like to eat until I'm full.

So here were the people on the shore of the Sea of Galilee. They had been hungry, Jesus was feeding them, and they kept on putting it away until they were full.

"Oh, could I have another piece of that bread? It's so fresh! Tastes like it just came out of the oven. And what is it about that fish? Best I've ever tasted. Just a little more, please."

Where was it all coming from? How was this miracle

accomplished? Have you ever tried to visualize how it took place? Maybe you picture Him standing with His hands outstretched over these little loaves and fishes and saying, "Be multiplied!" And then in the blink of an eye, there's this mountain of food.

No, I don't think it was anything as dramatic as that. I think the disciples would go out, distribute a basketful, come back, and there would be more. Then they would hand that out, and there would be more. And more and more and more, until everyone was satisfied.

God gives us what we need when we need it—not necessarily before and never after—but when it is needed.

You might find yourself struggling with some anxious situations in your life right now. And you say, "What would I do if *this* happens?" "How would I ever handle it if *that* happens?" Or maybe, "What would I do if this situation came or this opportunity arose?"

The lesson is simply this: the Lord will give you what you need when the need is there. For right now, He will give you what need for the moment. Your responsibility is simply to bring your loaves and fishes to Jesus.

"Fan into Flame"

God gives to each one of us certain gifts and abilities, and the simple fact is, gifts don't come from God fully developed. You have to *use* them. You have to apply them. You have to practice and gain experience. Sometimes discovering your abilities and gifts is as simple as discovering what you're *not* good at.

It may be a humbling experience, but a lot of times we simply have to go out there, get our hands dirty in the work of the Lord, and find out what we're not particularly good at. You roll up your sleeves and try things. And after a while, with the help of the Holy Spirit and the counsel of others, you can determine how effective you are at what you do.

Then, after you've worked in several different capacities, you find out, "Hey, this is really working. I enjoy it. People are being blessed. God has made me good at this!" Then take that gift, develop it, and cultivate it.

That is what Paul was talking about when he wrote to young Pastor Timothy: "For this reason I remind you to fan into flame the gift of God, which is in you through the laying on of my hands. For the Spirit God gave us does not make us timid, but gives us power, love and self-discipline" (2 Timothy 1:6–7 NIV).

In other words, "Take that ability, take that spiritual gifting, and pursue ministry with all your heart!" God has given to each of us the ability to do certain things well. So get after it! I like the way the J. B. Phillips translation speaks to this in Romans 12:

> Through the grace of God we have different gifts. If our gift is preaching, let us preach to the limit of our vision. If it is serving others let us concentrate on our service; if it is teaching let us give all we have to our teaching; and if our gift be the stimulating of the faith of others let us set ourselves to it. Let the man who is called to give, give freely; let the man in authority work with enthusiasm; and let the man who feels sympathy for his fellows in distress help them cheerfully. (vv. 6–8)

The idea is, take the gift God has given you and use it for His glory.

So, the young boy in John 6 brought what he had to Jesus, and the Lord multiplied it in a way that has had people talking about it for two thousand years. How did the people react? I love the way it's worded in verses 14-15: "Then those men, when they had seen the sign that Jesus did, said, 'This is truly the Prophet who is to come into the world.' Therefore when Jesus perceived that they were about to come and take Him by force to make Him king, He departed again to the mountain by Himself alone."

To me, the whole idea is laughable. Take Him by force? "Hey, You're going to be our king whether You want to be or not. We just decided it!" Why were they doing this? Because these people wanted to use God instead of being used by God.

At this time, of course, they were under Roman occupation—and most loyal Jews wanted their freedom back again. They seem to be reasoning here that if they had Jesus on their side—this miracle worker—they could drive out the Romans.

It wasn't because they recognized Him as the Messiah or because they wanted to submit to His rule and reign. No, they were excited about a leader who could feed them! They were energized by the idea of someone who could work miracles and impress people.

People do this all the time, don't they? They use God for their own purposes. As we enter into an election cycle, we'll see more and more religious rhetoric from our politicians. You'll hear politicians talk about their faith in God, and you'll think to yourself, *Really? I didn't even know they went to church.* You'll see photo ops where they'll be standing in front of a church with a Bible in hand, because they're going after that coveted evangelical voting bloc.

I would simply say, don't be misled just because someone says, "Yes, I'm a Christian. And, oh yes, I believe in God." It's more important to look at their life and to look at their actual voting record than it is to hear nice Christian words coming out of their mouth.

Salespeople will do this too. They'll be cussing and using crude language, trying to sell you something. And then if they happen to find out that you're a believer, it's "Hey, praise the Lord, brother."

A young man might use God in an attempt to soft-talk an attractive Christian girl. He'll claim to have "seen the light" when all he really sees is her. And if she's not wise and very careful, she will be deceived.

The fact is, people will use God in an attempt to get what they want. And that's what these people in John 6 were doing. They wanted to take Jesus by force and make Him king. Why? So they could use Him against the Romans. In other words, they wanted Jesus on their terms, not His terms.

His response? He withdrew from them (see John 6:15). He simply walked away from them and all their schemes. God is no genie in a bottle. Jesus will not be used by us. *But He will use us* if we will come to Him and submit our lives to Him.

So what do we learn from this story? At least five things.

1. We need to show compassion to those who are in need

Knowing that these people were false at heart and would eventually reject Him, He served them anyway. He showed compassion anyway. The miracle in John 6, however, also was a demonstration for the sake of His disciples (and us): In meeting people's physical needs, we're also to minister to people's spiritual needs. Jesus showed this very clearly by immediately transitioning from the topic of physical bread to that of *heavenly* bread, from satisfying a hunger of the stomach to satisfying a hunger of the soul.

Many churches and ministries do wonderful things for people who are in need—feeding them, clothing them, giving them medical treatment, and even building homes for them. There's no doubt that this is Christlike behavior. Come to think of it, I have never seen an atheist relief ministry, have you? I've never witnessed an agnostic feeding program. On the contrary, these are usually the people who seek to mock, attack, and undermine such efforts. All over the world there are followers of Jesus Christ who have responded to deep physical needs of men, women, and children. It doesn't even matter if they are from our country or even if they are of our faith. We reach out in the name of Jesus to them and say that we care and that we want to help.

But let me add something to that. Any church or ministry that provides relief to people in need and fails to give them the gospel is failing in their mission. This is very important, and it's why I support organizations like Samaritan's Purse, with Franklin Graham. It's a relief organization that always brings the saving message of Jesus Christ wherever they go, whomever they serve.

It's a praiseworthy thing to pick someone up out of the gutter to feed and clothe him or her. It does them little good if you simply hand them a gospel tract, say, "Jesus loves you," and then walk away.

On the other hand, to simply help people out of the gutter without ever telling them how their lives can permanently be changed and transformed by Jesus Christ—and how they can have the hope of heaven in His name—misses the point! Every one of those people that I feed and clothe will have to stand one day before the throne of God and give an account for their lives. Apart from the salvation of Christ, they will be separated from God for all eternity.

That is why we can never separate our giving of physical bread to the hungry from our priority of giving them the Bread of Life, who will sustain them forever.

2. Overwhelming need points us to an all-powerful God

There always will be situations in life in which you and I will have neither the resources nor the ability to respond. These will be times when we'll be over our head, out of our depth, and beyond our capacity. Such times as these will serve as tests in our lives. Have we really learned anything about walking with a faithful, powerful, loving God? Have we learned to trust Him? Have we learned to walk by faith when the way seems dark before us?

The way to pass such a test is to see our utter inability to do anything on our own.

That's all Philip needed to do! All he had to say was, "Lord, I have no idea how to handle this situation, but You do. And You're here right now. I'm looking to You. What do You want to do about this, Lord?"

Sometimes you and I find ourselves in a set of circumstances that seem absolutely overwhelming, and we'll say to ourselves, *There's no way out of this one!"*

Those times will come to all of us. When that unexpected bill or expense pops up and you wonder, *How am I ever going to pay this?* When you have that crisis with your spouse and you wonder, *How will we ever get through this?* When that so-called perfect child of yours gets himself or herself into serious trouble, and you wonder, *How will we ever survive this?* Or maybe you're facing a problem at work that seems so far beyond your capacity to deal with that you say, *How am I going to make it through the day?*

Can you trust God? *You must.* God will allow us to enter situations where the only way out is Him. And then, after He enables us to escape the inescapable and accomplish the impossible, He will get the glory.

3. Nothing is too big—or small—for God to respond to

The Bible tells us, "Cast all your anxiety on him because he cares for you" (1 Peter 5:7 NIV).

Which anxieties do we cast on Him—our anxieties for the mountain-sized problems or the gigantic dilemmas in our lives? Yes, but we're also to cast on Him our anxieties over those little worries, nagging fears, and nettlesome problems that buzz around our head like a swarm of bees. It's been said that a person can bleed to death from a thousand paper cuts. In other words, the little worries and burdens in our lives, as more and more of them weigh on our shoulders, can bring us down as effectively as the big issues.

He wants *all* our anxiety. Why? Because He cares for us.

4. Bring all of your abilities and resources to Jesus

Your talents may seem insignificant to you. Your resources may seem ridiculously small in your own eyes. But God can do so very much with so very little!

Just ask the little boy with the sack lunch . . . whose meager little snack, in the hands of Jesus, fed a multitude.

5. Jesus himself sustains us in the ultramarathon of life

I began this chapter by talking about ultramarathons and what people might eat to sustain themselves on a 50-, 60-, or 100-mile run. The fact is, the only way you and I will make it to the finish line is if we feed on Jesus himself.

He will save us. He will sustain us. He will keep us.

Jesus said, "I am the bread of life. Whoever comes to me will never go hungry, and whoever believes in me will never be thirsty" (John 6:35 NIV).

A little later, when the crowd grumbled about this truth, the Lord pressed it home again—just a little bit harder:

> "I am the bread of life. Your ancestors ate the manna in the wilderness, yet they died. But here is the bread that comes down from heaven, which anyone may eat and not die. I am the living bread that came down from heaven. Whoever eats this bread will live forever. This bread is my flesh, which I will give for the life of the world." (vv. 48–51 NIV)

He gave His life for us, and only by taking His life into ourselves will we live forever in heaven. Jesus himself is God's supernatural provision—both of eternal life and of all that we need to sustain our lives on earth.

Just as the Israelites ate manna every day to sustain them on their long journey to the Promised Land, so we need Jesus, the Bread of Life, on our daily journey through life. He is our strength, He is our provision, and He will keep us running and running the race of life until we hit that finish line.

In other words, Jesus is all we need.

WHO WILL FINISH THE RACE?

Back in the 1976, a young athlete named Fred Dixon entered a decathlon in Montreal.

This is an athletic event in which each competitor takes part in the same ten events over the course of two days: the 100-meter dash, long jump, shot put, high jump, 400-meter dash, 110-meter hurdles, discus, pole vault, javelin, and the 1,500-meter run. Traditionally, the title of "World's Greatest Athlete" has been given to the man who wins the decathlon.

Dixon had high hopes as he entered the competition and thought he might be in the running for a title.

But it didn't go the way he had hoped or planned.

Fred ran the first event and didn't do very well. He ran the next one and didn't do any better. He competed in the next event and did even more poorly. When he finally finished the fifth event at the end of the first day, he realized he had no chance at all of winning.

So he quit.

That night, alone with his thoughts, he asked himself what that surrender really meant. *Someday I'm going to have children,* he thought. *And they're going to read about the events in Montreal. And they're going to read that their daddy quit.*

Going back to the athletic field the next day, he pleaded with the officials to let him back into the competition—to let him finish the decathlon. Finally they relented, and Fred competed in the final five events.

In the year that followed, Dixon pushed his way up the charts to become America's number-one decathlete.[1]

If he hadn't gone back to the track the next day, Fred Dixon would have had three initials by his name in the record books: DNF.

Runners hate that acronym. It stands for "Did not finish."

What it means is that an athlete signed up for a particular race, paid an entry fee, clipped on an electronic monitor, lined up at the starting line, and started running with all the other participants at the sound of the starting gun.

But then . . . for some reason . . . he or she never comes across the finish line. When that runner's number doesn't show up, instead of getting a recorded time written in the blank by their name, they get a DNF.

Of course there are always a million excuses. Cramps, a pulled muscle, dehydration, intestinal woes, blisters, heat exhaustion—or maybe even an emergency cell phone call in the middle of the race. There are lots of reasons for not finishing a race, but the sad thing is, none of the excuses get into the record book. You don't get an asterisk with an explanation by your name when you drop out of a race.

You just get a DNF.

You intended to do something, you set a goal, and you started well . . . but somewhere along the way, you dropped out of the race. You didn't finish.

Now, that may be an embarrassing thing for a person who draws his or her identity from being a runner. But it's infinitely worse when you're talking about someone who started a race with Jesus Christ, but then bailed somewhere along the way.

When it comes to the spiritual life, you never, never want a DNF.

Finishing What You Start

Finishing what you start is a major theme in the New Testament, and Jesus himself spoke to that theme in several different ways.

He talked about a builder who didn't finish a tower and became a laughing stock. He talked about a king who thought about going to war, but then changed his mind when he saw he might be outnumbered. He talked about a man who put his hand to the plow to cultivate a field, but then turned back and never got the job done.

He also talked about a farmer scattering seeds and why some of those seeds were productive . . . but others fell short.

"Falling short"—those are two words you never want to hear if you're in an athletic contest. You don't want to hear that your football team lost by a field goal in double overtime. You don't want to watch your favorite baseball team lose in the ninth inning because of an errant throw. You don't want to give up on a marathon at mile twenty-four because of a blister.

In an athletic event, you want to push on through, win the day, and stay the course. In the parable of the sower, Jesus used a story from nature to talk about those who finish . . . and those who don't.

When they sowed seed back in those days, they reversed the familiar practice and did the plowing *after* the sowing. It's the idea of a farmer walking along with a bag of seed and just flinging it out as far as he can, letting the wind pick it up. Then he would come back and do the plowing later.

That's the explanation as to why this seed is falling on different types of soil. The passion of the farmer is to scatter that seed as far and wide and in as many nooks and crannies as it can possibly go. Will it all grow and bear fruit? He knows it won't. But he does everything he can as he sows to increase that possibility.

That's a good picture of our job as believers—to get the gospel out to as many people as we can, whenever and wherever we can. Will all our efforts be successful? Obviously not. But it's also true that the more we sow, the more we will reap.

To briefly change metaphors, it's a bit like fishing with a huge net, dragging it through the ocean. You'll get all kinds of stuff if you do that—fish, beer cans, and maybe a couple of snorkelers—just whatever happens to be there.

When our team goes into an area and does our Harvest Crusades, we get all kinds of people filling the stadiums or arenas. Some come because a friend has invited them. Others have noticed a poster or a flyer. And some just hear the crusade from a distance—as people did at our Central California Crusade on youth night.

The music was *loud* that night. We heard later about a man who had been mowing his lawn a few blocks away and heard the noise coming from the campus where we held our event. Out of curiosity, he came to see what it was all about. He ended up hearing the gospel and went forward during the invitation time and gave his life to Christ.

A number of years ago, a man was about to rob a liquor store in Anaheim and saw the lights on at Angel Stadium, where we were holding a Harvest Crusade. It perplexed him, because he knew the Angels weren't playing at that time. So he went to check out what this was all about. He, too, ended up hearing the gospel and gave his life to Christ that night.

So here's the idea: you just throw out that net, and you catch all kinds of people. Time will tell if they are real converts, but we want to reach as many people as we possibly can.

Why Do People Respond the Way They Do?

You pray for certain people, invite them to church or an evangelistic event, and they refuse—perhaps even with hostility. Why is that? Why is it they "just don't get it"?

Here are some other questions: Why is it that someone seems to be radically converted and then just suddenly falls away? Was this person really saved? If so, have they lost their salvation? For that matter, why do people fall away from the Lord to begin with? What steps can I take to make sure I won't fall away from the Lord myself? And what is the secret of going forward spiritually and producing lasting fruit in my life? How can you and I make sure we don't get a DNF for the most important race in our lives?

The answers to those questions and others are found in the account we're about to explore:

> And when a great multitude had gathered, and they had come to
> Him from every city, He spoke by a parable: "A sower went out to

sow his seed. And as he sowed, some fell by the wayside; and it was trampled down, and the birds of the air devoured it. Some fell on rock; and as soon as it sprang up, it withered away because it lacked moisture. And some fell among thorns, and the thorns sprang up with it and choked it. But others fell on good ground, sprang up, and yielded a crop a hundredfold." When He had said these things He cried, "He who has ears to hear, let him hear!"

Then His disciples asked Him, saying, "What does this parable mean?" And He said, "To you it has been given to know the mysteries of the kingdom of God, but to the rest it is given in parables, that 'Seeing they may not see, and hearing they may not understand.'

"Now the parable is this: The seed is the word of God. Those by the wayside are the ones who hear; then the devil comes and takes away the word out of their hearts, lest they should believe and be saved. But the ones on the rock are those who, when they hear, receive the word with joy; and these have no root, who believe for a while and in time of temptation fall away. Now the ones that fell among thorns are those who, when they have heard, go out and are choked with cares, riches, and pleasures of life, and bring no fruit to maturity. But the ones that fell on the good ground are those who, having heard the word with a noble and good heart, keep it and bear fruit with patience. (Luke 8:4–15)

There's an interesting statement in this parable. Jesus cried out, "He who has ears to hear, let him hear!" Another way to state it? *Listen up.*

Jesus is saying, "You really need to pay attention to what I am telling you in this parable . . . *because it applies to you.*" And so it does. It's a story that has application to every one of our lives, reminding us how vital it is to listen in the right way to God's Word.

I'm reminded of an account from the life of President Franklin Roosevelt, who often had to endure long greeting lines at the White House—people wanting to meet the president, get a photo with him, and so forth.

One day he told one of his aides, "No one ever listens to a word that I say." To prove his point, he tried an experiment. To each person he met in one of the endless lines going by one day, he murmured the words, "I murdered my grandmother this morning."

So an individual would shake his hand and say, "Mr. President, it is an honor to meet you." And Roosevelt would smile, nod, and reply, "I murdered my grandmother this morning."

Person after person went by. He said it again and again and again. And it wasn't until the end of the line, when greeting a foreign diplomat, that his words were actually heard. With a smile and a twinkle in his eye, the diplomat leaned over and said, "She probably deserved it, Mr. President."[2]

So at least one guy was listening.

The truth is, we all need to learn how to listen when God speaks to us in His Word. That's what we really see in this parable: It's a story of how different people listened to or received the Word.

Now let's look at four categories of hearers.

Category 1: The Highway Hearers

> "Those by the wayside are the ones who hear; then the devil comes and takes away the word out of their hearts, lest they should believe and be saved." (v. 12)

Whenever and wherever the Word of God is going out, the devil will be there to oppose it. That is a simple fact of spiritual life, and we ought to know it and never be surprised by it.

Who are the people the Lord refers to in this verse? These are the people who hear the Word of God but never allow it to actually take root in their lives.

Jesus illustrates this by the birds that descend on the fields and scoop up the loose seed. You've no doubt seen the little birds that hang out at fast-food restaurants, just waiting for some crumbs to hit the pavement, so they can swoop in and gobble them up. Sometimes the little beggars get greedy and hop right up on the table.

Now, we all love birds, but in this parable, the Lord uses them to depict evil. They are a picture of Satan and his evil hordes who try to steal away the Word of God that has just been sown in a person's life.

It's a picture of an individual who seems to be friendly and receptive to your witness, but it just doesn't compute. You invite him or her to church, and no, they don't want to go. And they'll offer up a plethora of excuses.

The bottom line is they simply don't want to expose themselves to the Word of God. Why? Jesus gave the answer in John 3:19. He said, "This is the verdict: Light has come into the world, but people loved darkness instead of light because their deeds were evil" (NIV).

They'll tell you, "The church is full of hypocrites." Or, "I have to work on Sunday." Or it will be something else, some other excuse. But the real reason they don't want to go is because they don't want their evil deeds to be exposed. They don't want to change their lifestyle.

Why have they become so hard? Because of sin. Sin truly does harden the heart, and the hardened heart sins even more. There is nothing that you or I will say that will convince them.

Paul says in 2 Corinthians 4:3–4, "If the Good News we preach is hidden to anyone, it is hidden from the one who is on the road to eternal death. Satan, who is the god of this evil world, has made him blind, unable to see the glorious light of the Gospel that is shining upon him or to understand the amazing message we preach about the glory of Christ, who is God" (TLB).

So what do you do with people like this? You pray for them. You pray that God will open their eyes, and you don't give up on them.

And here's something important to remember: Sometimes there are people who appear to be this category, appear to be hard, cynical, or disinterested, who are, in reality, wide open. In fact, that was the case with me. Before I became a Christian, I had a façade that I always hid behind. And my façade was that "I'm not interested and don't care about anything you might have to say to me."

But it was all a sham. In reality, I was very interested. In fact, I longed for someone to come and share with me what it meant to know God. But no one ever did.

There are people who will hide behind such a façade, and outwardly, they'll seem as hard as sunbaked clay. But the truth is, they're just waiting for someone who will care enough about them to persist a little with the message.

Consider the woman at the well, in John 4. When Jesus first approached her, she was flippant, sarcastic, even disrespectful. But Jesus pressed on, and He won a convert on that hot afternoon in Samaria.

You and I need to pray for discernment and wisdom from the Lord to know whom we should speak to.

But this first category, these "highway hearers," just don't get it. We need to pray that, finally, they will.

Category 2: The Rocky Road Hearers

> "But the ones on the rock are those who, when they hear, receive the word with joy; and these have no root, who believe for a while and in time of temptation fall away." (v. 13)

In contrast to the hardheartedness or indifference of the highway hearers, we now consider hearers who initially get excited about the truth but quickly fall away.

The picture Jesus uses is of a plant shooting up rapidly—and perhaps even flowering—but never really taking root.

If you ever visit Israel, you'll notice right away that there are lots and lots of rocks. Rocks are everywhere—on top of the soil, right beneath the soil, and deeply imbedded in the soil. And so it was in the days when Jesus walked that land.

The idea in verse 13 is of a seed that hits the soil, immediately germinates, and begins to shoot up in the bright sunlight. But because there is a rock directly beneath it, it never can get its roots down. As a result, it just withers away in the sun.

This is the picture of the person who seems to be converted but really never is. In contrast to the person who won't even go with you to a crusade, this person not only goes, but they respond when the invitation is given.

The next day—oh my goodness—all that joy, all those changes! All they can talk about is Jesus, and they seem so passionate about it. You take them to church on Sunday, and they sing louder than anyone else. They lift their hands higher than anyone else. They may even become a bit impatient with others who aren't quite as passionate as they are! You think to yourself, *Wow. That's one of the most dramatic conversions I have ever seen.*

And then one day, out of the clear blue, they suddenly drop off the radar. You don't see them in church, and the next thing you know, they are back into full-blown sin again. You wonder, *What happened?*

In addition, I have found that those in this category frequently will become the most hardened and cynical about the Christian faith. They'll say (dismissively), "Oh yeah, I went through that whole Christianity phase." The truth is, however, their faith never took root. They never got a correct foundation. Their response to the truth was purely intellectual or emotional. It's not that they were converted and became "unconverted." *They never were really saved to begin with.*

You say, "Greg, why would you say such a thing?"

I say it because, if they had been saved, they would have stayed on board. In the little book of 1 John, we read these words: "These people left our churches, but they never really belonged with us; otherwise they would have stayed with us. When they left, it proved that they did not belong with us." (2:19 NLT)

I'm not saying that a Christian won't stumble or even become a prodigal and wander for a time. But I am saying that if you profess faith in Christ, then turn your back on Him and never follow Him after that, you are not a person who lost your salvation; you are a person who never was saved to begin with. If you truly had been born again, there would have been changes in your life. You would have stuck with it, and your conversion would have stood the test of time. That's how we know who the real converts are.

Some people are simply impulsive by nature. If you don't believe me, just drive down any neighborhood street on a Saturday afternoon. People have their garage doors open, and you can see all those expensive treadmills and exercise machines claiming valuable garage floor space. And how often do you see someone in there working out on the exercise machine? Never! More likely, you'll see things hanging on them or stacked on top of them.

That's how it is: People feel discouraged about their weight or physical condition and suddenly decide to "do something about it," impulsively buying exercise equipment or a big hardcover book on the XYZ Diet. But if there's no follow-through, it's only a waste of money.

In the same way, in the spirit of "I think I'll try this. I think I'll try that," people will say, "I think I'll be a Christian." But it's only a shallow, surface sort of thing, not a genuine life surrender.

Why do people shoot up like plants and then fade away in a day? It's because they never have truly rooted themselves in Christ. Or when the first temptation comes their way, they give in and never follow through with their decision to surrender to Jesus.

Our Lord speaks of "these [who] have no root, who believe for a while and in time of temptation fall away" (v. 13). Temptation, of course, will come into the life of every Christian. The devil will always seek to entice people away from their allegiance to Jesus. He always will be there, challenging the work that God has done.

It's been said that Christians are a lot like tea bags: You don't know what they're made of until you put them into hot water. And every Christian will be put into the hot water of temptation, testings, and trials.

In Matthew's version of the parable of the sower, Jesus said, "For when tribulation or persecution arises because of the word, immediately he stumbles" (Matthew 13:21).

Some believers who experience persecution for the first time recoil and say, "Hey, I don't want this! I didn't sign up for this." Nevertheless, if you are a true follower of Jesus, you will experience some form of persecution. The Bible says, "Yes, and all who desire to live godly in Christ Jesus will suffer persecution" (2 Timothy 3:12).

I remember when I was a brand-new Christian and told all my buddies how I had accepted the Lord. Basically, they mocked me and laughed at me. So you know what I did? I traded them in on a new set of friends, because I realized these guys were dragging me down.

You might want to think a little bit about the people you call your friends, and ask yourself if they are encouraging you or discouraging you in your relationship with God. If they are dragging you down, if they are pulling you away, then you need some new friends too. You need friends who love the Lord and will encourage you to do the same. The Bible tells us to "flee also youthful lusts; but pursue righteousness, faith, love, peace, with those who call on the Lord out of a pure heart" (2 Timothy 2:22).

Find some godly friends who can lift you up. And be a godly friend that can lift others up as well.

It may be the challenge of discipleship that turns a potential follower of Christ away. In the Gospel of John we read that after Jesus laid down some pretty direct statements, many of His disciples turned away and deserted Him. Turning to the Twelve, Jesus said,

> "Do you also want to go away?" But Simon Peter answered Him, "Lord, to whom shall we go? You have the words of eternal life." (John 6:67–68)

Jesus told us to count the cost of being His disciple. That's why Paul wrote to Timothy and said, "Endure hardship as a good soldier of Jesus Christ" (2 Timothy 2:3).

The Christian life is not a stroll through the park. It's not a playground; it's a battleground. Some people are rocked back on their heels when they realize that. "Wow, this is harder than I thought it was going to be. I'm going to be tempted . . . I'm going to be persecuted . . . people are going to give me a hard time."

Some new believers fall away when they hit their first emotional low. That's why I don't really like it when people talk about "getting high on Jesus." That is not going to work . . . and it certainly won't last.

Certainly, many people report a real emotional experience when they come to Christ or when they're worshiping Him. That's very good, and those are experiences to be treasured. But what about those times when you won't feel any emotions at all? What will you do then? Will you still be "high on Jesus" or will you look for a high someplace else? The fact is, Jesus is not a drug or an additive or even an "experience." He is God. He is the Lord. And He wants you to worship Him and conform your life to His plan and purpose for you—which may or may not give you an emotional buzz every day.

So what will you do? Walk away from Jesus because you can't feel Him on a given day? Or, will you learn what it means to walk by faith and not by feeling? The Bible says, "The just shall live by faith" (Romans 1:17).

The "rocky road hearers" are those whose eyes have been opened to a spiritual need and have moved in that direction but have never sunk their spiritual roots into Christ himself. Yes, there may be some temporary changes in their lives, but they will not be the most important changes.

Category 3: The Thorny Hearers

> "Now the ones that fell among thorns are those who, when they have heard, go out and are choked with cares, riches, and pleasures of life, and bring no fruit to maturity." (v. 14)

I have always been amazed by weeds and how quickly they grow. You can have your little plants that you nurture and fertilize and water and talk to, and you wonder if they are ever going to grow. Then in the same amount of time it took your plant to grow a quarter of an inch, some ugly weed sprouts up through a crack in the sidewalk and grows thirteen feet high!

If you've ever dealt with weeds, you know they don't suddenly burst out of the soil, lunge at the stem of the flower, and shake it violently. No, it is not like a mugging; it's more like slow, gradual intimidation. The weed grows faster than your plant and seems to move closer to it every day. Then one morning, you notice that it's intertwined around your plant, choking the life out of it.

So who is Jesus talking about here? He's speaking of people who make a commitment to Christ but, over a period of time, other things crowd Him out. What other things? Jesus calls them "the cares, riches, and pleasures of life." He doesn't specifically say "sin," though the implication could include that.

Actually, these "cares, riches, and pleasures" may not even necessarily be bad things in and of themselves. It is not always the bad things that bring us down! It has been said that more have been killed by food than by poison. The bottom line here is that the second best often becomes the mortal enemy of the best.

This is not a person who necessarily would say, "I don't want to read the Bible. I don't want to go to church." This would be a person who would say, "I have every intention of reading the Bible. I plan on going to church." They just never get around to it.

You'll say, "Let's go to church this Sunday."

And they will reply, "Thanks, but I can't."

"Why not?"

"Because I'm golfing."

"Okay. Let's go the next Sunday."

"No . . . I can't."

"Why?"

"Because I have a triathlon."

"Oh. Well, let's go the Sunday after that."

"I can't."

"Why?"

"It's Super Sunday! The big game is on TV."

"Wait a second. I thought you said you wanted to go to church."

"I do."

"Well, let's read the Bible."

"I can't."

"Why?"

"Just too busy."

You see, it is not that these are evil things that crowd out the good seed, it's just *other* things. It seems like anything is more important to them than the most important consideration of all. They have time in their busy schedule for everything but that which matters most.

Gradually, like a weed entwining its tendrils around the stem of a growing plant, the physical becomes more important than the spiritual, and the temporal becomes more important than the eternal. Catching that favorite TV show is more important than the Bible. Taking in that new movie seems more appealing than church.

This individual may pay lip service to the importance of spiritual things, but when push comes to shove, he or she always will prioritize other activities or commitments over setting time aside to seek the Lord.

The truth is, if you have really met God, you will have a hunger for His Word. One of the key traits of the first century church was they "continued steadfastly" in the apostles' doctrine and in the breaking of bread and in prayer and so forth (see Acts 2:42). And that term "continued steadfastly" speaks of a real passion. These were people who deeply cared about what they were doing. And if you really love the Lord, then you will hunger for the Word of God and long to be with the people of God.

One of the first things a doctor will ask you if you're not feeling well is, "How's your appetite been?" The reason the doctor will ask that question is because a hungry person most likely will be a healthy person. (Which is how I know I'm so healthy right now!)

In the spiritual sense, too, a hungry person will be a healthy person (if he or she consumes the right things!). A hungry believer longs for more and more of the Word of God. As Peter writes, "Like newborn babies, crave pure spiritual milk, so that by it you may grow up in your salvation" (1 Peter 2:2 NIV).

Do you long for God's Word? If you've missed a day, do you experience a strong desire to spend time in its pages, letting the Holy Spirit speak to you through the words?

In Psalm 1, David tells about those who "delight in doing everything God wants them to, and day and night are always meditating on his laws and thinking about ways to follow him more closely" (Psalm 1:2 TLB).

That's a hungry man, a hungry woman. And you can step back and just watch them grow right before your eyes.

Category 4: Fruitful Hearers

> "But the ones that fell on the good ground are those who, having heard the word with a noble and good heart, keep it and bear fruit with patience." (v. 15)

Having heard the word, these hearers *retain* it. They hold on to it, letting it root deeply in their lives, and they do something with it.

That's one reason why you and I aren't going to know who the real believers are until much later.

I often say there will be three surprises when we get to heaven. First, the people we thought would be there won't be there. Second, the people we never thought would be there are there. Third, we will be there! (I'm just kidding on that last one, because I fully expect to be there.)

In this parable, Jesus says that you determine what kind of soil your heart will resemble by how you hear and respond to the Word of God. God's desire is for us to be receptive to His Word—not just as a hearer, but as a doer.

Jesus put it this way as He wrapped up His Sermon on the Mount.

> "Therefore whoever hears these sayings of Mine, and does them, I will liken him to a wise man who built his house on the rock: and the rain descended, the floods came, and the winds blew and beat on that house; and it did not fall, for it was founded on the rock. But everyone who hears these sayings of Mine, and does not do them, will be like a foolish man who built his house on the sand: and the rain descended, the floods came, and the winds blew and beat on that house; and it fell. And great was its fall."
> (Matthew 7:24–27)

Everything hinges on what you *do* with the Word of God after you have heard it! So . . . what are you going to do with the Word of God you just encountered in this story?

It's up to you. Do you want to follow through on this and become a fruitful believer? If you do, if that is your heart and your desire, then that is just what will happen in the Lord's timing.

Looking back on this parable, what kind of heart do you have? Which category would you fit into? Are you category number one: indifferent to the love of God and His offer of salvation? I doubt it—or you wouldn't be reading this book. But it's possible.

Are you category number two? Perhaps you're a person who once seemed to make a commitment to Christ, crowded up close to the Light, and experienced and felt some initial excitement and joy. But now you wonder if you ever really knew the Lord at all.

Are you category number three, where you have told people that you're a Christian, but find that you simply have no time in your life for God, His Word, and His people?

Or are you in category number four, where you're seeking to follow the Lord with all your heart and soul, loving Him, and hungering for His Word? No, you're definitely not perfect, and you're still making more mistakes every day than you would like, but you are seeking to become more like Jesus each and every day.

In fact, it's your choice!

If you *want* to sink your roots into the soil of God's Word and become a blooming, vibrant, fruit-bearing plant, then God himself will help you.

Jesus is a Master Gardener, and you will be His special delight.

And you won't cross the finish line empty-handed.

"IT IS FINISHED!"

Iremember someone telling me about running his first marathon. It was in Hawaii, and over the course of the twenty-six-plus miles, the heat and humidity became almost too much to bear.

Finally, he saw the finish line up ahead, somehow summoned the last ounce of his strength, and staggered across the line he had been dreaming about for hours and hours—a line that at times seemed he would never, ever reach.

But it wasn't the finish line.

What he had imagined to be his goal was something else . . . and he had several hundred yards left to go. Uphill.

He did finish. In spite of his mistake, he crossed the real finish line just a little while later. But it must have been the most difficult stretch of ground he had ever covered!

For every runner, there is that last mile, the last lap, the last few yards.

In a similar way, for every person who walks this earth, there will be a last meal, a last breath, and, of course, a last statement.

Sometimes, what we say at the end will be an insight into what we were in life—what we stood for, what we lived for. Because generally we will die as we have lived.

Consider the final words of American patriot Nathan Hale, who was hung by the British for spying. Right before he was executed, his final words were, "I only regret that I have but one life to lose for my country."[1]

Nathan Hale knew what his last words would be, and that was the final statement he wanted to give. Many of us, however, won't get to choose those last words, because we won't see the end coming.

In another example, the attending physician of American Revolutionary War General Ethan Allen was apparently trying to comfort his dying patient when he told him, "General, I fear the angels are waiting for you."

Allen snapped, "Waiting are they? Waiting are they? Well, let 'em wait!"[2] And then he passed on.

Then there were the final words of "Buckey" O'Neill. William "Buckey" O'Neill was quite a character. Throughout his lifetime he was an Arizona lawyer, a miner, a cowboy, newspaperman, a sheriff, a congressman, and a gambler. He was also one of the members of Teddy Roosevelt's Rough Riders during the Spanish-American War. O'Neill was a tough, fearless, man's man right to the end.

On the field of battle, prior to Roosevelt's famous charge up Kettle Hill, Buckey O'Neill stood on the battle lines smoking a cigarette and joking with his troops. When Spanish forces on the ridge delivered a burst of withering fire, one of O'Neill's sergeants shouted to him above the noise, "Captain, a bullet is sure to hit you!"

O'Neill responded, "Sergeant, the Spanish bullet isn't made that will kill me."

Guess what happened next? You guessed it. And those were O'Neill's "famous last words."[3]

Death is no respecter of persons. We're all going to give that final statement one day—be it hours or just seconds before our passing. We may know it, and see it coming, as Nathan Hale did. Or we may have no clue that death is near, like "Buckey" O'Neill. But it's going to happen.

The Gospels give us the final words of our Lord Jesus Christ— easily the most important last words given by any person at any time ever.

The fact that Jesus finished His race, completing what He set out to do on earth, is for you and me the most important truth that ever could be.

If He hadn't finished, we would be lost forever.

But because He did finish, the very doors of heaven have swung open to us.

What did He say as crossed that finish line? To find out, we must step into those final hours, after Jesus had been arrested and turned over to the Roman authorities.

"Behold the Man"

Then Pilate called together the leading priests and other religious leaders, along with the people, and he announced his verdict. "You brought this man to me, accusing him of leading a revolt. I have examined him thoroughly on this point in your presence and find him innocent. Herod came to the same conclusion and sent him back to us. Nothing this man has done calls for the death penalty. So I will have him flogged, and then I will release him."

Then a mighty roar rose from the crowd, and with one voice they shouted, "Kill him, and release Barabbas to us!" (Barabbas was in prison for taking part in an insurrection in Jerusalem against the government, and for murder.) Pilate argued with them, because he wanted to release Jesus. But they kept shouting, "Crucify him! Crucify him!"

For the third time he demanded, "Why? What crime has he committed? I have found no reason to sentence him to death. So I will have him flogged, and then I will release him."

But the mob shouted louder and louder, demanding that Jesus be crucified, and their voices prevailed. So Pilate sentenced Jesus to die as they demanded. As they had requested, he released Barabbas, the man in prison for insurrection and murder. But he turned Jesus over to them to do as they wished. (Luke 23:13–25 NLT)

Notice that Pilate said, "I will have him flogged." And that's what he did, directing his soldiers to give Jesus thirty-nine lashes across the back with the Roman cat-of-nine-tails. Pilate, hoping that would appease the bloodthirsty crowd, said, "Behold the Man!" (John 19:5). In other words, "Have a little mercy people. Come on, have you had enough?"

But no. They still wanted Him crucified.

Finally, the governor, who was very uneasy about pronouncing sentence on Jesus, called for a bowl of water and washed his hands in front of everyone. "I am free from this," he basically told them. "I am not responsible."

But of course he was.

In Luke 23, we read: "Now as they led [Jesus] away, they laid hold of a certain man, Simon a Cyrenian, who was coming from the country, and on him they laid the cross that he might bear it after Jesus. . . . There were also two others, criminals, led with Him to be put to death. 33 And when they had come to the place called Calvary, there they crucified Him, and the criminals, one on the right hand and the other on the left" (vv. 26, 32–33).

Before they crucified Him, the soldiers amused themselves by mocking Jesus. They pretended to bow before Him as king, slipping a royal robe over His lacerated shoulders. Then someone had the idea to weave a crown of long-spiked thorns and press it down onto His head. Someone else handed him a stick and said, "That's your scepter, King." Then they took the stick and beat Him with it and beat Him in the face with their fists.

Have you ever been hit in your face with a fist? We've all seen it a million times in the movies, and it doesn't look that bad, does it? Some guy gets smacked in the face with a haymaker and pops back up like it didn't really bother him.

Have you seen the *Rocky* movies? You've got to love Rocky's strategy, which seems to be "wear your opponent out with your face." Toward the end of the fight, the big, bad opponent is always pummeling poor Sylvester Stallone's face like it was a punching bag. His eyes are swollen shut, he's bleeding like crazy, and he's yelling, "Yo! Adrian, I love you!"

But if you have ever really been hit in the face, then you know what that's like. It's traumatizing. It's shocking. It *hurts*. And that's what these sadistic legionnaires were doing to Jesus.

When they made Him hold a fake scepter, it was as if to say, "All right, King Jesus, where's Your army? Why aren't they protecting You?"

Oh, little did they know.

Little did they know how *easily* He could have gotten out of that situation.

Angel Armies on Standby

Where were His armies?

They were on standby. There were angels there, no doubt with swords drawn, just waiting for the word. When Jesus had been arrested in the Garden of Gethsemane, Peter tried to defend Jesus with a sword. The Lord told him to put it away. And looking Peter right in the eyes, He said, "Do you think that I cannot now pray to My Father, and He will provide Me with more than twelve legions of angels?" (Matthew 26:53).

How many angels are in a legion? A Roman legion was comprised of six thousand soldiers. Essentially, Jesus was saying, "Look, I have twenty-two thousand angels at My disposal right now."

And just in case you might be wondering what a powerful force that might be, we read in the Old Testament of a single angel killing one hundred eighty-five thousand enemy soldiers in a night. So you might imagine that twenty-two thousand angels—protecting their King—could do some serious damage.

But the angels remained on standby, because Jesus didn't call them. He took the beating, the abuse, the mockery, and the systematic destruction of His body, because that is why He came. That is why He was born in that stable in Bethlehem. One of the wise men who paid honor to the young Christ child recognized this by offering Him the gift of myrrh, an embalming element. He was born to die.

So now we read in verse Luke 23:26, "They led Him away." They might have thought they were forcing Him to walk that road to the cross. But the truth is, nothing could have kept Him from it. As it tells us in the Book of Isaiah, Jesus "set [His] face like a flint" toward His great purpose and destiny (Isaiah 50:7).

He even had to carry His own cross. No small thing, because

that crude instrument of execution probably weighed between two hundred and four hundred pounds—with no wheels at the bottom for ease of transport.

Maybe if you're a body builder, you've dealt with some pretty heavy weights in the gym. But chances are you didn't have to lift that weight after being up all night, being beaten with fists, and having the skin torn off your back and your muscles lacerated by a Roman scourging.

Jesus, the true man's man, carried his own cross as far as He could. So much for the pale, anemic, wimpy versions of Jesus that we often see depicted in religious art.

Let me put it in the vernacular: Jesus was one buff dude. He was tough. He wasn't persevering through this ordeal in His strength as the Son of God; He was carrying that cross as a Man—a Man who had bled, suffered, and endured horrific physical abuse. Understandably, He eventually fell under the weight of it.

That's where a simple bystander named Simon entered the picture.

> A certain man from Cyrene, Simon, the father of Alexander and Rufus, was passing by on his way in from the country, and they forced him to carry the cross. (Mark 15:21 NIV)

For a few steps, we don't how exactly how far, this man Simon was able to relieve some of the suffering of Jesus, by carrying His cross. Now at the time, Simon probably didn't want to do this. But what he wanted mattered nothing, because you didn't say no to the Roman soldiers. There are, however, some Bible scholars who assert that as a result of this experience, Simon and members of his family ended up becoming believers. Mark calls him "the father of Alexander and Rufus," who were well-known members of the church at Rome in later years.

I would like to have done that for Jesus myself. If I could go back in time, if I could get in a time machine and be there at that moment, my desire would be to carry the cross for Jesus, if only for just a few feet. I wish I could have been Simon, and I think quite a number of us who love Jesus feel that way.

Here is some news for you: You *can* carry that cross today. And you must. "Greg," you might reply, "what are you saying? That we should all get crosses and carry them through streets?"

Yes, in a way I am saying that—not literally, but metaphorically. Because Jesus said, "If anyone desires to come after Me, let him deny himself, and take up his cross, and follow Me" (Matthew 16:24).

What does that mean? He went on to explain: "For whoever desires to save his life will lose it, but whoever loses his life for My sake will find it" (v. 25)

So when Jesus tells us to take up our cross as Christians today, it means that we are to place God's will above our own. It means that we take our plans and our aspirations and offer them to God. It means that we will stand up for Him and speak well of Him when it's definitely not popular or politically correct to do so. It means we obey His Word and do what He tells us to do. It means we will love God more than anyone or anything else. To take up the cross and follow Jesus is a willingness to make any sacrifice He asks.

Are you taking up your cross? You don't have to go back in time and wish you were Simon of Cyrene. You can and you must carry the cross today.

And when you do, that's when you begin to live life at its fullest! I know that sounds contradictory, because when we think of someone carrying a cross, we think, "Oh, that is a hard life . . . a miserable life . . . a life of deprivation and sadness."

Well, no.

Actually Jesus said, "Whoever loses his life for My sake will find it." In other words, when you offer your life to God and look for His plans for you, then you will discover that His plans for you are far, far better than your plans for yourself!

That is why Paul wrote, "I have been crucified with Christ; it is no longer I who live, but Christ lives in me . . ." (Galatians 2:20).

So take up your cross and follow Jesus. Simon did just that, and so can we.

The Dreaded Moment

> And when they had come to the place called Calvary, there they crucified Him. . . . (Luke 16:33)

Luke gives no further explanation here, because none was needed. Back in the New Testament times, everybody knew about crucifixion. Everybody had seen crucifixion. It was a very, very dark—but not unusual—occurrence.

The fact and the manner of Christ's death fulfilled many Old Testament prophecies. In Psalm 22, in particular, we see graphic glimpses into the physical anguish of crucifixion—written a thousand years before the first such execution had ever taken place!

> My God, My God, why have You forsaken Me? Why are You so far from helping Me, and from the words of My groaning? . . . All those who see Me ridicule Me; they shoot out the lip, they shake the head, saying, "He trusted in the Lord, let Him rescue Him; let Him deliver Him, since He delights in Him! . . . I am poured out like water, and all My bones are out of joint; My heart is like wax; it has melted within Me. My strength is dried up like a potsherd, and My tongue clings to My jaws; You have brought Me to the dust of death. . . . They pierced My hands and My feet; I can count all My bones. They look and stare at Me. They divide My garments among them, and for My clothing they cast lots. (vv. 1, 7–8, 14–18)

Here is Jesus now. His back already has been shredded open, and He is lying on a crude wooden cross. A nail is driven through each hand and then His feet—His left foot would have been pressed together against the right foot, and a nail driven through both.

People who were crucified did not die by the crucifixion itself. In fact, crucifixion was really death by slow suffocation, because you became (eventually) unable to breathe. The executioners put a little step at the base of the cross, which the crucified man could use to put his weight on, pushing up, in order to get breath into his lungs. Obviously, with nails through your hands, a nail through your feet, and a back ripped open by a Roman whip, that in itself would cause pain almost beyond comprehension. And so Jesus was experiencing the worst kind of trauma at this point.

I read a doctor's report on crucifixion, where physicians had studied what happened physically to crucified persons. Physical symptoms include a swollen tongue, a congestion of the blood in the head, lungs, and heart, and the swelling of virtually every vein. How do you even describe such agony?

Again from Psalm 22, in *The Living Bible*:

> My strength has drained away like water, and all my bones are out of joint. My heart melts like wax; my strength has dried up like sun-baked clay; my tongue sticks to my mouth, for you have laid me in the dust of death. The enemy, this gang of evil men, circles me like a pack of dogs; they have pierced my hands and feet. I can count every bone in my body. See these men of evil gloat and stare; they divide my clothes among themselves by a toss of the dice. (vv. 14–18)

Somehow, hanging on that cross, Jesus found the wherewithal to speak. Breathing was hard. Speaking was harder. And yet Jesus gave seven statements from the cross, each one significant, each one poignant with meaning. We will focus in on just three of these in this chapter.

"Father, Forgive Them . . ."

> Then Jesus said, "Father, forgive them, for they do not know what they do." (Luke 23:34)

Had the first words of Jesus been, "My God, My God, why have You forsaken Me," or "I thirst," we would have understood. But His first words from the cross were "Father, forgive them. . . ." Forgive who? *Forgive the ones who did this to Me. Forgive the ones who betrayed Me. The ones who tried Me. The ones who sent me here on false charges. The ones who scourged Me. That ones who hit Me. The ones who crucified Me. The ones who stare at Me now, and gloat over Me.*

As He prayed, He didn't put His family and loved ones first. No, the first thing He did was to pray for His enemies.

This is exactly what Jesus taught us to do. In the Sermon on the Mount, He told us in Matthew 5:44, "But I say to you, love your enemies, bless those who curse you, do good to those who hate you, and pray for those who spitefully use you and persecute you." And that is precisely what He was doing. He was praying for them.

Have you ever prayed for an enemy?

"Yeah," you reply. "I prayed for them all right: *Lord, kill them!*" But that is not a prayer; that is called a curse! Jesus prayed. "Father, forgive them. . . ." *Help them to come to their senses. They don't realize the enormity of what they are doing.*

Yes, Pilate and the Sanhedrin were fully aware there were no legitimate charges against Jesus. The soldiers could see an injustice had been done, yet they gleefully participated in brutalizing Him. But did they really understand that they were torturing, murdering, and crucifying the very Son of God?

At least one of them did . . . afterward! When the Roman centurion in charge of the execution saw the dark skies, the earthquakes, and the way in which Jesus had died, he said, "Truly this was the Son of God!" (Matthew 27:54).

It's so strange. Many of those who had cried out for the crucifixion of Jesus had experienced His miracles firsthand. He had taken their children into His arms, He had healed people in their midst, He had taught them truths beyond anything they had ever encountered before.

But now they were crying for His blood.

Paul wrote in 1 Corinthians 2:8, "None of the rulers of this age understood it, for if they had, they would not have crucified the Lord of glory" (NIV).

Jesus prayed, "Father forgive them," because they needed forgiveness so desperately—forgiveness for committing a sin that was wicked beyond all comprehension, black beyond their realization.

Interestingly, we see an answer to this prayer on the Day of Pentecost. After the Holy Spirit was poured out on the church and the rapidly assembling crowd heard the apostle Peter preach a powerful sermon, they were moved by what he said. And then Peter made this statement in Acts 2:36: "Therefore let all the house of Israel know assuredly that God has made this Jesus, whom you crucified, both Lord and Christ."

And their response to Peter's words?

"Now when they heard this, they were cut to the heart, and said to Peter and the rest of the apostles, 'Men and brethren, what shall we do?' " (v. 37).

"Cut to the heart" is an unusual term, used only once in the Bible. It literally means to be stabbed in the heart and speaks of something that is both sudden and radical. The people in Peter's audience that day came under intense conviction by the Holy Spirit and called out, "What shall we do?"

Peter told them to believe in Jesus and be baptized in His name. And three thousand of them did!

Can you imagine what it would have been like to be one of the people who actually crucified Him? I have always found the "Who killed Jesus?" debate rather ridiculous. The Jews killed Jesus. The Romans killed Jesus. *You* killed Jesus. *I* killed Jesus. It's absurd to try to lay the blame of the death of Christ on a race of people or even a particular group of people. It was our sin that put Him on the cross.

So we don't need to be looking for a scapegoat here unless we want to just look in the mirror.

"Today You Will Be with Me in Paradise"

Two criminals had been crucified with Jesus, one on either side of Him. We often call them "thieves," but the original word used to describe them in the text implies more than simple thieving. They probably were guilty of murder and some kind of anarchy. Rome generally didn't crucify thieves, but if you were an insurrectionist or tried to lead a revolt against Rome, you could count on dying a horrible death like this.

So these were hardened criminals on each side of Him. And initially, the men on the other crosses joined in the taunting and derision of Jesus:

> Then two robbers were crucified with Him, one on the right and another on the left. And those who passed by blasphemed Him, wagging their heads and saying, "You who destroy the temple

and build it in three days, save Yourself! If You are the Son of God, come down from the cross." Likewise the chief priests also, mocking with the scribes and elders, said, "He saved others; Himself He cannot save. If He is the King of Israel, let Him now come down from the cross, and we will believe Him. He trusted in God; let Him deliver Him now if He will have Him; for He said, 'I am the Son of God.'" Even the robbers who were crucified with Him reviled Him with the same thing. (Matthew 27:38–39)

You would think, if you were hanging on the cross and facing death, that the last thing you would be doing is mocking somebody else. But that is exactly what both of them were doing.

But then as that dark, terrible day dragged on, one of the crucified felons suddenly experienced a change of heart:

Then one of the criminals who were hanged blasphemed Him, saying, "If You are the Christ, save Yourself and us." But the other, answering, rebuked him, saying, "Do you not even fear God, seeing you are under the same condemnation? And we indeed justly, for we receive the due reward of our deeds; but this Man has done nothing wrong." Then he said to Jesus, "Lord, remember me when You come into Your kingdom." And Jesus said to him, "Assuredly, I say to you, today you will be with Me in Paradise." (Luke 23:39–43)

That is how quickly conversion can happen. Sometimes we imagine it as a process that takes months. People will tell me, "I'm in the process of converting to Christianity."

Friend, either you are or you aren't. Either you're converted or you aren't converted.

Conversion can happen so quickly that I don't know that we can measure it by human time. The man on the cross believed right on the spot, not because of the miracles he had witnessed or the teaching he had heard, but because of what he saw of Jesus on the cross that day. He saw Him forgive the very people who had crucified Him, though He had been unjustly accused and had done no wrong.

And so he rebukes the other criminal on the cross: "What are you talking about? We deserve to be here. This Man is innocent."

I love the zeal of a new convert, don't you? I wish I could bottle it up sometimes, because it is so intense right after a person comes to faith. And here is this brand-new convert, heart overflowing with zeal, believing in Jesus, even as his time on earth draws to a close.

He says, "Lord, remember me when You come into Your kingdom." Note that he didn't say, "Lord, remember me *if* You come into Your Kingdom." It wasn't "if" but "when." He believed that Jesus was God and that He was leaving this earth for another kingdom. And he wanted to join his new Lord in that place.

Here were two men, both confronted with the truth of Jesus, and one believed while the other did not. It's interesting how two people can sit side by side in a pew and hear the same message, and one will believe and one won't.

Both of these crucified men were, in a sense, on their deathbeds. But one of those eternal souls resisted (as far as we know) to his last breath. The old expression is "there are no atheists in foxholes." But that isn't true. There are many atheists in foxholes, willing to die as they have lived. The sad fact is, if you harden your heart to God through your whole life, it's entirely likely that you will harden your heart in death as well.

One man on his cross proved how hard his heart had become. Even in the face of death, he continued to resist God's grace. But another man, on a cross just like his and as near death as he was, looked to Jesus for forgiveness, mercy, grace, and salvation.

And he received them.

Why Did This Have to Happen?

Maybe you saw Mel Gibson's cinematic portrayal of Christ's crucifixion, *The Passion of the Christ*. Some filmgoers complained that the movie was too graphic, too bloody, too violent. But the truth is, the movie portrayal probably didn't even come close to the horror and bloodshed of the real event.

Why did it have to happen?

Why can't we just talk about "gentle Jesus, meek and mild"? Why can't we remember Him as a baby in a manger and a wise teacher—or even a miracle worker?

Why all the blood and gore, all the pain and violence?

Why? Because this is exactly why Jesus came to Earth in the first place. He came to give His life. He came with the express purpose of going to a cross and dying a sacrificial death for the sins of the world.

But didn't He come teach us wonderful things about peace and brotherhood and social justice and spread good cheer?

No, He came to die.

He talked about it from the very beginning. He knew it was coming, and He knew it had to happen.

But why?

1. Jesus died to show us the love of God

You might say today, "Greg I don't think anyone loves me."

Listen, when you think God doesn't love you, take a long look at the cross.

> For God loved the world so much that he gave his one and only Son, so that everyone who believes in him will not perish but have eternal life. God sent his Son into the world not to judge the world, but to save the world through him. (John 3:16–17 NLT)

As the apostle Paul said, "Christ loved the church and gave himself up for her" (Ephesians 5:25 NIV). John agrees, saying He "loves us and has freed us from our sins by his blood" (Revelation 1:5 NIV).

He died to show His love for the world. He died to show His love for you and me.

2. Jesus died to absorb the wrath of God

If God were not just, there would be no demand for His Son to suffer and die. And if God were not loving, there would be no willingness for His Son to suffer and die.

But God is both just and loving. And because of these twin attributes, He created a plan that would both satisfy His justice and reach out to His lost creation in love.

God is all loving, *and* God is all just. That may be hard for us to wrap our minds around sometimes. Because of His perfect justice, He says in His Law that "the soul who sins shall die" (Ezekiel 18:4, 20), and that "the wages of sin is death" (Romans 6:23).

The bottom line? Someone has to pay a price here! And it either will be you, or it will be the sinless Son of God who gave His life for you, to pay the debt you could never pay. Jesus died to absorb the wrath of God.

Sometimes we will say, "Well, as far as sin goes, there are some biggies and then there are little sins."

The truth is, however, that no sin is small, because it is not committed against a small God. The seriousness of an insult rises with the dignity of the one insulted. For instance, if you insult a New York cab driver, I don't know what kind of trouble you'll get into. I think they almost expect you to insult them because of the way they drive (but that's another story).

If you insult a police officer, that's another matter entirely. I highly recommend that you do *not* insult police officers. If you get pulled over, whether you think you should have been or not, be courteous and compliant!

Now . . . what if you insult or threaten the President of the United States? You'll be in deeper trouble still!

You see, the seriousness of your insult rises with the importance and dignity of the one insulted.

And you and I have insulted God himself.

We all have. We insulted Him over and over again. We took His name in vain. We broke His commandments left and right with abandon. So Jesus absorbed the wrath of God that should have come to you and me.

3. Jesus died to cancel the legal demands against us

Conventional wisdom says, "God grades on the curve. So if your good deeds outweigh your bad deeds, you'll be okay. You'll slip through a side door into heaven."

Once again, "conventional wisdom" in this case is neither true nor biblical. There will be no salvation by balancing records; there is only salvation by *canceling* records. And Jesus took the charges against us and *canceled* them at Calvary.

Colossians 2:13–14 says, "You were dead because of your sins and because your sinful nature was not yet cut away. Then God made you alive with Christ, for he forgave all our sins. He canceled the record of the charges against us and took it away by nailing it to the cross." (NLT).

Our sins? *Forgiven.* The record of the charges against us? *Canceled, then destroyed.*

As the old hymn says so well, "Hallelujah, what a Savior!"

4. Jesus died to provide our forgiveness and justification

We are told in Romans 5:9 that we have been justified by His blood. To be justified means to be forgiven of all the wrongs you have ever done. The slate wiped clean! That's a wonder beyond imagination right there.

But that's only the beginning.

Justification also speaks of something being done for you: God will not only remove your sins and forgive your past, but He will deposit the very righteousness of Christ into your spiritual bank account! And so we have, as Peter put it, "everything we need for a godly life" (2 Peter 1:3 NIV).

What a gift! That is why Jesus came to this earth, and why He gave up His life for us.

He did it for me, and He did it for you.

And what were His *last* last words? In John 19:30, we read these words:

He said, "It is finished!" And bowing His head, He gave up His spirit.

The Greek word is *tetélestai,* and it means "paid in full."

Jesus finished the race He set out to run. He ran that last mile, though the way was hard beyond imagining. And He crossed the finish line with that mighty cry: *Paid! Done! Completed! Finished!*

Because He finished His race, you and I can finish ours. Because He crossed that line and paid that price, you and I can follow behind and enter into His victory.

He crossed the finished line. And because He did, we can too.

THE FINISH LINE . . . AND BEYOND

In my thirty-five years of pastoral ministry, I have talked about heaven countless times and have given an untold number of messages on life after death. I have counseled scores of people who lost loved ones.

My desire to be in heaven is greater now than ever before, and heaven is more real to me now than at any time I can remember.

Why? Because I have a major investment there now. My son Christopher left for heaven a few years ago, at the age of thirty-three.

The Bible tells us that when a believer dies, he or she immediately enters God's presence. There is great glory in that place, fullness of joy at God's right hand, and pleasures forevermore.

That doesn't mean you stop missing your loved ones. But it does mean that you know you will see them again. People often will say, "I'm so sorry you lost your son." I know what they mean, and I appreciate it. But the truth is, I haven't "lost" my son, because I know where he is, and I will join him one day. And all believers will join their loved ones one day soon:

> We tell you this directly from the Lord: We who are still living when the Lord returns will not meet him ahead of those who have died. For the Lord himself will come down from heaven with a commanding shout, with the voice of the archangel, and with the

trumpet call of God. First, the Christians who have died will rise from their graves. Then, together with them, we who are still alive and remain on the earth will be caught up in the clouds to meet the Lord in the air. Then we will be with the Lord forever.
(1 Thessalonians 4:15–17 NLT)

I saw a headline in a newspaper after my son's accident. It said: "Christopher Laurie Dead." But that's not true. He's not dead. He is more alive than he has ever been before, because Jesus said, "I am the resurrection and the life. He who believes in Me, though he may die, he shall live" (John 11:25).

When you are a believer in Christ, you will never die.

No, I'm not in major denial here. I understand that this body ceases to function and begins to decay. But the *real* you—your soul, your spirit—goes on to one of two places: heaven or hell.

People have asked me, "Are you angry at God?"

No, I'm not. How could I be mad at a God who holds my son safely in His arms at this very moment? The Bible says there is a time to mourn, and I am mourning. I understand what the psalmist said when he wrote, "Day and night I have only tears for food" (Psalm 42:3 NLT). And I know there will be more of that to come.

But at the same time, I am not as a person who has no hope. The Bible says we have hope as believers, no matter what the temporary circumstances of our lives might be. As I write these words, I am writing to myself too. We all need to be reminded that life is short, death is inevitable, and eternity is real.

What Do You Live For?

When you've had an encounter with death—a near-death experience of your own or the sudden passing of a loved one—it inevitably leads to a few essential questions.

What is life all about, anyway?

Why am I alive . . . and what am I really living for?

In other words, what gets you out of bed in the morning? What gets your blood pumping? Is it an alarm clock or a calling that gets you up each and every day? Every one of us needs some motivating passion, some ideal, something that gives our lives purpose, that drives us on. Unfortunately some people don't know what they're living for. A poll was taken among the viewers of *The Oprah Winfrey Show* some time ago. The question was asked, "What is your life's passion?" and 70 percent of the respondents had no idea!

Many people are merely enduring—instead of enjoying—their lives. Their favorite day of the week is "someday." Someday my ship will come in. Someday my prince will come. Someday it's all going to get better. Someday my life will change. A recent study revealed that 94 percent of the people surveyed were simply *enduring* the present, while waiting for something better to happen.

But here is what people don't plan on: they don't plan on death. And they never expect it to come around the corner unexpectedly.

Now when you're getting along in years as I am, death is at least in the back of your mind. You know that you have less years to live than you've lived already, and that death waits at the end . . . whenever that may be. But many younger people think they're invincible. Death happens to "other people." Cancer and heart attacks and fatal accidents happen to "someone else."

When you're young, you tell yourself, "I don't even have to think about that for another fifty or sixty years." And that may be true. But death knocks at every door. The Bible says that each of us has an appointment with death:

> People are destined to die once, and after that to face judgment. . . . (Hebrews 9:27 NIV)

> To everything there is a season, a time for every purpose under heaven: a time to be born, and a time to die. . . . (Ecclesiastes 3:1–2)

That "time to die" may come later than you expected. On the other hand, it may come much, much sooner.

Statisticians tell us that three people die every second, 180 every minute, and 11,000 every hour. That means that every day 250,000 people enter into eternity. Moses prayed, "Teach us to realize the brevity of life, so that we may grow in wisdom" (Psalm 90:12 NLT), and David wrote, "You have made my life no longer than the width of my hand. My entire lifetime is just a moment to you; at best, each of us is but a breath" (Psalm 39:5 NLT).

Philip of Macedon, who fought Alexander the Great, commissioned his servant to stand in his presence each and every day and repeat this statement: "Philip, you will die." In contrast, France's Louis XIV decreed that the word "death" could never be used in his presence. I'm afraid that most of us are more like Louis than Philip, denying death and avoiding the discussion. The subject makes us uncomfortable, and we don't want to think about it, let alone talk about it.

The truth is, only those who are prepared to die are really ready to live.

Maybe you're thinking, *This guy shouldn't be writing a book at this time of grief and mourning in his life. He should wait until he has a little more perspective.* No . . . this is the perfect time to write about hope for hurting hearts. Why? Because I have never been more filled and energized with the hope of life beyond the grave! Yes, I have the knowledge that my son is there with Jesus Christ ahead of me. But I also love the life I am living as a follower of Jesus, and I wouldn't trade it for anything this world has to offer. To know the Lord and walk with Him is the greatest life there is to live this side of heaven.

"For Me to Live . . ."

In a dungeon in Rome, facing imminent execution, the apostle Paul wrote:

> For to me, to live is Christ, and to die is gain. But if I live on in the flesh, this will mean fruit from my labor; yet what I shall choose I cannot tell. For I am hard-pressed between the two, having a desire to depart and be with Christ, which is far better. Nevertheless to remain in the flesh is more needful for you. (Philippians 1:21–24)

I love his statement, "For to me, to live is Christ."

But not everyone will love those words. Some will think a person who says, "To live is Christ" is nuts. They'll think, "This is a guy who's got his head in the clouds. He's a few clowns short of a circus!" Or maybe, "This is a woman who's so heavenly minded, she's no earthly good."

But that's not true. Far from it! Those who think of the next world do the most for this one. My concern is for people who are so earthly minded, they're no heavenly good!

The apostle Paul loved life. And the simple fact is, no one loves life more than the Christian. We can enjoy it, because we know it comes to us from the hand of a loving God. That beautiful sunset? That is the signature of my Father, who happens to be the Creator of all. That wonderful meal . . . the joy of love and marriage . . . the comfort of family and friends . . . the satisfaction of a hard day's work . . . all of these are beautiful gifts from the hand of our Father.

As James wrote:

> Whatever is good and perfect comes down to us from God our Father, who created all the lights in the heavens. He never changes or casts a shifting shadow. He chose to give birth to us by giving us his true word. And we, out of all creation, became his prized possession. (James 1:17–18 NLT)

But as blessed as we may be in this life, there is more . . . more than what we are experiencing on this earth. All the great things we do experience are just hints of heaven, of something better that will come for the man or the woman who has put faith in Jesus Christ.

C. S. Lewis, author of *The Chronicles of Narnia,* made this statement: "All the things that have ever deeply possessed your soul have been but hints of it—tantalising [*sic*] glimpses, promises never quite fulfilled, echoes that died away just as they caught your ear."[1] He went on to say, "If I find in myself a desire which no experience in this world can satisfy, the most probable explanation is that I was made for another world."[2]

Lewis concluded: "Earthly pleasures were never meant to satisfy it, but to arouse it, to suggest the real thing."[3]

There is another place, another time, another life. And life on earth, be it nine years or ninety years, is a nanosecond compared to eternity. Even so, it is here on this earth where we will decide where we will spend eternity. It is here on this planet that you decide between heaven and hell.

Now we love life as Christians. *To live is Christ*. Again, to quote C. S. Lewis, "Aim at heaven and you will get earth 'thrown in': Aim at earth and you will get neither."[4]

So here is Paul, and he says, "I long to go and be with Christ, which would be far better for me" (Philippians 1:23 NLT). I never understood those words . . . until now. I would read those words and say to myself, "Oh sure, I'd like to be in heaven. But then, I'm pretty happy here on earth too." But when you have loved ones on the other side—and perhaps someone who has just recently made that journey—then the promise and hope of reuniting in that place brings great joy and something to look forward to.

But we recognize that we have a job to do and a task to fulfill here on earth. And that is why I am writing these words. I am a dying man speaking to dying men, and I'm saying that eternity is real. And you get to decide where you will spend it.

My son Christopher is in heaven—not because he is my son, but because he believed in the Son of God and received Him into his life as Savior and Lord. That is why he is in heaven.

Fill in the Blank

Paul says, "For to me, to live is Christ." If you were to fill in that blank, what would you say? For me, to live is . . . what?

Some might say, "For me, to live is . . . to just live." In other words, they just take it a day at a time. Life for them is mere existence. They don't have any philosophy to speak of and don't like to contemplate the meaning of life. They just live for the moment, seeking to satisfy their desires, whatever they might be. This type of person is very uncomfortable with any discussion about life and its meaning. Their motto is, "Just live and let live."

Others would take it a step further and say, "Hey man, for me, to live is *pleasure*. To me, to live is parties . . . to go clubbing . . . to have this experience . . . do this or that . . . try this recreational drug or that one." They live and die for those things.

I know that particular train of thought all too well. Been there, done that, and bought the T-shirt. Before I was a Christian, I experimented with drugs, partied, and did all that stuff. And I knew the answer to my hunger for "more" in life was not in those things. In fact, one of the things that brought me to Christ was a simple process of elimination. I knew life wasn't in this, and I knew it wasn't in that. And I began to search and wonder, *What is the meaning of life? What is the purpose of my existence?* It seemed to me that I had spent more time waiting for a good time than actually having a good time.

It was sort of like being at an amusement park. You wait for two hours for a ride that lasts a minute-and-a-half. And that's the way it is with life before you come to Christ: you wait and wait to have your little pleasure. But the "fun" or excitement of that pleasure is short-lived at best and usually has a lot of guilt attached to it.

Others might be more noble, and say, "Ah, yes, for me, to live is to acquire knowledge." And they will say, "I have multiple degrees. I have studied, and I'm an intelligent person." That's all well and good. But if your pursuit of knowledge fails to take God into account, then you will end up empty.

The wisest man who ever lived was named Solomon. People came from all around the world to sit at his feet and glean his pearls of wisdom. Thousands of years ago, in the book of Ecclesiastes, Solomon wrote, "Look, I am wiser than any of the kings who ruled in Jerusalem before me. I have greater wisdom and knowledge than any of them" (Ecclesiastes 1:16 NLT).

But at the end of all his study and vast academic accomplishments, he concluded, "So I set out to learn everything from wisdom to madness and folly. But I learned firsthand that pursuing all this is like chasing the wind. The greater my wisdom, the greater my grief. To increase knowledge only increases sorrow" (vv. 17-18 NLT).

In 1966, a year before he died, the brilliant physicist J. Robert Oppenheimer made this statement. "I am a complete failure." This man had been director of the Manhattan Project, a research trained team that produced the atom bomb. He also served as the head of the Institute for Advanced Study at Princeton. Yet at the end of life, he looked back and declared it all meaningless. He said of his accomplishments, "They leave on the tongue only the taste of ashes."

The real answer to life is Paul's answer: "To live is Christ." No one who genuinely lives completely for Him will be disappointed.

Saul of Tarsus was hunting down Christians, putting them into prison, and even having some of them put to death. And guess who he met face to face? Jesus Christ himself. Jesus said to him, "Saul, Saul, why are you persecuting Me?" (Acts 9:4 NLT). And Saul essentially, said, "Who are You, Lord, and what do You want me to do?"

Saul later changed his name to Paul, and the world was a better place because of his conversion. From that moment on, Paul said, "For me to live is Christ. I'm going to serve Him and follow Him to the end of my days."

Paul's full quote in Philippians 1 is: "For to me, to live is Christ, *and to die is gain*" (1:21, emphasis added). Another translation says, "To die is better." How could anybody say such a thing? How could an individual in his or her right mind say that to die is better than living on this earth? It's because Paul understood what happens when a believer leaves this world:

> Yet what shall I choose? I do not know! I am torn between the two:
> I desire to depart and be with Christ, which is better by far.
> (Philippians 1:22–23 NIV)

The word he uses in this passage for "depart" is an interesting word that could be translated in several different ways. One definition means "to strike the tent." In other words, to break camp. You may or may not be a big fan of tent camping, but I can tell you that my favorite part of the whole experience is when we're getting ready to break camp and leave! That's when I get excited. I can hardly wait until I get home and get into that hot shower. In this passage, Paul says, "I'm ready to break camp. I'm ready to leave this place and move on, and let me tell you friends . . . *I can't wait.*"

This body that we're living in is a lot like a tent—just fabric stretched over some poles with pegs attaching us to the earth. It's not a permanent structure, and it wasn't meant to last forever.

The Bible says, "For we know that if the earthly tent we live in is destroyed, we have a building from God, an eternal house in heaven, not built by human hands" (2 Corinthians 5:1 NLT).

That word "depart" Paul used in Philippians 1:23 also could be used to describe a prisoner being released from shackles. Ironically, when Paul made this statement, he was actually chained up in a dungeon in Rome. His chains were made of iron, but perhaps you're dealing with chains of a different sort: an addiction to drugs, alcohol, or pornography. Whatever it is, Paul is saying there is a coming a day when I will be released from these shackles.

There is one additional way "depart" could be translated. The word was also used to describe untying a boat from its moorings . . . sort of like when you set sail.

We understandably feel great sadness when a loved one leaves us, and sometimes we feel sorry for that person. We say, "Oh, poor John. I wish he could be with us today."

But stop and think about it. Think about the port they have left, and the port they are heading for. If you stood on the wharf and said good-bye to someone sailing off in a leaky, rusty old freighter bound for Outer Siberia, well, that would be pretty sad. But if you went down to the dock and saw that they were boarding a beautiful new cruise ship destined for Tahiti, you might be more inclined to feel sorry for yourself instead! After all, you would be the one left standing on the shore, and your loved one would be on his or her way to a great adventure and a beautiful destination.

And heaven, in the presence of Jesus Christ, is exactly as Paul describes it: "better by far." Why? Because heaven is infinitely better than life on earth.

In Revelation 7, the Bible says of those in heaven, "They will never again be hungry or thirsty; they will never be scorched by the heat of the sun. For the Lamb on the throne will be their Shepherd. He will lead them to springs of life-giving water. And God will wipe every tear from their eyes" (vv. 16–17 NLT).

Why is heaven better than earth? It's better because we are moving from a tent to a mansion. The Bible compares heaven to a city, a garden, and a paradise. These are ideas that we can attempt to wrap our minds around. But then again, the majesty and beauty of heaven always will be difficult for a finite mind to grasp. The general idea, however, is that one day we will leave a broken-down shack with a leaky roof for a mansion far better than anything we could ever find on earth. There will be no more devil, no more temptation to sin, and we will be reunited with loved ones in the presence of Jesus Christ.

Here's the way the writer of the Book of Hebrews describes it:

> No, you have come to Mount Zion, to the city of the living God, the heavenly Jerusalem, and to countless thousands of angels in a joyful gathering. You have come to the assembly of God's firstborn children, whose names are written in heaven. You have come to God himself, who is the judge over all things. You have come to the spirits of the righteous ones in heaven who have now been made perfect. You have come to Jesus, the one who mediates the new covenant between God and people. . . . (Hebrews 12:22–24 NLT)

It sounds like a place where I'd like to be!

The reality of heaven is immediate after we leave this life. We will exhale our last lungful of earthly air and take the next breath of celestial air on the other side. Paul said, "I desire to depart and be with Christ." Notice he didn't say, "I desire to depart and go into a waiting room somewhere." Or, "I desire to depart and go into a state of suspended animation or soul sleep." No, he said, "Depart and *be with Christ*." The Bible tells us that to be absent from the body is to be present with the Lord (see 2 Corinthians 5:6).

Heaven is better, because when I get there, all of my questions will be answered. I heard about one woman's question for God. In an overly ambitious moment, she had invited a lot of people to a dinner party. And she was just frazzled. But at the dinner table, she thought it would be a good idea to ask her six-year-old daughter to say the blessing. So she said, "Sweetheart, why don't you say the blessing and pray a prayer over our meal?"

"Well, Mommy," she replied, "I don't know what to say."

The mother said, "Just say what you always hear Mommy say."

So the little girl prayed, "Lord, why on earth did I invite all of these people to dinner?"

We all have legitimate questions. Why did this happen? Why didn't that happen? And of course, I have mine too. But the truth is, even if we had some of the most troubling questions in our hearts answered, we wouldn't be satisfied. The answers would only raise more questions! The Bible doesn't promise us a peace that necessarily gives understanding, but it promises a peace that *surpasses* human understanding (see Philippians 4:7).

I received a letter from Warren Wiersbe, a great author and Bible teacher, after my son went to heaven. He said, "As God's children we live on promises, not on explanations. And you know as well as I do the promises of God." He went on to say, "When we arrive in heaven we will hear the explanations, accept them, and we will say, 'May God be glorified.' "

I have many questions in my heart in these days of grief and mourning, and I don't seem to have many answers. But here's what I know. I know my son, Christopher Laurie, is with the Lord. And I know one day that all of my questions will be answered. In one paraphrase of 1 Corinthians 13, we read, "We don't yet see things clearly. We're squinting in a fog, peering through a mist . . ." (v. 12 MSG). The King James Version says, "For now we see through a glass, darkly. . . ."

It reminds me of a car with tinted windows. Someone drives by, and you're straining to look through the glass. You're saying, "Who's in there?" That's how it is for us sometimes. We try to look at heaven. We try to figure out the big questions of life. And it's hard to make it out. Maybe we see a little silhouette, but we're not even sure about that.

But the Bible says we will one day be known even as we are known. To quote again from *The Message:* "We don't yet see things clearly. We're squinting in a fog, peering through a mist. But it won't be long before the weather clears and the sun shines bright! We'll see it all then, see it all as clearly as God sees us, knowing him directly just as he knows us!" (1 Corinthians 13:12 MSG).

Most importantly, heaven is better than earth, because Paul says, "I will be with Christ." And that is the greatest joy. Yes, we will be reunited with our loved ones. But we will be with Jesus and we will never be separated from Him again.

But then again, you don't have to go to heaven to find Christ. In fact, it's the other way around: *You go to Christ to find heaven.*

Here is what I can say to you. Take the worst-case scenario of life: finding out that a loved one—maybe even your child—has been suddenly taken from this life. My family and I have just lived that terrible scenario, and I can say this. *God was there.* I have hit bottom, and it is sound. God is there. His Word is true. You don't have to be afraid; God will be with you, no matter what you face in your life.

So often in this life we are crippled by our fears. What if this happens? What if that happens? Jesus says, "Do not be afraid; only believe" (Mark 5:36). I'm not saying it's easy. But I am saying the Lord was there, and He is there, and He will be there—for all of us—no matter what troubles we have.

What do you live for? Be honest now. If your answer is, "For me, to live is money," then to die is to leave it all behind. If you say, "For me, to live is fame," then to die is to be forgotten. If you say, "For me, to live is power," then for you, to die will be utter weakness. But if you say, "For me, to live is Christ," then you will also be able to say, "To die is gain."

And the day you end your race will be the most glorious moment of life.

CONCLUSION:
Consider the Winners

We have looked together at some unlikely winners and tragic losers in life's most important race. Some have run and fallen, never to rise. Others have fallen, hobbled to their feet, wiped away the dirt, mud, and blood, and got back into the race. Still others have run strong and steady from beginning to end.

If I had to pick one Scripture that best summarizes this whole book, I think Hebrews 12 says it very well:

> Therefore we also, since we are surrounded by so great a cloud of witnesses, let us lay aside every weight, and the sin which so easily ensnares us, and let us run with endurance the race that is set before us, looking unto Jesus, the author and finisher of our faith, who for the joy that was set before Him endured the cross, despising the shame, and has sat down at the right hand of the throne of God.
>
> For consider Him who endured such hostility from sinners against Himself, lest you become weary and discouraged in your souls. You have not yet resisted to bloodshed, striving against sin. And you have forgotten the exhortation which speaks to you as to sons: "My son, do not despise the chastening of the Lord, nor be discouraged when you are rebuked by Him; for whom the Lord loves He chastens, and scourges every son whom He receives." (Hebrews 12:1–6)

This passage gives us a few things we need to consider.

Lessons from Hebrews 12

1. We need to consider the winners

We are told there is "so great a cloud of witnesses." Think of people in the grandstands at a sports event. This verse describes those people whom Hebrews 11 lists as being in the hall of fame of faith. These are men and women who lived godly and obedient lives. They gave us an example to follow, a pace to keep, a template to apply.

2. We need to consider ourselves

When the race is difficult, we tend to blame circumstances, other people, or even God. We need to remember that if we stumble or fall in the race of life, it's our own fault. The Bible says, "His divine power has given us everything we need for a godly life through our knowledge of him who called us by his own glory and goodness" (2 Peter 1:3 NIV).

Hebrews tells us to "lay aside every weight, and the sin which so easily ensnares us." Do you see the distinction? Lay aside the weight and the sin. Sin is sin, no matter how you slice it or dice it. A weight may be something else.

I've mentioned this before, but it's worth repeating. Ask yourself about each thought, activity, idea, word: Is it a wing, or is it a weight? Is it something that speeds you on your way? Or is it something that slows you down?

A great concert violinist was asked her secret. She said it was "planned neglect." She explained, "Anything that would keep me from practicing and playing well must be neglected." Some of us could use some planned neglect in our lives. We carry around a lot more junk than we may realize. Periodically we need to jettison this excess weight and let it go. Lay aside both sin and weight.

3. We need to consider the race itself

What race should we run? *The race that is set before us.*

Remember that I'm not competing with you, and you're not competing with me. Our competition is the enemy—the world, the flesh, and the devil. Our goal is not to outrun each other. Our goal is to outrun those wicked influences that could bring us down.

You might justify your slow pace by saying a lot of people are still behind you on the track. True. But there are also probably a lot of people ahead of you. Don't concern yourself with who is behind or ahead of you. You are to run the race that is set before *you*. God hasn't called you to run my race, nor has He called me to run yours. He calls each to run his or her own race.

Today, are you running the race of life as well as you ought to? Or are you just offering a half-effort?

Back in the first chapter of this book, I quoted the apostle Paul's view of the daily running of our race. Writing from prison, he said: "I focus on this one thing: . . . I press on to reach the end of the race and receive the heavenly prize . . ." (Philippians 3:13–14 NLT).

Keep your eyes on your own lane. Run your race.

4. We need to consider Jesus Christ

> "Looking unto Jesus, the author and finisher of our faith, who for the joy that was set before Him endured the cross, despising the shame, and has sat down on the right hand of the throne of God."

This is what will keep you going in the race of life.

We are running for an audience of One. Jesus is watching us and rooting for us. He's even praying for us.

Remember, this is what gave young Stephen the courage to face death when his audience's anger boiled. Just before they stoned him, he said, "Look! I see the heavens opened and the Son of Man is standing at the right hand of God!" (Acts 7:56). The sight of Jesus gave Stephen the ability to run the race and finish it.

Keep your eyes on Jesus; look unto the Author and Finisher of your faith. Why? Because circumstances will disappoint and, at times, devastate you. People will let you down. Feelings will come and go. But Jesus is there standing before you, holding your reward, and saying, "Come on, you can do this! You can live this life. You can finish this race. I am here with you. Let's do it."

What do you want to be—a winner or a loser in this spiritual race?

Did Jesus Have an Advantage?

Jesus was the greatest winner of all. You may say, "Of course. He was God. He had a definite advantage over the rest of us." But there's more to it than that.

We sometimes think that because Jesus was and is God, it was relatively easy for Him to run His race and finish His work on earth. It wasn't. He lived the same way you and I must: by faith in God and obedience to His Word. Hebrews 5:8 says, "Even though Jesus was God's Son, he learned obedience from the things he suffered" (NLT). Don't forget that Jesus experienced rejection . . . deep sorrow . . . intense loneliness. Jesus felt every human emotion.

Even when He resisted the devil's temptations in the wilderness, Jesus responded in a way we can. When the devil tempted Him, Jesus didn't say, "Back off, Satan. I am Jesus Christ, the only begotten Son of God. You can't touch Me." Nor did He airlift himself out of the situation. He faced it as any human being could: He fought back with the Word of God.

Jesus has run before us. He is the ultimate winner. He is showing us how to do it. As Corrie ten Boom said years ago, "Look within and be depressed. Look without and be distressed. Look at Jesus and be at rest."

Are you looking to Jesus today? How are you doing in the race of life? Are weights slowing you down? Are sins tripping you up? If so, I urge you to follow the leader—Jesus.

Keep to your own lane, hold a steady pace, and that finish line will be at your feet any minute. I know you can do it.

And unless I see you sooner, I'll meet you in the victor's circle, just on the other side.

NOTES

Introduction

1. Larry King, *Remember Me When I'm Gone* (New York: Random House, Inc., 2004), 34.

2. Ibid., 26.

3. Ibid., 112.

4. Ibid., 123.

5. Ibid., 136.

6. Elisabeth Elliot, *Shadow of the Almighty* (New York: HarperCollins, 1979), 247.

Chapter 2

1. Charles R. Swindoll, *Growing Strong in the Seasons of Life* (Grand Rapids, Mich.: Zondervan Publishing House, 1983), 317.

Chapter 4

1. *Notable Quotes*, http://www.notable-quotes.com/l/longfellow_henry_wadsworth.html.

Chapter 6

1. Alan Redpath, *The Making of a Man of God: Lessons from the Life of David* (Grand Rapids, Mich.: Revell, 1962), 17.

2. Charles R. Swindoll, *David: A Man of Passion and Destiny* (Nashville: Thomas Nelson, 1997), 22.

3. Alvin Reid, *Introduction to Evangelism* (Nashville: B&H Publishing Group, 1998), 65.

Chapter 8

1. R. Kent Hughes, *Disciplines of a Godly Man* (Wheaton, Ill.: Crossway Books, 2001), 25.

Chapter 9

1. "More Sad Stories of Lottery Winners Ending Up Broke, Depressed and Lonely," *LifeTwo.com*, http://lifetwo.com/production/node/20070425-more-sad-stories-of-lottery-winners-ending-up-broke-depressed-and-lonely.

Chapter 11

1. Jeffrey Kluger, "Fear Not! For Millions of Sufferers of Phobias, Science Is Offering New Treatments—and New Hope," *Time*, April 2, 2001, http://www.time.com/time/world/article/0,8599,2047666,00.html.

Chapter 15

1. W. J. Conybeare, *The Life and Epistles of Saint Paul,* vol. 1 (New York: Charles Scribner, 1854), 57.

2. Henry Jacobsen, *The Acts Then and Now* (Wheaton, Ill.: Victor Books, 1973), 76.

Chapter 21

1. Deirdre Donahue, " 'The Other Wes Moore' Author Knows What Might Have Been," *USAToday.com*, May 7, 2010, http://www.usatoday.com/life/books/news/2010-05-06-wesmoore06_CV_N.htm.

Chapter 24

1. Charles R. Swindoll, *The Tale of the Tardy Oxcart: And 1,501 Other Stories* (Nashville, Tenn.: Word Publishing, Inc., 1998), 210–11.

2. Skip Heitzig, *Godprint: Making Your Mark for Christ* (Alachua, Fla.: Bridge-Logos Foundation, 2009), 31–32.

Chapter 25

1. *Dictionary.com*, http://dictionary.reference.com/browse/i+only+regret+that+i+have+but+one+life+to+lose+for+my+country.

2. *UncovertheNet.com*, http://www.uncoverthenet.com/quotes/listing/28.php.

3. "Last Words of Real People," http://www.sanftleben.com/Last%20Words/lastwords-r-n.html

Chapter 26

1. C. S. Lewis, *Made for Heaven: And Why on Earth It Matters* (New York: HarperCollins Publishers, 2005), 19.

2. C. S. Lewis, *Mere Christianity* (New York: HarperCollins, 2001), 136–37.

3. Ibid., 137.

4. Ibid., 134.

ALLEN DAVID BOOKS

**Other AllenDavid Books
Published by
Kerygma Publishing**

A Handbook on Christian Dating
Are We Living in the Last Days?
As I See It
Better than Happiness
Daily Hope for Hurting Hearts Devotional
Dealing with Giants
Deepening Your Faith
Discipleship: The Road Less Taken
Essentials: Foundational Topics for Christians in Today's World
For Every Season: Daily Devotions
For Every Season, volumes 1, 2, and 3
God's Design for Christian Dating
His Christmas Presence
Hope for Hurting Hearts
How to Know God
"I'm Going on a Diet Tomorrow"
Living Out Your Faith
Making God Knowns
Marriage Connections
Married. Happily.
Secrets to Spiritual Success
Signs of the Times
Strengthening Your Faith
Strengthening Your Marriage
Ten Things You Should Know about God and Life
The Great Compromise
The Greatest Stories Ever Told, volumes 1, 2, and 3
Upside Down Living
What Every Christian Needs to Know
Why, God?

Visit: www.kerygmapublishing.com
www.allendavidbooks.com